THE WATER PARADOX

THE WATER PARADOX

Overcoming the Global Crisis in Water Management

EDWARD B. BARBIER

YALE UNIVERSITY PRESS
NEW HAVEN AND LONDON

For information about this and other Yale University Press publications, please contact:
U.S. Office: sales.press@yale.edu   yalebooks.com
Europe Office: sales@yaleup.co.uk   yalebooks.co.uk

Set in Adobe Caslon Pro by IDSUK (DataConnection) Ltd
Printed in Great Britain by TJ International, Padstow, Cornwall

Library of Congress Control Number: 2018957474

ISBN 978-0-300-22443-6

A catalogue record for this book is available from the British Library.

10 9 8 7 6 5 4 3 2 1

CONTENTS

FIGURES, TABLES AND BOXES

Figures

vi

Tables

Boxes

PREFACE

When the history of the early twenty-first century is written, scholars will be perplexed by a puzzling paradox. With overwhelming scientific evidence pointing to growing overuse and scarcity of freshwater, why did the world not mobilize its vast wealth, ingenuity and institutions to avert this crisis?

Explaining this water paradox—and offering possible solutions to resolve it—is the purpose of the following book. The main message is straightforward. The global water crisis is predominantly a crisis of inadequate and poor water management.

In the near future, many countries, regions and populations may face rising costs of exploiting additional water resources that could constrain growth as well as make it increasingly difficult to meet the needs of those poor populations and countries that face chronic water insecurity. If unchecked, water scarcity could increase the likelihood of civil unrest and conflicts.

There is also a risk of disputes over the management of transboundary water sources and "water grabbing" acquisitions. Yet this crisis could be avoided. Inadequate policies, governance and institutions, coupled with incorrect market signals and insufficient innovations to improve efficiency, underlie most chronic water problems. This process has become a vicious cycle. Markets and policy decisions currently do not reflect the rising economic costs associated with exploiting more freshwater resources. This in turn leads to freshwater infrastructure and investments that are accompanied by higher environmental and social damages. These damages are reflected in increased depletion of water resources, pollution, degradation of freshwater ecosystems and, ultimately, rising water scarcity. But, because the economic costs of this scarcity continue to be ignored in decision making, the consequences for current and future wellbeing are underestimated. The end result is what I call the chronic *underpricing of water*.

Unraveling this vicious circle and turning it into a virtuous one is one of the biggest challenges facing humankind. It starts with designing water governance regimes and institutions that are suitable for managing the rapidly changing conditions of water availability and competing demands, including the threat posed by climate change. Ending the underpricing of water also requires reforms to markets and policies to ensure that they adequately capture the rising economic costs of exploiting water resources. These costs include not only the full cost recovery of water infrastructure supply but also environmental damages from degrading ecosystems and any social impacts of inequitable distribution. Incorporating these costs will ensure that all water developments will minimize environmental and social impacts, which in turn will lead to more water conservation, control of pollution and ecosystem protection. The result will be efficient allocation of water among its competing uses, fostering of water-saving innovations, and further mitigation of water scarcity and its costs.

Such a transformation is very difficult, yet there are encouraging signs that it is starting to happen in many places around the world. Of course much more needs to be done, and the obstacles are great. As the early chapters of this book document, today's water paradox did not just happen over a few years or even decades. Its roots have a long history, which has impacted our key market, policy and governance institutions and has affected major technical innovations. As a consequence, in today's economies, water use management, and its accompanying institutions, incentives and innovations, is still dominated by the "hydraulic mission" of finding and exploiting more freshwater resources.

By drawing on many examples from around the world, this book explains that our approach to managing water can and must be changed if we are to avoid a global water crisis. By developing appropriate governance and institutions for water management, instigating market and policy reforms, addressing global management issues, and improving innovation and investments in new water technologies, we should better protect freshwater ecosystems and secure sufficient beneficial water use for a growing world population.

E. B. B.

Fort Collins, Colorado

July 2018

ACKNOWLEDGMENTS

I am grateful to Taiba Batool for proposing that I write this book, and for her helpful suggestions and comments on how to develop and improve it.

During the process of writing this book, I benefited from the support of my colleagues in the Department of Economics and College of Liberal Arts, University of Wyoming, and the Department of Economics, College of Liberal Arts and the School of Global Environmental Sustainability, Colorado State University.

As always, I have benefited greatly from the insights, comments and suggestions of Joanne Burgess, and the support of my family.

INTRODUCTION
The Water Paradox

If water is valuable and scarce, why is it so poorly managed?

Up to now, we have adopted only one approach to resolving this water paradox. We ignore the signs of growing water scarcity, until sudden and unexpected shortages force us to take drastic measures to curtail excessive use. This is proving to be a costly response to water crises—as the following example illustrates.

In 2017, for the first time in 2,000 years, Rome turned off its iconic drinking fountains. Faced with a prolonged drought in the spring and summer of that year which inflicted over €1 million worth of agricultural damages, city authorities decided to stop the flow of water to Rome's 2,800 public fountains.[1] Such a decision is unprecedented in Rome's history.

Ancient Rome pioneered the invention of the modern urban water system, which included its famous aqueducts and elaborate city fountains.[2] Rome's water system was designed to carry large volumes of water into the city, which was made freely available to citizens through its elaborate network of public drinking fountains. Many of modern Rome's fountains are still stamped with the initials SPQR—*Senatus Populusque Romanus* (the Senate and People of Rome)—to denote their symbolic link to the original public water system built by the Roman Empire.[3]

Since the first aqueduct conveyed water to public fountains at the ancient city's cattle market, there has always been water to supply Rome's fountains. Through centuries of wars, conflicts, revolutions and other human and natural catastrophes, the tradition of free fountain water in Rome has continued unabated, until the devastating 2017 drought. One of the city's principal water sources, Lake Bracciano, suffered rapidly falling levels, and, with Italy's farmers facing crippling water shortages, free public water for the city had to be sacrificed. There was simply not enough water for both uses.

The tradeoff that Rome faced—water for its fountains versus averting a catastrophic drought for farmers—is likely to occur again, as agricultural, municipal and industrial uses of water arise and climate change makes dwindling supplies even more variable. Moreover, it is a tradeoff that may increasingly confront many countries and regions around the world. For the entire globe, the era of plentiful water appears to be over.

Forget energy price shocks, mass unemployment, fiscal crises and financial failures. Even biodiversity loss, ecosystem collapse, human-made environmental catastrophes or the spread of infectious diseases pale in comparison. According to the World Economic Forum's annual report *Global Risk 2016*, over the next decade the biggest threat to the planet will be a global water crisis.[4] What is more, this is the fifth year in a row that water has been identified as a top global risk to economies, environments and people. In 2015, respondents to the World Economic Forum's Global Risks Perception Survey ranked water shortages as the greatest threat in terms of impact over the next ten years.

Water problems are also strongly linked to two other prominent global risks—climate change and food insecurity. By 2050 more than 40 percent of the world's population will be living in water-stressed regions, which is around 1 billion more people than live in such areas today.[5] Around 2.7 billion people are also affected by water shortages each year.[6] Meanwhile, 663 million people—one in ten of the world's population—lack access to safe water and 2.4 billion—one in three—do not have use of a toilet.[7] These water stresses and shortages will only worsen with the rising temperatures, more frequent droughts and variable rainfall that will accompany global warming. Growing water scarcity will, in turn, magnify the economic and environmental impacts of climate change.

Global agriculture and food security depend on water. Irrigation, which accounts for 40 percent of agricultural production globally, currently consumes 70 percent of the world's freshwater supplies.[8] And irrigation keeps expanding with growing populations and demand for food. Total harvested irrigated area is expected to increase from 421 million hectares in 2000 to 473 million by 2050. But people need water, too, for overcoming water shortages, meeting nonagricultural uses such as houses, sanitation and industries, and even new agricultural demands, such as biofuel production. These growing demands for water plus the vagaries of global climate change will place increasing pressure on using scarce water resources for agriculture and may threaten global food security.

Why Should We Be Surprised?

First, water is essential to life. All life forms on our planet require water to survive. Thus, it should not be surprising that, as demand by humans for water increases—for food, drinking, sanitation, industrial use and so forth—there is less water available to meet these diverse and growing needs in the future. This also means less water for all the remaining life on earth, which lies at the heart of the global problem.

Second, freshwater on our planet has always been limited. Freshwater is defined as having a low salt concentration or other dissolved chemical compounds—usually less than 1 percent. It is this low sodium content that makes freshwater fit, and necessary, for human consumption. However, only around 3 percent of the world's water is "fresh," and 99 percent of this supply is either frozen in glaciers and pack ice or found underground in aquifers. Freshwater ecosystems account for the remaining 1 percent of the world's freshwater sources. Lakes and rivers, which are the main sources for human consumption of freshwater, contain just 0.3 percent of total global reserves.[9]

In other words, freshwater ecosystems, which comprise ponds, lakes, streams, rivers and wetlands, are the main source of accessible water supply for humans on our planet. This would suggest that, if water is the most valuable commodity for humans and it is growing scarcer because of its increasing use, then we ought to be taking care of its main source—freshwater ecosystems.

Instead, for thousands and thousands of years, our approach to managing water supplies has been just the opposite. Instead of viewing water as a scarce resource, our perception of water is that it is abundant, freely available and easily accessible. We have used it copiously for agriculture, domestic use and industries. We have built massive and sophisticated engineering structures—dams, dykes, pipelines and reservoirs—to move water from where it is abundant, and sometimes unwanted, to cities, farms and populations that have growing demands. We treat, recycle and redistribute wastewater to prevent contamination of natural sources of freshwater and to extend its consumption. We are now extracting water from the sea and removing the salt to extend freshwater supplies even further.

Freshwater Ecosystems—A Vital Resource under Threat

Unfortunately, the consequence of our action and neglect is that our principal source of water—freshwater ecosystems— is under increased pressure and even destruction from both human impacts and environmental change (see Figure 0.1).

Ironically, the main human threats to these ecosystems stem from our attempts to manage water and extract more of it for our various uses: modification of river systems, other inland waters and their associated wetlands, and water withdrawals for flood control, agriculture or water supply.[10] Pollution and eutrophication by agricultural, industrial and urban waste, overharvesting of inland fisheries, and the introduction of invasive alien species are further degrading freshwater ecosystems and biodiversity.[11]

Significant environmental impacts to freshwater ecosystems occur through climate change, nitrogen deposition and shifts in precipitation and runoff patterns. Such environmental changes impact global freshwater ecosystems directly, and are increasingly interacting with human threats to magnify the dangers to these dwindling resources in many parts of the world. The increasing pressure on freshwater ecosystems from human activities combined with environmental change poses a grave risk to water security while simultaneously endangering freshwater biodiversity and healthy ecosystem functioning.[12]

The global decline and loss of freshwater ecosystems should be of concern because they are essential for a diverse

Figure 0.1 Major Human and Environmental Threats to Freshwater Ecosystems

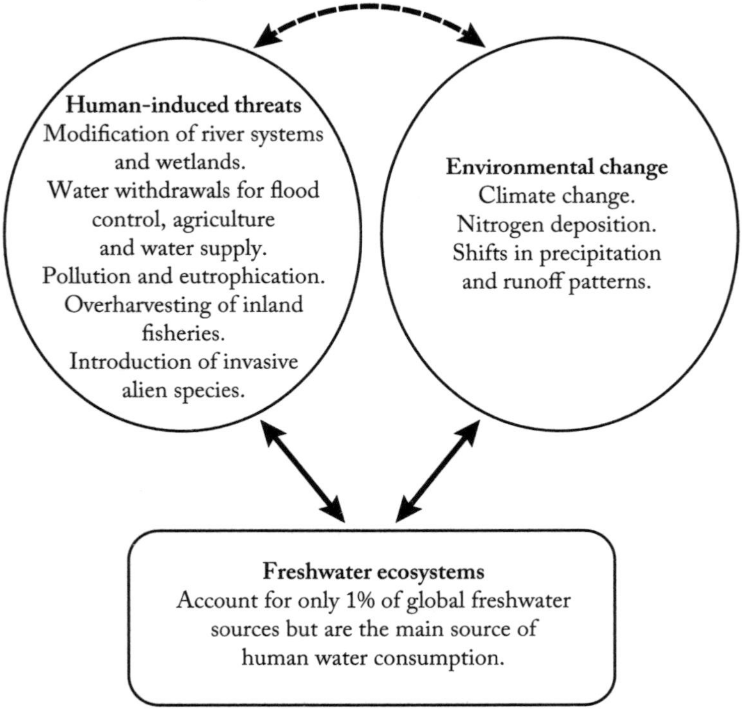

Human-induced threats and environmental change impact directly (solid line) on freshwater ecosystems as well as interact (dotted line) to magnify these impacts.

range of human uses in addition to water supply and security for human consumption. For example, these ecosystems are vital for inland capture fisheries, which contribute about 12 percent of all fish consumed by humans; irrigated agriculture, which supplies about 40 percent of the world's food crops; and hydropower, which provides nearly 20 percent of the world's electricity production.[13] Lakes, ponds, rivers and other freshwater systems are also used to cool industrial and energy processes, and for washing, flushing or other sanitation purposes.

The intensity of recent human-induced and environmental impacts on freshwater ecosystems is exacerbating chronic difficulties of water availability in some regions. Modifications of rivers and other inland waters may have increased the amount of water available for human use, but more than 40 percent of the world's population experience high or extreme water stress, measured in terms of annual withdrawals of water availability, with this percentage expected to increase to almost 50 percent by 2025.[14] Over 1.4 billion people currently live in river basins where the use of water exceeds minimum recharge levels, and most of these critical basins are in the developing world.[15] In 201 basins, with 2.67 billion inhabitants between them, during the period 1996–2005 there was severe water scarcity during at least one month of each year.[16] The pollution and degradation of surface and underground sources of water by agricultural, industrial and urban waste are further aggravating the global availability of freshwater.[17]

Already, increasing uses of freshwater supplies are exacting a noticeable toll globally. In recent decades, many countries have experienced a sharp decline in per-capita water availability, which is expected to worsen with growing populations and economies.[18] Although water use is expanding everywhere, the most significant growth in global water demand will occur mainly in developing countries.[19] The world is currently experiencing increased freshwater withdrawals of about 64 billion cubic meters (m^3) a year.[20] Global water demand is also anticipated to rise significantly, from about 3,500 cubic kilometers (km^3) in 2000 to nearly 5,500km^3 in 2050, primarily due to increased use for manufacturing, electricity and domestic purposes.[21] However, water withdrawals are predicted to increase by 50 percent by 2025 in developing countries, as compared to 18 percent in developed countries.[22]

As a consequence, many countries of the world will be experiencing high or extreme water stress by 2040 (see Table 0.1). Thirty-five countries will be withdrawing 80 percent of their available freshwater supplies for agricultural, industrial and municipal uses, and another thirty-one countries will be withdrawing 40–80 percent of their available supplies. A number of these countries that will experience high or extreme water stress in 2040 are developing economies today. Many are from the chronically water-short Middle East and North Africa region. However, there are also a number of prominent and large emerging market economies that will be suffering from high or extreme water stress by 2040. These include India, Pakistan, Turkey, Mexico, Indonesia, Iran, South Africa and the Philippines.

Social and Economic Implications

A global water crisis will have a number of economic and social implications, which are likely to raise the costs of exploiting additional water resources, constrain economic

Table 0.1 Projected Water Stress in Countries, 2040

Extreme water stress (> 80%)	High water stress (40–80%)	Medium to high water stress (20–40%)
Afghanistan	Algeria	Argentina
Antigua & Barbuda	Andorra	China
Bahrain	Armenia	Estonia
Barbados	Australia	Haiti
Comoros	Azerbaijan	Ireland
Cyprus	Belgium	Luxembourg
Dominica	Chile	Macedonia
East Timor	Cuba	Malaysia
Iran	Djibouti	Monaco
Israel	Dominican Republic	Nepal
Jamaica	Eritrea	North Korea
Jordan	Greece	Ukraine
Kazakhstan	India	United Kingdom
Kuwait	Indonesia	United States
Kyrgyzstan	Iraq	Venezuela
Lebanon	Italy	
Libya	Japan	
Malta	Lesotho	
Mongolia	Mexico	
Morocco	Peru	
Oman	Philippines	
Pakistan	Portugal	
Palestine	South Africa	
Qatar	South Korea	
St. Lucia	Sri Lanka	
St. Vincent & Grenadines	Swaziland	
San Marino	Syria	
Saudi Arabia	Tajikistan	
Somaliland	Tunisia	
Trinidad & Tobago	Turkey	
Turkmenistan	Vatican City	
United Arab Emirates		
Uzbekistan		
Western Sahara		
Yemen		

Table 0.1 Projected Water Stress in Countries, 2040 (cont.)

Low to medium water stress (10–20%)	Low water stress (< 10%)	
Albania	Austria	Latvia
Angola	Bangladesh	Liberia
Belize	Belarus	Liechtenstein
Botswana	Benin	Malawi
Bulgaria	Bhutan	Mali
Canada	Bolivia	Mauritania
Costa Rica	Bosnia &	Montenegro
Czech Republic	Herzegovina	Mozambique
Ecuador	Brazil	Myanmar
Egypt	Brunei	Niger
El Salvador	Burundi	Nigeria
France	Cambodia	Norway
Gabon	Cameroon	Panama
Georgia	Central African	Papua New Guinea
Germany	Republic	Paraguay
Guatemala	Chad	Republic of Congo
Guyana	Colombia	Romania
Kosovo	Côte d'Ivoire	Rwanda
Lithuania	Croatia	Senegal
Madagascar	Denmark	Serbia
Moldova	Equatorial Guinea	Sierra Leone
Namibia	Ethiopia	Slovakia
Netherlands	Finland	Slovenia
New Zealand	Gambia	Somalia
Nicaragua	Ghana	South Sudan
Poland	Guinea	Sudan
Russia	Guinea-Bissau	Suriname
Sweden	Honduras	Taiwan
Switzerland	Hungary	Togo
Tanzania	Iceland	Uruguay
Thailand	Kenya	Zambia
Vietnam	Laos	Zimbabwe

Water stress measures total annual water withdrawals (municipal, industrial and agricultural) expressed as a percentage of the total annual available freshwater supplies. Higher values indicate more competition among users.
Source: Tianyi Luo, Robert Young and Paul Reig (2015), "Aqueduct Projected Water Stress Rankings," World Resources Institute, August, http://www.wri.org/sites/default/files/aqueduct-water-stress-country-rankings-technical-note.pdf (accessed June 7, 2018).

growth and development, worsen inequality, and increase the likelihood of civil unrest and conflicts.

Many regions and countries will be unable to escape the rising economic costs of harnessing more water resources for their growing economies and populations. As existing freshwater supplies dwindle, it will become increasingly expensive to develop alternative sources of supply and to deliver water to where it is needed most. New technologies for augmenting freshwater supplies, such as removing salt from seawater through desalination, are still not cost-effective on a large scale for many parts of the world. Instead, as available water from freshwater ecosystems and surface supplies fails to keep up with demand, the only cheap alternative is to extract "groundwater," the water found underground in aquifers. But available groundwater supplies are rapidly disappearing too, and the remaining supplies are harder to find and more costly to extract.

Simply put, in the near future, regions facing greater water stress and declining per-capita availability of supplies should expect the economic and social costs of exploiting more water resources to rise. The economic consequences for these affected regions are summarized by Meena Palaniappan and Peter Gleick:

> Because the costs of transporting bulk water from one place to another are so high, once a region's water use exceeds its renewable supply, it will begin tapping into non-renewable resources such as slow-recharge aquifers. Once extraction of water exceeds natural rates of replenishment, the only long-term options are to reduce demand to sustainable levels, move the demand to an area where water

is available, or shift to increasingly expensive sources, such as desalination.[23]

There is considerable evidence that the growing stresses on surface water supplies and freshwater ecosystems are leading to significant pressure on the "backstop" resource—groundwater. Some have argued that groundwater depletion is endangering global water security and, as a consequence, we already face a "global groundwater crisis."[24] Groundwater already accounts for one-third of total water withdrawals worldwide, and over 2 billion people rely on aquifers for their primary water source.[25] Unlike most surface water, however, groundwater often consists of fixed or isolated stocks that are consumed far faster than their slow rate of recharge. Thus, rapid depletion of these underground aquifers is a major concern worldwide.

There is also concern that the rising environmental and social costs of increasing water use and scarcity will deter economic growth and development. As water becomes increasingly scarce and remaining supplies less accessible, appropriating additional surface water requires more expensive investments in dams, pumping stations, pipelines and other supply infrastructure. Groundwater depletion also leads to rising costs, as falling underground levels require the digging of deeper wells and increased pumping of water.[26] At some point, the mounting environmental and social costs will become a "drag" on the overall economy, outweighing the productive benefits of increase water use and adversely affecting economic growth and development.[27] In many countries, and especially in developing economies, the problem is further exacerbated by socially inefficient water policies which fail to take into account the increasing costs of water use and scarcity.[28]

Growing global water scarcity and stress will also worsen inequality. As noted previously, significant numbers of the world's population still have inadequate water security. One in ten people lack access to safe water, and one in three do not have basic sanitation.[29] This suggests that huge disparities in access to and use of freshwater exist globally. While most populations in developed countries have achieved water security, the number of people who have adequate drinking water sources and sanitation varies widely among developing countries. Improving global coverage of these vital water services will mean further stress on available freshwater supplies in many countries and regions. Or, as is more likely, as the economic and social costs of securing future supplies increase, the disparities will grow even larger between those populations who can afford plentiful supplies for their drinking, sanitation and domestic needs and the poor without basic water and sanitation amenities.

We will also see increasing disputes over water, both within countries and between them. A major complication in global water management is that many countries share their sources of water, as river basins, large lakes, aquifers and other freshwater bodies often cross national boundaries. Such transboundary water sources are important for global supply. For example, two out of five people in the world live in international water basins shared by more than one country;[30] three or more countries share the water of fifty-three river basins worldwide; the Amazon River has seven countries sharing it, the Nile ten countries and the Danube seventeen.[31] Although the potential for armed conflict between countries over shared water resources remains low, cooperation to resolve disputes over water is often lacking.[32] In some cases, such as the shrinkage of Lake Chad in sub-Saharan Africa, the lack of cooperation is having a detrimental effect on the shared water system.[33] In south Asia, the 1996 Ganges River Treaty between India and Bangladesh may be in serious jeopardy because of projected future water uses relative to basin supply, unless it is extended to allow augmentation of river flows through water transfers from Nepal.[34] Equally worrisome, many international river basins and other shared water resources still lack any type of joint management structure, and some international agreements over joint management need to be updated or improved.[35]

A related problem is the increasing prevalence of "water grabbing" across the globe.[36] Countries with scarce water resources, large populations and sufficient wealth are investing in other countries to acquire fertile land and water resources to grow crops that can then be exported back to their own countries for domestic consumption. If countries in which freshwater is scarce, especially for growing food, can ease the demand on their water supplies by acquiring land in water-abundant countries, then such purchases or long-term leases lead to more efficient use of water and land for agricultural production globally. However, too often, the amount of water "grabbed" in this way is excessive, and there can be adverse impacts on food security and even malnourishment in the countries and regions that are the targets of water grabbing.[37] In addition, some of the countries that engage in water grabbing and trade do not face water scarcity or agricultural production constraints, and the large-scale investors and companies behind water grabbing are simply looking to make substantial profits from acquiring cheap water resources to grow exportable crops.[38] In the future, we should expect that a growing number of these land and water acquisitions will generate considerable conflict, through disputes about the legality of the expropriation, the basis of compensation, meeting the needs of local people for water, protecting the environmental integrity of ecosystems, and ensuring food security in targeted countries.[39]

To summarize, the rising costs of exploiting additional water resources will constrain economic growth and development, worsen inequality and increase the likelihood of civil unrest and conflicts. Averting a global water crisis is becoming increasingly difficult, and there is no simple solution. As the journalist H. L. Mencken once said, "For every complex problem there is an answer that is clear, simple, and wrong."[40]

But before we can begin formulating solutions, we have first to admit that such a problem exists. And, on top of that, we need to start urgently finding sensible solutions to managing water. However, no solutions are possible if we fail to heed the warning signs of our current mismanagement and use. In fact, this is the mystery of our relationship with water in the twenty-first century. Why we continue to ignore the impending threat of a global water crisis—despite water being the most essential resource for human existence and survival—is the great *water paradox* facing humankind today.

The Water Paradox

If the world is facing increasing risk of harmful water shortage and stress, then why are countries not mobilizing institutions, policies and technological innovations to avert this crisis? Water is growing increasingly scarce, yet we continue to act as if it will always be abundant.

Explaining this *water paradox* is the focus of this book. The main message is straightforward: The global water crisis is largely due to *inadequate and poor water management*. How this crisis came about, why it persists today, and what we can do to overcome it are the main topics that will be explored in subsequent chapters.

At the heart of the crisis in global water management is the persistent *underpricing of water*. The increasing environmental and social costs associated with freshwater scarcity are not routinely reflected in markets. Nor have we developed adequate policies and institutions to handle these costs. This means that economies do not have the correct price signals or incentives to adjust production and consumption activities to balance water use with supply, protect freshwater ecosystems and support necessary technological innovations. All too often, policy distortions and institutional and governance failures compound water scarcity by encouraging wasteful use of water and ecosystem degradation.

As depicted in Figure 0.2, this process has become a vicious cycle. Markets and policy decisions currently ignore the rising economic costs associated with exploiting more freshwater resources. This in turn leads to freshwater infrastructure and investments that result in higher environmental and social damages. These damages are reflected in increased depletion of water resources, pollution, degradation of freshwater ecosystems and, ultimately, rising water scarcity. But because the economic costs of this scarcity continue to be ignored in decision making, the consequences for current and future wellbeing are underestimated. The outcome is a vicious cycle, which poor institutions and inadequate governance structures perpetuate.

Figure 0.2 The Vicious Cycle of Excessive Water Use and Scarcity

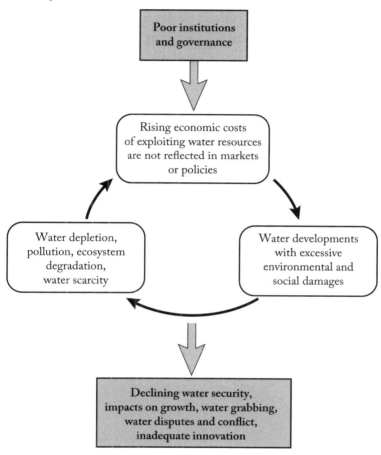

Exploring the key factors underlying this vicious cycle of water use and scarcity is the main aim of this book. Identifying these factors is important, but it is only one step toward formulating solutions. Unravelling the vicious cycle outlined in Figure 0.2 requires addressing some important questions. How can we reduce water depletion, pollution, ecosystem degradation and ultimately water scarcity, despite growing demand and competing uses for water? What are the institutions, governance and policies we need in order to ensure that markets adequately take into account the costs of excessive water exploitation? How do we foster the correct technological and engineering innovations to mitigate water scarcity?

Addressing these questions comes down to one fundamental objective: allocating scarce water resources to meet growing and competing uses. This requires assessing trade-offs and choices, which is what economics is all about. Thus, the first step in unravelling the vicious cycle of water use and scarcity is to take an "economic" approach to water management. To do this, we need to examine further the main economic characteristics of water that are essential to understanding the management challenges.

1

WATER AS AN ECONOMIC GOOD

In the past several decades, there has been greater recognition that how we manage water scarcity and its competing uses must change.

In January 1992, a group of experts met in Dublin, Ireland, to discuss water and its relationship to sustainable development. Called the International Conference on Water and the Environment (ICWE), the meeting was concerned with the growing problems of water scarcity, overexploitation and conflict. As it sought to grapple with the economic and social implications of these problems, the ICWE turned out to be a significant landmark in transforming humankind's approach to managing water.

This new perspective is reflected in the ICWE's 1992 Dublin Statement on Water and Sustainable Development, which declared as one of its core principles: "Water has an economic value in all its competing uses and should be recognized as an economic good."[1]

What does it mean to view water as an "economic good," and how does this characterization help us understand and overcome the challenges facing global water management? The Dublin Statement offers the following explanation: "Past failure to recognize the economic value of water has led to wasteful and environmentally damaging uses of the resource. Managing water as an economic good is an important way of achieving efficient and equitable use, and of encouraging conservation and protection of water resources."

This explanation may seem a little puzzling, especially given the mounting concerns over growing global water use that were outlined in the Introduction. If water is becoming increasingly scarce and a global water crisis is imminent, why has there been "past failure to recognize the economic value of water"? After all, water is the most essential of all natural resources for human life. We also have many valuable uses for water, as explained by the water economist Robert Griffin:

> Water is employed for such a great variety of things. We use it in our homes, businesses, and industries. We transport goods on it. We apply it to our crops and serve it to our livestock. We swim in it, fish in it, and recreate on it. We take pleasure in seeing and listening to it flow by. We directly generate power with it and cool our fossil fuel plants with it. We dump our wastes into it, relying on natural forces to transport and assimilate what we discard. Commercial fisheries, even offshore ones, depend on fresh water availability. Water is a vital substance for the maintenance of the environment, and the environment is similarly vital for supporting humankind.[2]

As we saw in the Introduction, these competing uses for water are growing worldwide, as populations increase and economies develop. In addition, water is not the free and abundant resource that it once was. Soon there may not be enough freshwater resources to meet all its uses. As a result, comparisons are being made between the "limits" to continuing water use and those of another economically vital natural resource—oil. And, increasingly, such comparisons suggest that we should be much more worried about the problem of water scarcity, as noted by water experts Meena Palaniappan and Peter Gleick:

> Real limits on water are far more worrisome, because water is fundamental for life, and for many uses, it has no substitutes. Absolute limits on affordable, accessible water will constrain the ability of regions to do certain things: in particular, limits to the availability of freshwater typically lead to the inability of a region to produce all the food required to meet domestic needs, and hence lead to a reliance on international markets for food.[3]

In sum, water has many valuable uses, yet there may not be enough available for all these uses, or at least not without incurring more and more costs. Such a situation is a familiar one in economics—the allocation of a scarce resource to meet competing uses. It requires considering the tradeoffs involved in choosing how best to allocate water among its different uses. For example, if we want to increase the amount of water for agricultural irrigation, there will be less available for urban domestic, business and industrial use. And, if we want to expand freshwater supplies to meet both growing agricultural and urban demand, we should take into account all the economic and environmental costs of increasing and delivering these supplies to meet this demand. That is, if freshwater is less affordable and accessible, then we would expect this rising scarcity to be reflected in higher costs for all uses of water.

If water is an "economic good," then our institutions for managing water—markets, policies and governance—should ensure that scarce water is allocated to its most valuable competing use. Rising freshwater scarcity would mean that all users of water would pay higher costs. In such a situation, freshwater scarcity would not get worse or impose limits on water use. Instead, any increasing scarcity would be temporary, and, as the Dublin Statement points out, the resulting higher costs would be "an important way of achieving efficient and equitable use, and of encouraging conservation and protection of water resources."

Unfortunately, as discussed in the Introduction, humankind is facing a water paradox. While water has so many valuable uses, our basic market, policy and governance institutions are failing to manage it adequately to meet these uses. That is why the global water crisis is really a crisis in global water management. At the heart of this crisis is persistent underpricing—the failure to treat water as an economic good. The increasing environmental and social costs associated with freshwater scarcity are not routinely reflected in markets. Nor have we developed adequate policies and institutions to handle these costs. This means that economies do not have the correct price signals or incentives to adjust production and consumption activities so as to balance water use with supply, protect freshwater ecosystems and support necessary technological innovations. All too often, policy distortions and institutional and governance failures compound water scarcity by encouraging wasteful use of water and ecosystem degradation.

Physical and Economic Attributes of Water

One reason why it has been difficult to develop adequate policy, market and governance institutions to manage water resources is the nature of the resource itself. Water has an unusual set of physical and economic attributes that makes it different from most commodities, including other natural resources. This is easily seen by comparing water to another strategically important natural resource in modern economies—oil.

Oil is, for example, a fully marketable commodity. The rights to extract and produce oil are purchased by private companies, it is an international commodity traded in markets, and there is generally a well-defined price for the resource all over the world. Which means, when there is conflict in the Middle East, a rise in gasoline demand, an extremely cold winter, an expansion in electricity generation or any other factor that causes physical supplies of oil to fall short of rising demand, that all users of oil will face higher prices. In other words, the price that most users pay for oil will reflect its scarcity value.

In contrast, as explained by the economist Michael Hanemann, water is marketed and priced very differently, and, as a consequence, the "price" paid for using water has little to do with its scarcity:

It is important to emphasize that the prices which most users pay for water reflect, at best, its physical supply cost and not its scarcity value. Users pay for the capital and operating costs of the water supply infrastructure but, in the USA and many other countries, there is no charge for the water per se. Water is owned by the state, and the right to use it is given away for free. Water is thus treated differently than oil, coal, or other minerals for which the USA government requires payment of a royalty to extract the resource. While some European countries, including England, France, Germany and Holland, do levy an abstraction charge for water, these charges tend to be in the nature of administrative fees and are not generally based on an assessment of the economic value of the water being withdrawn. Thus, in places where water is cheap, this is almost always because the infrastructure is inexpensive, or the water is being subsidized, rather than because the water per se is especially abundant.[4]

To understand why water is so different from oil and other natural resource commodities, it is worth exploring further the contrasting physical and economic characteristics of water compared to oil.

The Physical Resource

Oil is a finite, fixed resource that is a classic example of a non-renewable (stock) resource. Once underground reserves of oil are discovered, and drilling begins, the oil is extracted as a flow from this fixed stock. As a non-renewable underground stock, oil is not very mobile, and oil reserves do not naturally fluctuate in supply.

In contrast, with water, only groundwater supplies—those found in underground deposits or aquifers, in sands, gravels and rocks —are considered non-renewable stocks because of their slow recharge rate. Much of our available freshwater resource lies above ground, in lakes, rivers, streams and other water bodies. And this surface water is generally viewed as a renewable resource, because it is frequently renewed through local water cycling and flows.

Water is also highly mobile and available supplies fluctuate considerably. Water does not stay in one place: it flows, evaporates, seeps and transpires. This makes it difficult to measure and even capture the resource, and means that its available supplies fluctuate wildly, especially for surface water. The seasonal cycles of precipitation and stream flows that replenish water bodies are difficult to predict and control. This variability in turn means that there can be times when there is too much water, which can lead to disasters such as flooding, or there may be too little water, in which case there is a risk of prolonged drought. In the case of groundwater, the resource may not fluctuate seasonally, but it is often difficult to know how much water is contained in underground aquifers or how fast they are naturally recharging.

Another unusual feature of water is that it is highly solvent. That means a lot of substances—from human and animal sewage to toxic chemicals—are easily dissolved in it. This makes water an ideal medium for assimilating pollution and waste. Unfortunately, water quality can vary substantially in different locations. Thus, water that is plentiful in supply may not be of sufficient quality for some important uses, such as for human or animal consumption or for use in irrigation.

The Economic Resource

These physical features of water have important economic implications. Because water is so highly variable and mobile, it is difficult to locate, measure and capture. As a result, claiming or enforcing exclusive property rights over water can be problematic, which makes it hard to "market." Even when rights can be established, if there is uncertainty over the availability of water, it is challenging to know how much to extract and sell. Equally, some uses for water, notably irrigation in agriculture, are often intermittent. Crops need to be watered only in certain periods or seasons, and the amount used may fluctuate significantly. This encourages farmers to share their access to water, and discourages one individual from claiming exclusive ownership to supply it to other farmers.

In addition, like many liquids, water is extremely bulky and thus difficult to transport long distances. Some of these commodities, such as oil, are worth a lot of money—today (July 11, 2018), oil is $65 a barrel—and thus are worth the expense of transporting all over the world. Unlike oil, however, the value of water relative to its weight tends to be extremely low. Thus its transportation costs are very high compared to the value of most of its end uses. Compared to transporting a more valuable liquid such as oil, developing expensive transportation networks to transport water a long way across regions and even countries is too costly.

The high cost of storing, conveying, transporting and distributing water means that it is susceptible to *scale economies*. The problems of mobility and variability of water can be overcome by investing in facilities to store, convey and distribute it in large quantities, but such infrastructure is too expensive for many individual users. The only way to manage such costs is to build the necessary infrastructure on a sufficient scale so that the fixed costs of these investments are spread over larger amounts of stored and distributed water. This will ensure that the average costs of delivering water to users will fall. But achieving such scale economies requires large upfront investments that only a public authority or a single private entity can afford. Consequently, water is generally supplied publicly or through regulation of a single private investor (i.e., a monopoly).

How water is used is also unique to the resource. Oil is completely consumed when it is used, especially if it is burned to provide energy. This also means that the amount of oil consumed by one user is not available for someone else. In contrast, much water use is sequential, and it is not often fully consumed by the first user. For example, the water contained in a river may be extracted by many users as it flows from the upper watershed to its eventual end in a floodplain or ocean. Water may be withdrawn from the river by upstream users, through pumping, diversion and other methods of extraction, but there can also be a lot of return flow of water back to the river during upstream use. This return flow to the river is then available for other users further downstream. In fact, some uses of water, such as hydroelectric power generation, transportation and recreation, do not require any withdrawals of surface water. Water for these purposes is neither withdrawn from the source nor consumed.

However, the sequential use of water may have another impact, which is to affect the quality of the water. The return flow of water from upstream users on a river may be significantly degraded in quality, if it is polluted or its temperature is changed. This may create significant problems for downstream users, especially if they require water to be sufficiently clean for health and sanitation reasons. Thus, the quality of water available after sequential use may be even more important than the quantity.

Water Can Be Both a Private and a Public Good

Many of these characteristics of water mean that it is sometimes a *private good* but it can also be a *public good*. Economists usually distinguish such goods based on two properties: *rivalry* and *excludability* in use or consumption. When a good is *rival*, then one person's use of the good reduces the amount available for everybody else. When a good is *exclusive*, then one user can exclude others from consuming the good at the same time. Private goods have both these properties. But if a user can neither exclude another from using a good nor reduce the amount of that good that is available to everybody, then that commodity is a public good.

Again, oil is a good example of a private good. The gasoline I purchase for my car is exclusive for me to use, and the amount I consume means less gas is available for other car owners.[5] In comparison, whether water is a private or a public good will depend on how it is used and the specific context for that use.

For example, once water is delivered and used in homes, factories and farms, it has the characteristic of a private good. Each user has exclusive rights to the water, and how much is used reduces the amount available to others. Any water in the reservoir or delivery network is also a private good. Use of this water is exclusive, and there is less available in the reservoir or network for others. However, the storage capacity of the reservoir is likely to be a public good. It is maintained by natural water flow, possibly from a river discharging into the reservoir. Although this flow may vary with season and precipitation, continual use of the storage capacity over a period of time should not diminish the amount of total capacity available. And, assuming there is sufficient capacity, there is no exclusion of users of this capacity. In fact, a large reservoir could be employed for a variety of uses simultaneously, such as for drinking water, sanitation, industrial use, recreation and navigation.

Many nonconsumptive uses of water are also public goods. Water-based recreation and navigation on rivers and lakes do not rely on water withdrawals, and even hydroelectricity generation may not necessarily involve permanent extraction of water. These uses do not preclude the same water being employed for other purposes, and have negligible impact on the total water available. Water is also an important aquatic habitat for plants and wildlife, which an individual may enjoy without excluding others or diminishing their enjoyment.

One of the most important public goods is improvement in water quality, such as through abating pollution, removing sediment or controlling temperature extremes. Some aquatic habitats might provide these services naturally, through purifying water, regulating temperature and trapping eroded soils. Often, human treatment and sanitation infrastructure is required to improve water quality. Regardless of how it occurs, however, any resulting improvement in water is generally a public good. If I live by a lake that has had a reduction in pollution, any benefits I receive from the cleaner lake water do not reduce the benefits of the clean water to others, and all of us are free to enjoy these benefits simultaneously.

In some cases, water may be neither completely a private nor a public good, but something in between.[6] For instance, under certain circumstances, water may still be rival but not exclusive, in which case it is a *common pool resource*. Two important cases of this situation that we will explore throughout this book are groundwater depletion and river management.

Recall that groundwater stocks often recharge slowly, and thus they are effectively a nonrenewable resource. On the one hand, this means that extracting water from aquifers for irrigation or household use will reduce the amount available for others to use. But the size and extent of groundwater stocks beneath the surface are often unknown. It is difficult for one farmer who is extracting groundwater for irrigation to exclude other famers from using the same resource. Equally, many homes could be simultaneously drilling wells to use groundwater from a single aquifer. Thus, many groundwater sources are common pool resources.

Rivers also have a long history of being treated as common pool resources, mainly to keep them free for navigation or to prevent individual users from controlling the supply. In addition, rivers are the most variable and mobile of surface water resources, and, as a result, it is often difficult to identify, measure or even capture the resource. Establishing exclusive ownership by an individual or even a group of individuals is nearly impossible. In fact, since Roman times, claiming exclusive ownership of rivers has been legally prohibited. For rivers and other flowing waters, and even sometimes lakes, these resources may not be owned but can only be used. In some cases, these "rights of use" are strictly allocated and regulated, but in other circumstances and locations they are not, which in turn can complicate the management of these common pool resources.

Treating water resources and uses as public goods or common pool resources has two important consequences: they will be *undersupplied* by individuals and *undervalued* in markets. Take the example of cleaning up lake pollution. If I pay for the removal of pollution from a lake, then I will benefit from the resulting improvement in water quality. But so will other users of the lake. The difference is that they will have little incentive to pay for the pollution removal, because I will have already done so. I may decide that it might be worthwhile making such an investment anyway. But, more often than not, because removing pollution from water is likely to be an expensive process, and I know that I am not able to charge others for this benefit, I will probably not be willing or able to invest in reducing lake pollution. As other individuals using the lake will probably reach the same conclusion as I have, the pollution cleanup will not occur. Or, to use the language of economics, water quality improvement will be undersupplied, if left to individuals to make such an improvement.

Public goods are also undervalued in markets, which exist for private goods but rarely for public goods. For example, aquatic habitats such as wetlands provide diverse benefits that are often public goods, including breeding or refuge for unique species, recreation, hunting and tourism, or purification of water supplies. These benefits are enjoyed simultaneously by many people and are provided to them for "free" by the natural functioning of the wetlands. As a result, there is no "market" and thus no "price" for these public good uses of wetlands. But the actual value of these services is not zero. Because many people benefit from these services, their value is the total additional benefits of all individuals who enjoy provision of these services by wetlands. This value could be huge, even though there is no apparent "market price" for these wetland services. This gap between the (zero) price for wetland services and their actual value to all beneficiaries indicates how much these public goods are undervalued in markets.

Finally, individuals who do not use a water resource for irrigation, recreation or drinking supplies may still additionally benefit if the resource is not degraded or depleted. These individuals may still value the resource, even though they may never use, visit or even see it, simply because they value its existence or they believe the resource should be available for use by future generations. Such *non-use values* also have no "market" or "price," yet they can be significant especially for some unique water resources and habitats—such as the Great Lakes in the US and Canada, the Okavango Delta in Africa and the Danube River in Europe. For these habitats and other important water resources, the non-use values could be substantially large components of the benefits provided by such public goods.

Use It or Lose It

One implication of the unique physical and economic characteristics of water is that it has encouraged a "use it or lose it" approach worldwide. Because it is so difficult to establish exclusive property rights over water, and there are so many competing uses, the "first user" of water has a strong incentive to hoard and use as much as possible. By obtaining initial access to the water, the first user may also have priority in use over others. However, unless this water allocation is fully utilized, the right to use the water might be revoked. Another user will then claim first rights over it. Hence, the "use it or lose it" incentive is ingrained in all potential users of water.

In some parts of the world, including throughout the western United States and in many developing countries, this "use it or lose it" approach to water rights is enshrined in law. For example, the United States has the doctrine of *prior appropriation*, which was adopted for surface water by every western state beginning in the nineteenth century. Called the "first in time, first in right" rule, prior appropriation allows individuals to claim, divert and use water based on priority of claim. The priority, or most senior, water right goes to whoever first diverts water from a lake, river or stream and puts the water to beneficial use. Subsequent claimants on the water have lower priority, or junior rights. The result is a "ladder of water rights." In times of drought, for example, users of a body of water that are more junior may be left without any water if the first claimants exercise their prior right over any available water. But claims on water are also established on the basis of "beneficial use," whereby all priority users must demonstrate that the amount claimed is necessary for some "approved" application, such as irrigation for crops, watering livestock, mining, domestic, industrial and municipal supplies, and so forth. As noted by the economist Gary Libecap, "beneficial use, however, contributes to waste as rights holders devote intensively to low-marginal value 'approved' applications in order to maintain ownership and neglect higher-marginal value uses that may not be considered consistent with the doctrine, which is a political decision."[7]

The "use it or lose it" incentive also pervades management of *transboundary water resources*. A major complication in global water management is that many countries share their sources of water, as river basins, large lakes, aquifers and other freshwater bodies often cross national boundaries, and such transboundary water bodies are an important, and growing, source of water for many people, countries and regions.[8] With transboundary waters, and especially international and regional rivers, "first use" is invariably determined by geography. A country, state or province that is located in the upper watershed, or upstream, will have first claim on the water by default. This priority can be easily established through building the necessary infrastructure to capture, store and thus retain water that flows through its territory. In contrast, the political entities located in the lower watershed, or downstream, can claim only the remaining water that is released by the upstream claimant. The upstream country, state or province therefore has an incentive to use as much of the water as possible, which also yields an advantage in any subsequent negotiations with downstream neighbors over managing the transboundary water source.

Prior appropriation law and transboundary water resources are just two examples where the "use it or lose it" incentive deters effective and efficient water management. This incentive is symptomatic of the general failure to allocate available freshwater resources to meet growing and competing beneficial uses, and poses a major challenge to more efficient and equitable water management. Before we address this challenge, it is helpful to explore how humankind's complex relationship with water evolved historically to create today's water paradox. As we shall see in the next chapter, the historical roots of this relationship are a significant reason why our current institutions for managing water—markets, policies and governance—fail to ensure that scarce water today is treated as an "economic good."

2

HUMANKIND AND WATER

Today's water paradox did not just happen over a few years or even decades. Its roots have a long history. Exploring this history is important, as humankind's complex relationship with water has changed considerably. These changes have impacted our key market, policy and governance institutions, and have affected major technical innovations. Understanding how the incentives, institutions and innovations that govern our use of water in the present day evolved from past eras is critical to overcoming our current failure to manage water as a valuable and scarce resource.

There is a significant difference between how water is managed and used for economic development today compared to past eras. Starting with the Agricultural Transition around 10,000 years ago, economic development was spurred by harnessing more water resources. Rather than threatening sustainable development, exploiting and controlling water resources was the key to building successful and long-lasting economies. This historical relationship between water and development is summarized by Steven Solomon:

> Throughout history, whenever water resources have been increased and made more manageable, navigable, and potable, societies have generally been robust and long-enduring. Those that succeeded in significantly increasing their command and supply were regularly among the few that broke out of history's normative condition of changelessness and bare subsistence to enjoy spurts of prosperity, political vigor, and even momentary preeminence. Often major water innovations leveraged the economic, population and territorial expansions that animated world history. Those unable to overcome the challenge of being farthest removed from access to the best water resources, by contrast, were invariably among history's poor.[1]

Although the relationship between exploiting water resources and economic development has changed, many of our water institutions and innovations have not. Water may appear to be cheap, but it is only artificially so. Instead, our current market, policy and governance institutions underprice it, and so we continue to use water excessively as if it were not scarce. Most of our innovations are also geared toward expanding our command and control of water resources, not toward reducing use as our economies develop.

As we shall see in this chapter, our current water institutions and innovations are largely relics of past historical eras, when development was dependent on finding and exploiting more water resources. The overarching premise was that water is always abundant, available and necessary for fostering development. The persistence of these water institutions and innovations means that they are inadequate and insufficient for managing our current global water problems, which are a reflection of growing freshwater scarcity. As economic historians have emphasized, institutions tend to be the "carriers of history," and in the case of water, this institutional "path dependency" works against sound management today.[2]

To illustrate this process, this chapter highlights key historical changes in water institutions and innovations that continue to shape water and development. In essence, we will explore how humankind's complex relationship with water evolved historically to create today's water paradox.

The Agricultural Transition and the Rise of Early Civilizations

A good starting point is the Agricultural Transition, when the emergence and spread of agriculture globally were tied to access to water resources as well as innovations in irrigation and other nascent water infrastructure.[3] The transition to agriculture, which gradually unfolded from 12,000 to 5,000 years ago, has been described as "the most important of all human interventions to date," even surpassing trade and manufacture in its economic significance.[4] Almost all of today's domestic crops and animals originate from this era, in which agriculture first emerged as the predominant global food production system. Although very gradual, so profound were the changes that occurred during the Agricultural Transition that it is usually associated with the start of human economic and social development, as noted by the archaeologist and prehistorian Steven Mithen:

38

Human history began in 50,000 BC ... Little of significance happened until 20,000 BC—people simply continued living as hunter-gatherers, just as their ancestors
had been doing for millions of years ... Then came an
astonishing 15,000 years that saw the origin of farming,
towns and civilizations. By 5000 BC the foundations of
the modern world had been laid and nothing that came
after—classical Greece, the Industrial Revolution, the
atomic age, the Internet—has matched the significance
of those events.[5]

Starting around 10,000 years ago, domestication of plants
and animals occurred independently over thousands of years
in various parts of the ancient world: the Fertile Crescent of
southwest Asia, the Yellow and Yangtze river basins of China,
central Mexico, the central Andes and Amazonia, and the
eastern United States.[6] From these original "homelands"
agriculture spread to other parts of the world, by hunter-
gatherers either acquiring and adopting agricultural methods
or being displaced by migrating farmers. Between 10,000 and
3,000 years ago, farming proliferated widely, limited only by
"natural barriers" imposed by oceans, mountains, deserts and
inhospitable climates.

Changing climatic conditions, coupled with access to
water-rich habitats, influenced the transition to agriculture
in at least three regions, the Fertile Crescent, the eastern
United States and sub-Saharan Africa.[7] For example, the
archaeologist Bruce Smith argues that cooler and drier
weather during this era "contributed to a steepening of the
environmental gradients between rich waterside habitat areas
and outlying dryer zones less able to sustain hunter-gatherer

societies, especially sedentary ones."[8] The result is that the landscape for human habitat became patchy: relatively affluent and sedentary hunter-gatherer societies became concentrated in low-lying resource-rich zones located near rivers, lakes, marshes and springs with abundant animals, plants and aquatic species, surrounded by more arid and resource-poor environmental zones that were sparsely populated. Eventually, populations located in some favorable water and resource-rich zones would begin "to search widely for ways of reducing long-term risk," and one obvious strategy would be "to experiment with ways of increasing the reliability of promising species." These conditions may have occurred at different times in the Fertile Crescent, the eastern United States and sub-Saharan Africa, but Smith concludes that the outcome was ultimately the same: "In these three areas, seed plants were domesticated by affluent societies living in sedentary settlements adjacent to rivers, lakes, marshes and springs, locations that would have offered both abundant animal protein—in the form of fish and waterfowl, for example—and well-watered soils for secure harvests."

Smith also suggests that "other regions of the world seem to fit this general pattern." For example, early millet and rice farmers emerged among relatively prosperous societies settled along the resource-rich river and lake systems of the Yangtze and Yellow river basins. The south-central Andes might also fit this pattern, where the main center of domestication appears to have been river and lake environments at lower elevations compared to the high sierras. Similarly in Mexico, "the evidence of domestication recovered from higher-elevation caves sites such as those in Tamaulipas and Tehuacán reflects a transition to a farming way of life that took place largely in a lower-elevation river valley setting rich in resources."

Once agriculture was established in these various regions, it spread rapidly to neighboring areas and beyond. Environmental conditions appear to have played an important part in determining this diffusion, with the most critical factor again being rainfall and access to water-rich habitats. For example, the spread of agriculture in Africa from Lake Victoria to Natal occurred despite a 30-degree change in latitude across climate zones that varied from tropical to temperate; however, rainfall seasonality changed very little across these zones. Similarly, the movement of agriculture from central Mexico to North America involved a 12-degree change in latitude and required skirting desert barriers, but it was facilitated by similar rainfall conditions throughout the region. In comparison, the expansion of farming from Baluchistan to Haryana occurred along the same latitude but was hampered by a change in rainfall seasonality.[9] Thus the proximity of regions with abundant land rich in favorable soils and rainfall, and access to water resources suitable for early farming techniques, appears to have spurred the rapid spread of agriculture.

In the rich and productive floodplains of southwest Asia, innovations such as irrigation and the development of key agricultural commodities led to the creation of surpluses that were instrumental to the beginnings of urbanization, manufacturing and trade. By around 5,000 BC, these favorable water-rich regions developed agricultural-based economies that could support large, urban-based populations engaged in non-food production activities such as manufacturing, commerce and defense. Irrigation and other water innovations became instrumental to harnessing more water resources, in response to growing population and economic pressures on limited land and water resources.

For example, vast irrigation networks were developed in the Tigris–Euphrates river basin and the Nile River valley to support the emerging city-states around 5,000 years ago. However, over the next millennium and a half, population pressures coupled with climatic changes required a range of innovations. These included new irrigation projects and canals, subterranean water systems to harness groundwater for irrigation and supply water to cities, facilities for storing grain surpluses, the draining of marshes and lakes to expand agricultural land area, and the construction of terraces and other conservation structures to prevent erosion on existing arable land. Rainfed agriculture and herding in the surrounding semi-arid areas also had to adapt to the changes in climate and seasonal rainfall. Throughout the Near East, in response to drier conditions and prolonged periods of drought, "each of the human societies underwent profound changes and was forced to invent new methods to cope with the scarcity of water and food."[10] Innovation in response to this scarcity continued to be a key factor in the rise of Islamic states that precipitated the "Golden Age of Islam" (AD 1000–1492).

Diverting water for irrigation was also critical to the rise of early imperial dynasties in China. Early millet and rice farmers first emerged along the relatively resource-rich river and lake systems of the Yangtze and Yellow river basins. Settlement in these fertile regions was based largely around floodplain agriculture initially, which became the basis for the first empires in China around 4,000 years ago.[11] Floodplain agriculture and settlements in the upland river basins were systematically augmented through drainage and cultivation of the huge inland marshes and eventually linked by a system of artificial canals and waterways. However, with the growing demand for agricultural land for rice cultivation, reclaiming land from the lowlands and river deltas in south China became the only option. Starting in the tenth century AD, the establishment of dams and artificial reservoirs not only controlled flooding and provided fresh drinking water to sustain large farming populations in the reclaimed lowlands and deltas but also enabled the large-scale supply of regulated irrigation water. These developments led over the next 400 years to the conversion of the lowlands into rice paddy systems by the construction of enclosures. The resulting water-led boost to rice production, agricultural development and transportation became the dominant economic "engine" sustaining the great Chinese empires from AD 1000 to 1500.[12]

The development of irrigated rice cultivation was also critical to the emergence of powerful Indian states in the Ganges River valley from 800 to 500 BC.[13] This region was largely covered by tropical forests, which were impenetrable to farmers until iron tools were widely available. Once cleared, the land in the lush floodplains with plentiful surface water was ideal for irrigated rice cultivation, through the use of the same terraced paddy rice techniques employed by the Chinese. The result was a highly productive, sedentary agricultural system that could support and sustain a new urban-based civilization— perhaps the first of its kind based on large-scale agricultural conversion of a natural tropical forest ecosystem.

The historian Karl Wittfogel has emphasized the key role of scarce water supplies, irrigation and large-scale agricultural development in the rise of early city-states and empires.[14] His "hydraulic hypothesis" maintains that the need to control scarce water supplies for agriculture in semi-arid environments was critical for the growth and social development of highly centralized and despotic empires. That is, because irrigation under such environmental conditions required substantial and centralized control, elites monopolized political power and dominated the economy, resulting in the emergence of stratified and complexly organized societies. Although many small-scale irrigation societies also evolved around the world without developing into large, irrigation-based empires, most civilizations comprised agricultural-based and centralized states dependent on harnessing vast amounts of water.[15] In other words, the beginning of human "civilization"—and thus modern economies and societies—stems fundamentally from managing water for large-scale agricultural production.

Because the control and use of water resources were critical to the rise of the first great city-states and civilizations, many of these early agricultural-based empires were prone to water overuse and mismanagement, which meant they were frequently vulnerable to climate change, drought, soil salinity, river and canal silting, and flooding. Table 2.1 provides examples of major early civilizations that experienced a number of environmental stresses, including water-related impacts. Often, these stresses were interlinked and arose through complex patterns of climate change and environmental degradation over decades and even centuries. For example, from 2500 to 500 BC, the climate of southwest Asia became warmer and drier. Annual rainfall declined and droughts became more frequent. As a result, the areas of fertile land suitable for agriculture diminished and were restricted mainly to river valleys and floodplains. Even these fertile lowland areas were prone to land degradation from the increase in

Table 2.1 Civilizations and Major Environmental Stresses, 3000 BC–AD 1000

Civilization	Period	Major sources of environmental degradation
Sumer, southern Mesopotamia *	2200–1700 BC	Soil salinity; land degradation; deforestation; river and canal silting
Egypt, Nile Valley †	2200–1700 BC	Deforestation; land degradation; soil salinity; wildlife extinction
Harappa, Indus Valley *	1800–1500 BC	Land degradation; overgrazing; salinity; deforestation; flooding
Greek city-states *	*ca.* 500–200 BC	Deforestation; soil erosion; river silting; flooding; pollution
Chin and Han dynasties, China ‡	221 BC–AD 220	Deforestation; flooding; erosion; river silting; wildlife extinction
Roman Empire *	AD 200–500	Land degradation; deforestation; soil erosion; river silting; air and water pollution; lead poisoning; wildlife extinction
Various dynasties, China Δ	AD 600–1000	Deforestation; flooding; erosion; river silting
Various empires, Japan *	AD 600–850	Deforestation; flooding; erosion; river silting
Maya, Central America ≈	AD 830–930	Land degradation; erosion; deforestation; river silting; weed incursion

Notes: Period refers to either the approximate period of decline of the civilization and/or when evidence of extensive human-induced environmental damage is cited.
Sources: * Sing C. Chew (2001), *World Ecological Degradation: Accumulation, Urbanization, and Deforestation 3000 BC–AD 2000* (Walnut Creek, CA: Altamira Press).
† Sing C. Chew (2006), "Dark Ages: Ecological Crisis Phases and System Transition," in Barry K. Gills and William R. Thompson, eds., *Globalization and Global History* (New York: Routledge), pp. 163–202; Donald J. Hughes (2001), *An Environmental History of the World: Humankind's Changing Role in the Community of Life* (London: Routledge).

‡ Mark Elvin (1993), "Three Thousand Years of Unsustainable Growth: China's Environment from Archaic Time to the Present," *East Asian History* 6, 7–46; Hughes (2001).
Δ Elvin (1993); and John R. McNeill (1998), "Chinese Environmental History in World Perspective," in Mark Elvin and Liu Ts'ui-jung, eds., *Sediments of Time: Environment and Society in Chinese History* (Cambridge, England: Cambridge University Press), pp. 31–49.
≈ T. Patrick Culbert (1988), "The Collapse of Classic Maya Civilization," in Norman Yoffee and George L. Cowgill, eds., *The Collapse of Ancient States and Civilizations* (Tucson: University of Arizona Press), pp. 69–101; Hughes (2001).

crop cultivation. Overirrigation led to salinization of arable land and saltwater intrusion in water tables. Changing river courses and periodic drought affected the availability of surface water for farming, and the rivers and canals constructed to divert water gradually became silted.[16]

It is possible that such a process of environmental degradation was an important factor in the collapse of the first great civilization of Sumer in southern Mesopotamia. As the various city-state empires of Sumer emerged, grew and expanded their territory between 3400 and 1000 BC, the limited irrigated land along the Tigris and Euphrates rivers struggled to sustain production to feed the growing population. Drier climates and variable rainfall not only reduced river flow and limited the availability of arable floodplain area but also contributed to the increased salinity of irrigated agricultural lands by raising groundwater levels. Despite their declining agricultural productivity and the limited availability of arable land, the floodplains nonetheless remained sufficiently fertile compared to the surrounding desert regions to attract repeated incursions by the growing number of neighboring nomadic peoples. It was these invasions that ultimately doomed Sumer.[17]

Changing environmental conditions, including climate change and water scarcity, may have precipitated numerous nomad invasions to find new lands through conquering agricultural-based empires. As first noted by the historian Arnold Toynbee, changing climate and environments were often responsible for the repeated incursions by Eurasian steppe nomads into Europe and west Asia that began in the second millennium BC.[18] Warmer and wetter periods led to better grazing and thus to increased herd sizes and populations of nomads; on the other hand, a reduction in arid conditions on the steppes also encouraged encroachment by sedentary agricultural populations seeking new land suitable for crops and pasture. A shift to drier and cooler conditions could also cause conflicts. In such periods, rival nomadic peoples would fight for dwindling grazing, forage and water resources. The losers would be forced to migrate to new territory, and this would often be inhabited or controlled by sedentary agriculture societies and civilizations. Similar environmental changes are thought to have spurred nomadic tribes from the surrounding desert to periodically invade the Nile valley of ancient Egypt.[19]

Innovations and Institutions in Water-Abundant and Water-Scarce Regions

Appropriating and harnessing water resources became important to the success of many early civilizations and empires. Those with access to abundant freshwater supplies became adept at developing new innovations and institutions to aid this process. For those societies in more water-scarce regions, adapting to harsh and changing environmental conditions became important for avoiding overuse and mismanagement of water that could precipitate major social catastrophes and even collapse.

In water-abundant regions, an important innovation was the establishment of dams, artificial reservoirs, canals and waterways to control flooding, provide fresh drinking water for growing urban populations, transport people and produce, and, above all, supply large-scale regulated irrigation to promote agricultural expansion. These innovations were especially crucial to sustaining successive Chinese empires from AD 1000 to 1500, starting with the rich and powerful centralized empire created by the Sung Dynasty from 979 to 1276. Its first priority was management of China's interior waterways and rivers.[20] Development of canals, waterways and an inland water transport system, as well as investments in flood control, dams, land reclamation projects and irrigation networks, were publicly funded ventures. The main source of these public investments was government tax revenues, virtually all of which came from levies on agricultural production. The investments in turn provided cheap and safe transportation along China's waterways, facilitated the movement of agricultural products over long distances across the empire, and provided greater incentives for expansion of agricultural cultivation into new frontier areas. And, of course, the resulting increases in agricultural output meant more revenues for the imperial state.[21] Investments in improved transportation, especially of waterways, facilitated the marketing and taxation of surpluses, increasing the demand for money as a "medium of exchange" and the expansion of commercial services and trade.

Ancient Rome also pioneered several important innovations, including the vertical water wheel for grinding grain into flour, hydraulic pressure for mining, and the use of water for concrete. The latter invention was also instrumental in the development of one of the most famous Roman inventions— the aqueduct. As noted by Steven Solomon, the city-state built "an extensive network of aqueducts that enabled Rome to access, convey, and manage prodigious supplies of wholesome freshwater for drinking, bathing and sanitation on a scale exceeding anything realized before in human history and without which its giant metropolis would not have been possible."[22] The aqueduct system not only sustained and housed a population of around 1 million but also provided each inhabitant with 570–760 liters per day to use, which compares favorably to water availability in urban centers up to modern times.[23] The Romans also quickly learned that the abundant flow of water into the city also facilitated the outflow of wastewater. They developed gravity-fed sewer systems that carried waste away from the city on a constant supply of flowing water to rivers.[24] This system of aqueduct water supply and sewage system was replicated in emerging urban centers throughout the Roman Empire, and remained largely unrivaled until more modern times.

Innovation and institutions in response to scarce freshwater supplies were also essential for sustaining important empires in arid and semi-arid regions, most notably the rise of Islamic states to global economic dominance from AD 700 to 1500. By the time of his death in 632, the prophet Mohammed had succeeded in uniting under Islam almost the entire Arabian peninsula. Within the next hundred years, his followers established a large Islamic empire from India and central Asia across the Middle East and north Africa to Spain. This empire, which quickly splintered into a loose collection of independent states, or "caliphates," included the former centers of ancient civilizations, the Tigris–Euphrates river basins and the Nile River valleys. Thus the new Islamic empire faced the same freshwater scarcity problems as the older civilizations that it had assimilated: how best to manage these scarce water resources to sustain growing populations and economies.

These severe freshwater constraints were overcome through several key innovations that facilitated the development and diffusion of new crops and farming systems ideally suited to the limited water resources available for irrigated agriculture across north Africa, the Middle East and west Asia.[25] The new crops varieties included fruit trees (e.g., citrus, banana, plantain and mango), cash crops (e.g., sugar cane, coconut palm, watermelon and cotton), grains (e.g., sorghum, Asiatic rice and hard wheat) and vegetables (e.g., spinach, artichoke and eggplant). The Islamic states also grew new plants cultivated chiefly as sources of fibers, condiments, beverages, medicines, narcotics, poisons, dyes, perfumes, cosmetics, wood and fodder. Growing these industrial and food crops on a large scale in turn required major improvements in irrigation systems, especially during the peak summer months of the growing season when rainfall was scarce. This led to state-led investments and innovations in constructing dams, water storage and other hydraulic improvements, developing new techniques for catching, channeling, storing and lifting surface water, and tapping aquifers through wells, underground canals and pipes. The rulers of the Islamic state benefited greatly from these hydrological investments through two sources of additional revenues: taxes on the additional water use and taxes on the additional cultivated land and harvests resulting from irrigation.[26]

Agricultural production and land expansion were also promoted through changes in land use and taxation. Private ownership of land was protected by law, and agricultural land became a fully marketed commodity. Water rights, especially access to irrigation, were also marketable. Such commercialization facilitated the selling off of inefficient large estates into smaller units. As noted by the historian Andrew Watson, "The end result was to endow the early Islamic world with an extensive patchwork of irrigated lands . . . The available water resources were generally used to the full extent allowed by known technology. In many regions it would be only a slight exaggeration to say that there was hardly a river, stream, oasis, spring, known aquifer or predictable flood that was not fully exploited—although not always by irrigators, who had to compete with urban and domestic users."[27]

Agricultural development in western Europe from the eleventh through the thirteenth centuries also depended on the rapid expansion of new farming lands, mainly for cultivating cereal grains. This occurred particularly in the floodplains of northwestern Europe through the draining of fens, marshes and other wetlands, and the building of dams and dykes along the North Sea and Baltic coasts.[28] Along with agricultural commercialization came improvements in transporting food and other surpluses to market. Like China, Europe benefited from numerous, navigable inland waterways.[29] Merchants and sailors throughout western Europe became adept not only at navigating the seas and coastal waters that surrounded three-quarters of the continent—from the Baltic and North seas to the English Channel and the Atlantic coastal waters, and, finally, to the Mediterranean Sea—but also at utilizing the various rivers, canals, lakes and other waterways located throughout water-abundant Europe.

To induce such settlement and land clearing in flood-plains and along waterways on a grand scale, other measures were also adopted. One important incentive was that rural settlers were sometimes allowed by local lords to build, own and operate their own water mills for grinding grain, one of the most important—and profitable—capital outlays of the medieval European rural economy.[30] But the use of this new technology was further adapted as a consequence of the Black Death, wars and other catastrophes beginning in the mid-fourteenth century, which depopulated the countryside, caused massive labor shortages, and led to long spells of declining cereal production. Before the Black Death, mills and mill sites were used exclusively for the grinding of grain. With the collapse of the grain economy in many rural regions, water mills were converted to other uses, such as the fulling of cloth, the operation of bellows and the sawing of wood.[31] This was the start of basic manufacturing in Europe that ultimately led to the Industrial Revolution centuries later.

An important parallel institutional innovation was the evolution of common and riparian water law, which was also fundamental to the agricultural and transport development of Great Britain and other European countries from the thirteenth through the eighteenth centuries.[32] One of the key contributions of the new laws was to sort out the growing and competing uses of water, especially between exploiting rivers for agriculture and powering mills as opposed to transport and fishing. The biggest legal obstacle to overcoming such private conflicts was the resource itself: compared to land and other fixed resource endowments, the flowing water of streams and rivers cannot easily be appropriated and possessed to exclude others from using it. In other words, land can be owned but water cannot. To resolve this problem, English common law evolved to establish riparian property rights for water use.[33] That is, water rights became associated with or connected to the land adjacent to the body of water, and thus it became sufficient to own and occupy riparian land in order to appropriate the benefits of the nearby running stream or river.[34] At first, this riparian law was invoked mainly to protect ancient, or hereditary, uses of water attached to riparian lands. But, eventually, the law facilitated and protected growing agricultural and water power uses that began flourishing in preindustrial Britain.[35] At the same time, water laws also enshrined the Roman legal precedence for protecting the common property right of using rivers and waterways for fishing, navigation and transportation, ensuring that rights of access for transporting goods and people could not be obstructed by other water users. Thus, in premodern Britain, these legal innovations facilitated the rapid expansion of economic development, as agriculture, hydropower for mills and waterway transportation flourished. The stage was set for the next major leap in social and economic development—the Industrial Revolution.

Water and the Industrial Revolution

The legal historian Joshua Getzler captures the importance of expanding uses and quantities of water for the industrialization of Great Britain:

> Water was not only an energy source for the Industrial Revolution, it was also a crucial raw material for production

and urbanization. Water was necessary for brewing and food manufacture, and especially for manufacturing processes requiring washing and draining such as the textiles, dyeing, printing, chemical and mining industries. Moreover, water resources were essential to the transport revolutions of the same period: it was the construction of an intricate inland navigation system of improved river-channels in the 1730s and man-made canals from the 1780s which enabled the heavy raw materials of the emergent mineral-based economy and its finished products to be moved across regional spatial barriers. Water thereby contributed to the creation of a vast internal free-trade area, lessening the need for small-scale autochthonous production as an insurance against dearth, and helping to develop regional comparative advantages in agriculture and industry with the benefits of economics of scope, scale and specialization.[36]

The role of such water-based developments in spurring industrialization in Great Britain was pivotal to the spread of similar developments throughout Europe and the Western world. For example, the first phase of the Industrial Revolution occurred over the period 1750–1830, and centered on key inventions during this time, such as the steam engine, cotton spinning, railroads and steamships. Such innovations helped propel Great Britain to global economic and political domi-nance, and they had lasting economic impacts on all industri-alizing economies up until 1900. Most accounts of this phase focus on the innovative role of the steam engine, Britain's advantage in terms of abundant and accessible resources to power these engines, and the emergence of fossil fuels as the driver of industrialization.[37] Although coal resources and steam were fundamental to the Industrial Revolution, the importance of inland waterway transportation and factories powered by water in the initiating industrialization in Great Britain and eventually all of Europe cannot be overlooked. Before canal and river networks were established for waterborne transport, in premodern times most goods and people had to travel by land or via coastal seas. Similarly, up to the nineteenth century, the iron industry in Britain and Europe was entirely dependent on hydro-power, and thus initially located near streams and rivers. Indeed, as pointed out by the social historian Terje Tvedt, "steam engines could not have been built in the first place without waterwheels to drive the equipment that was needed to smelt the iron and form the cylinders and other metal parts of the steam engine."[38]

Eventually, the spread of steam engines and the use of coal resources and other fossil fuels did supplant the predominance of water power for industrial processes, and the development of the steam locomotive meant that railroads displaced rivers and canals as the main transportation network for goods and people. In the first half of the nineteenth century, steam engines began taking over industrial processes; for example, by 1839 Britain's textile industry operated 2,230 waterwheels and 3,051 steam engines.[39] The replacement of water as a source of power for industries and canals and rivers as the main inland transport network continued during the second phase of major innovations during the Industrial Revolution, which occurred from 1870 to 1900.[40] These innovations included electricity, the internal combustion engine and improved sanitation, which in turn fostered most of the important industrial and transportation advances in the twentieth century. The resulting rapid pace of innovation, industrial development, population growth and urbanization had lasting global economic impacts until 1970 and led to the rise of the United States as the world's premier advanced economy.

But the Industrial Revolution did more than simply displace water as a source of industrial power and internal transportation in modern economies: it made water more accessible and easy to exploit than ever before in human history. The uses of water may have been changed by the Industrial Revolution, but the ability to access, extract and divert freshwater resources more cheaply than previously possible meant that the fundamental relationship between economic development and harnessing more water resources intensified rather than diminished. As Brian Fagan notes, "By the mid-nineteenth century, water was an industrial commodity to be pumped, bought and sold, and redistributed in ways that were unimaginable in earlier times."[41] Thus, the Industrial Revolution was instrumental in ensuring that the innovations, institutions and incentives of modern economies are geared toward expanding our command and control of water resources, not toward reducing use as our economies develop and populations grow. This relationship between water and modern economic development was further cemented through enabling exploitation of global water frontiers, developing modern urban water systems, and relying increasingly on large-scale public supply and provision of water supplies.

Exploiting Global Water Frontiers

The era from 1500 to the beginning of the twentieth century was associated with an unprecedented global expansion in land use, economic development, trade and population migration. The historian Walter Prescott Webb has suggested that the hallmark of this unique period of global economic development was exploitation of the world's "Great Frontier," which comprises present-day temperate North and South America, Australia, New Zealand and South Africa. According to Webb, exploitation of this land-abundant but sparsely populated resource was instrumental to the "economic boom" experienced in the "Metropolis," or modern Europe: "This boom began when Columbus returned from his first voyage, rose slowly, and continued at an ever-accelerating pace until the frontier which fed it was no more. Assuming that the frontier closed in 1890 or 1900, it may be said that the boom lasted about four hundred years."[42]

Over this period, from 1500 to 1900, the exploitation of global land and resource frontiers, the Industrial Revolution and the rise of the modern economy were inexorably linked. The economies of western Europe clearly benefited from these developments. Through its unrelenting exploitation of previously underdeveloped land and natural resources, western Europe obtained a vast array of natural wealth, in the form of land frontiers for settlement as well as fisheries, timber, plantations, mineral ores, precious metals and other valuable natural resources. New land in sparsely populated temperate regions of the Great Frontier not only provided an outlet for poor populations emigrating from Europe and other regions in search of better economic opportunities but also yielded a large resource windfall that benefited the development, trade and industrialization of European economies.

The Great Frontier economies also developed significantly. For example, along with the United States, Canada, temperate

Latin America, Australia, New Zealand and South Africa benefited from the global agricultural and raw material trade boom of the late nineteenth and early twentieth centuries, and in response, engaged in rapid cropland expansion.[43] In addition, the Great Frontier regions attracted vast foreign investment flows as well as immigrants from Europe. However, the United States was the clear winner of all economies. In the late nineteenth and early twentieth centuries, it experienced the most extensive territorial and frontier land expansion of any country or region in the world. For example, over 40 percent of the increased cropland area that occurred outside of western Europe from 1870 to 1910 took place in the United States.[44] However, neither cropland expansion nor the development of agriculturally related industries was responsible for the phenomenal rise of the United States as a global industrial power. In just over half a century, the United States was transformed from one of several emerging manufacturing nations to the leading global industrial power, surpassing even the United Kingdom.[45] Instead, the economic ascendency of the US was attributable to exploitation of its vast energy and mineral wealth, which fostered the expansion of its resource-based manufacturing exports, notably from the iron and steel industry, copper manufactures and refined mineral oil.

However, this unprecedented global frontier and land expansion could not have taken place without a parallel development and exploitation of key water frontiers. In the case of the United States, its emergence as a global economic power in the twentieth century was facilitated by its harnessing for industrial and urban development of the water-abundant eastern states and the Mississippi River, its exploitation of the maritime trade potential of its Atlantic and Pacific coasts, and the economic development and settling of its water-scarce regions west of the Mississippi.[46] Although the first two developments were essential for the rise of the US as the world's leading industrial and trading nation, as indicated by Steven Solomon, "even greater impetus was generated by the water innovations that transformed its inhospitably arid, virgin, western frontier lands into a cornucopia of irrigated agriculture, mining and hydroelectric-powered industry."[47] The key to this approach was to develop a massive network of dams and reservoirs across the western United States to collect the available freshwater from major rivers and channel it for agricultural irrigation and growing cities and industries. This was facilitated by the development of engineering techniques and the concrete industry to build enormous dams, pipelines and aqueducts.

Although the improved ability to capture, channel and distribute scarce freshwater on a large scale from rivers, streams, lakes and other surface water was an essential innovation, equally important was the development of a new water institution—the doctrine of prior appropriation. The concepts of first possession and prior appropriation emerged from allowing acquisition of a water right through diverting water for a beneficial use, such as irrigated agriculture, mining or transportation, and may have had their roots in colonial Spanish water law and English common law.[48] First possession ensures that claim of ownership or use of a resource should remain with the person that initially gained control before other potential claimants. It was an ideal way of establishing land, and especially water, rights in sparsely populated frontier regions located far from government administration and large settlements. As these regions become more settled, ownership of available surface water is allocated through the rule of first possession or priority of claim. Thus, first possession became extremely important to the "great land rush" that transformed North America, Australia, New Zealand and South Africa from 1650 to 1900, and which in turn laid the foundation for the association between access to freely abundant water and expansion of economic activities.[49]

In the western United States, this approach quickly evolved in the nineteenth century into the doctrine of prior appropriation, which allows a water user to divert water from a river or stream for delivery and use on non-riparian lands. Used initially to obtain the best unoccupied ranching or agricultural land with prime access or location with regard to nearby surface water, the doctrine was essential for the establishment of mining, agricultural and ranching interests across western US states and territories. Moreover, the doctrine legally sanctioned a hierarchy of rights based on prior claims of beneficial use, or "first in time, first in right." The first person to divert and use water productively has the highest priority, or "senior" water right, and those with subsequent claims have lower priority, or "junior" water rights.

The Development of Modern Urban Water Systems

Industrialization also brought rapid expansion of cities and urban populations, leading to additional demands for increased water use and sanitation. During the eighteenth and nineteenth centuries, private companies emerged to provide drinking and other water supplies to growing cities. For example, by the mid-nineteenth century, only 10 of the 190 municipal councils in Great Britain controlled their cities' water supplies.[50] However, shortages of water were pervasive, and water supplies remained insufficient to meet the needs of increasing urban populations. In addition, spreading urbanization and rising population densities caused major pollution problems for the available water, and deadly water-borne diseases, such as cholera and typhoid, became a growing threat. As cities in Europe, North America and the rest of the industrializing world grew, they struggled to provide adequate clean water and sanitation on a large scale for their numerous residents.

Fortunately, scientific advances in water and sewage treatment, especially the combination of filtration and chlorination of drinking water, allowed the development of modern urban water systems that in turn fueled the continued growth of cities.[51] These breakthroughs were essential, because ancient urban water systems—including those based on the Roman gravity-fed aqueduct and wastewater disposal network—could not cope with the onslaught of global industrialization and urbanization from the nineteenth century onward. These innovations were largely in response to the health crisis caused by water-borne diseases in the densely populated and rapidly expanding cities worldwide. For example, in response to cholera and typhoid outbreaks in Lawrence, Massachusetts, and Hamburg, Germany, local engineers developed improved sand filtration methods to purify drinking water. The health benefits of this method soon saw it spreading to urban areas throughout the United States and Europe, including major cities such as New York, Chicago, London and Paris. In the early twentieth century, the addition of chlorine as a low-cost and proven disinfectant further enhanced the development and effectiveness of drinking water treatment. By World War II, the one-two punch of filtration followed by chlorination became the basis of modern urban water supply systems.

Overall, the development of modern urban water systems was both a consequence of and a necessity for the growth of large cities, increasing urban populations and industrial expansion. More importantly, it solidified the modern mindset that solving the problem of large-scale water use and waste disposal is largely an engineering matter. The bigger the city and its population, the more clean drinking and other water supplies must be found, and the quicker and more efficiently the resulting volumes of wastewater must be channeled away and disposed of away from urban areas.

Public Provision of Water Supply

The advances in urban water systems from the mid-nineteenth century onward also signaled another important consequence of the expansion of water use after the Industrial Revolution, which was the growing dominance of public provision of water supply. Industrialization, new engineering methods, fossil fuel power, and advanced materials and processes allowed the harnessing of available water supplies on a massive scale never previously imagined. Huge volumes of water could be diverted from rivers and other major surface-level sources, stored and distributed, and sent long distances for use in irrigation and industry and by the populations of growing cities. The large investments required and the economies of scale of such operations meant that water supply, its treatment and distribution, and the consequent disposal of polluted waste were beyond the ability of private companies to finance and manage. Water services in the modern economy quickly became the exclusive obligation of the public sector.

The growing influence of the public sector on water provision began soon after industrialization. Starting early in the nineteenth century, in Great Britain canal companies, municipal corporations and water companies were given state powers by Parliament to appropriate land and water for waterworks and to protect water supplies from pollution and diversion to alternate uses.[52] Eventually, as demand for urbanization and industries increased, state intervention increased to provide legal protection of private investors' capital in water supply, the guarantees of this supply and water services to the public, and the regulation of prices and rates of return as private companies increasingly coalesced into large monopolies. Eventually, as discussed previously, with even large monopolies struggling to supply adequate clean water and sanitation on a scale sufficient for their numerous residents, the public sector became increasingly responsible for water supply and services in modern economies.

Similarly, the enormous dam and distribution systems required to supply water to fast-growing economies, especially in water-scarce areas such as the US western states, increasingly became public works. This included massive irrigation projects along the Colorado and Columbia rivers and numerous distribution networks. In addition, as populations expanded across the United States, new settlements and towns increasingly called on the federal government to assist with large-scale flood control projects, including the vast systems developed for the Mississippi and Ohio rivers. A third important impetus was the increasing demand for large-scale dams to generate hydroelectricity, which spread rapidly in the late nineteenth and early twentieth centuries in the western United States.[53] Finally, the expansion and control of navigation, which had always been the responsibility of the federal government, also became an important reason for public investments in controlling and diverting water. By the early twentieth century, the federal government became principally responsible for building large dams for multiple purposes and services—river navigation, electrical power, irrigation, flood control and municipal water supplies— throughout the United States.

Thus, the stage was set for the twentieth century, an era of unprecedented expansion of economics, populations and cities worldwide made possible through harnessing yet more water resources for human use.

As we shall see in the next chapter, these trends have continued to the present day. As industrialization continued to spread globally, the United States not only emerged as the leading economy but also became the model of development for other economies. Consequently, many countries also followed the US approach to managing its water resources. The result is the present day "water paradox": The institutions, incentives and innovations of today's economies are geared toward expanding our command and control of water. They are incapable of reducing use as our economies develop and populations grow, but water sources become increasingly scarce.

3

WATER IN THE MODERN ERA
Toward a Global Crisis?

As we saw in the previous chapter, the genesis of the water paradox today lies in how we have managed water for many centuries. Our current water institutions and innovations are largely relics of past historical eras, when development was dependent on finding and exploiting more water resources. Throughout human history, economic progress has been linked with increased water appropriation, control and use. The global spread of industrialization from the 1900s onward further cemented this association. As a consequence, in today's economies, institutions, incentives and innovations are geared toward finding and exploiting more freshwater resources. The result is an emerging global water crisis, which is predominantly a crisis of inadequate and poor water management.

This chapter examines the use of water in the modern economy, focusing on the period from the 1900s to the present day. During this period—which we will refer to as the *modern era*—the global model for economic development has been the United States, and subsequently, many countries emulated the US approach to harnessing its water resources. Thus, how water management evolved in the US and other economies during the modern era has set the stage for today's "water paradox."

We begin by exploring some of the key trends of water use in the modern era. These include the growth in water use as populations and economies have expanded, the continuing dominance of agriculture as the major user of water, and growing demands from trade, urbanization and industrialization.

Population and Water

One reason for the increased stress on global water resources has been the exponential rise in populations during the modern era. Figure 3.1 shows how both global population and total water withdrawals have increased from 1900 to the present day. The figure also indicates likely projections to 2050.

Overall, as populations worldwide have expanded during the modern era, water use has increased significantly. This trend is especially noticeable post-World War II. In 1900, the world's population was just over 1.6 billion, and water withdrawals were around 580 billion m³ per year. By 1950, there were over 2.5 billion people, and annual global water use was around 1,400 billion m³. In 2010, as the number of people approached 7 billion, water withdrawals amounted to 3,000 billion m³ annually. By the time the world population tops 9 billion in 2050, annual water withdrawals will total 4,300 billion m³.

Figure 3.1 also shows that, since the 1970s, the growth in water withdrawals has not kept pace with the expansion of

Figure 3.1 Global Population and Water Withdrawals, 1900–2050

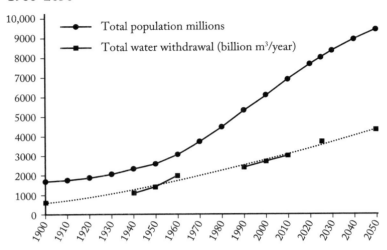

Sources: Total population from 1900 to 1940 from Max Roser and Esteban Ortiz-Ospina (2018), "World Population Growth," published online at OurWorldInData.org. Available at https://ourworldindata.org/world-population-growth (accessed July 10, 2018).
Total population from 1950 to 2050 from U.S. Census Bureau, international database. Available at https://www.census.gov/data-tools/demo/idb/informationGateway.php (accessed July 10, 2018).
Total water withdrawal from 1900 to 1960 from Igor A. Shiklomanov and Jeanna A. Balonisnikova (2003), "World Water Use and Water Availability: Trends, Scenarios, Consequences," in *Water Resources Systems: Hydrological Risk, Management and Development*, IAHS Symposium Proceedings, pp. 358–364.
Total water withdrawal from 1990 to 2010 from AQUASTAT Main Database, Food and Agriculture Organization of the United Nations (FAO), http://www.fao.org/nr/water/aquastat/data/query/index.html?lang=en (accessed June 12, 2018).
Total water withdrawal projections for 2025 and 2050 (most plausible) from Upali A. Amarasinghe and Vladimir Smakhtin (2014), *Global Water Demand Projections: Past, Present and Future* (Colombo, Sri Lanka: International Water Management Institute).

population worldwide. This trend is expected to continue in the near future. The result is that global per-capita water withdrawals have stabilized, and are expected to remain around 400m³ per person per year to 2050. Yet individual water use is still higher than levels at the beginning of the modern era in 1900, when per-capita water withdrawals were around 350m³. We have managed to stop people's water use from rising, but not to reduce it.

Thus, one of the most important legacies of the modern era is that the world is consuming more water per person than ever before in global history. As global populations continue to grow, a key question is whether the world can continue to use more and more freshwater. Will it even be possible by 2050 to withdraw 4,300 billion m³ of water annually, and can that level of water use be sustained, or even expanded, as the world's population approaches 10 or 11 billion people by the end of the twenty-first century?

Economy and Water

Trends in global average water use can be misleading, as there is considerable variation in per-capita water use across countries. During the modern era, industrialization and economic wealth have spread across the world, increasing use of water. As countries urbanize, develop and become richer, they tend to use much more water compared to countries that are poorer, more rural and less developed.

Table 3.1 compares water use for twenty-four countries, which encompass high-income, emerging market and developing economies. The eight rich countries in the table have average annual incomes of just over $46,000 per person. The

Table 3.1 Water Withdrawals per Person, Selected Countries

	Year	Total water withdrawal per capita (m³/person/year)	GDP per capita (constant 2010 US$), 2016
High Income Countries			
United States	2010	1,543	$52,195
Canada	2009	1,113	$50,232
Italy	2008	900	$34,284
Australia	2013	824	$55,671
Japan	2009	641	$47,608
France	2012	476	$42,013
Germany	2010	411	$45,552
United Kingdom	2012	129	$41,603
Average		*754*	*$46,145*
Emerging Market Economies			
Pakistan	2008	1,034	$1,182
Philippines	2009	849	$2,753
Mexico	2011	658	$9,707
India	2010	602	$1,861
Turkey	2008	561	$14,071
China	2013	432	$6,894
Russia	2013	425	$11,099
Brazil	2010	370	$10,826
Average		*616*	*$7,299*
Developing Countries			
Bangladesh	2008	231	$1,030
Bolivia	2009	141	$2,458
Haiti	2009	141	$729
Ethiopia	2016	106	$511
Kenya	2010	76	$1,143
Nigeria	2010	74	$2,458
Mozambique	2015	53	$515
Uganda	2008	18	$662
Average		*113*	*$1,188*
Total Average		*495*	*$18,211*

Source: AQUASTAT Main Database, Food and Agriculture Organization of the United Nations (FAO), http://www.fao.org/nr/water/aquastat/data/query/index.html?lang=en; "World Development Indicators," World Bank, http://databank.worldbank.org/data/reports.aspx?source= world-development-indicators (both accessed June 12, 2018)

emerging market economies, which are rapidly industrializing countries with large and growing populations, average around \$7,300 per capita. The eight developing countries are predominantly rural low- and lower middle-income economies, with average annual income of almost \$1,200 per person.

Across all twenty-four countries, per-capita water use averages nearly 500m³ annually. However, there are great differences across these countries. At one extreme, people in the United States use over 1,500m³ of water each year, whereas individuals in Uganda withdraw less than 20m³. Water use per person appears to go up dramatically as countries become wealthier. For example, average annual water withdrawal is over 100m³ per person for the eight developing countries listed in Table 3.1, but exceeds 750m³ per capita in the eight rich countries. Emerging market economies are quickly catching up with high-income countries. The eight industrializing economies depicted in the table withdraw on average over 600m³ per person each year, and people in Pakistan use over 1,000m³.

As most of the world comprises developing economies, a key issue is whether there are sufficient global freshwater supplies to meet growing water demand as these countries industrialize and urbanize and begin to match water use levels in richer countries.

However, richer countries also have greater water productivity, in terms of the value of the production gained from water use, compared to poorer countries. As shown in Figure 3.2, the amount of gross domestic product (GDP) generated per cubic meter of freshwater withdrawal has increased worldwide over the past four decades, from around $3 to $18. But high-income economies produce almost $50 per cubic meter of water used compared to less than $10 per cubic meter in developing countries. A major concern is that water productivity has not increased significantly worldwide in the twenty-first century, and appears to be fluctuating around a long-run trend of about $20 per cubic meter of total freshwater withdrawal.

Figure 3.2 Global Water Productivity, 1977–2014

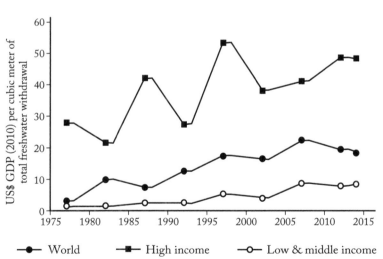

Sources: "World Development Indicators," World Bank, http://databank.worldbank.org/data/reports.aspx?source=world-development-indicators (accessed June 12, 2018).
Gross domestic product (GDP) is in constant US$ 2010.

Agriculture and Water

Across the globe, the predominant use of water today is still for agriculture (see Figure 3.3). It accounts for around 70 percent of freshwater withdrawal worldwide, and 81 percent in low-income countries.[1] Almost two-thirds of water use worldwide occurs in Asia, which allocates 80 percent of its freshwater to agriculture. In Africa, which is dominated by low- and middle-income (or developing) economies, agriculture also accounts for around 80 percent of freshwater withdrawals.

The main reason why water continues to be used principally for agriculture is that most of the world is composed of developing countries. For these economies, agriculture still contributes significantly to development, employment and food security. Consequently, water demand for irrigated crops, livestock and aquaculture remains high and growing. Irrigation is an especially important use of water. Irrigation covers 20 percent of all cultivated land globally and accounts for 40 percent of agricultural production. Total irrigated area is expected to increase even more, from 421 million hectares in 2000 to 473 million by 2050. This expansion is necessary to feed more people and animals. For example, 53 percent of cereal production growth during 2000–2050 is likely to be from irrigation. Much of this additional production will be used as animal feed to meet the increasing demand for livestock production, especially in Asia. As incomes rise and diets change, there is likely to be greater demand for other water-intensive crops, such as sugar cane, horticultural crops, and fruits and nuts.[2]

In Europe and the Americas, more water is used for industry and municipal purposes than for agriculture (see

Figure 3.3 Water Use by Sector and Major Regions

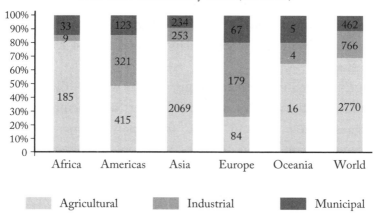

Total water withdrawal by sector (billion m³)

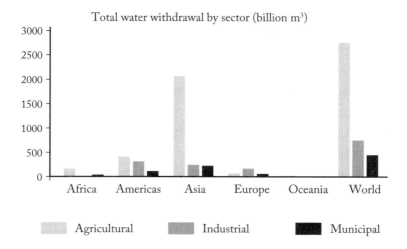

Total water withdrawal by sector (billion m³)

Source: AQUASTAT Main Database, Food and Agriculture Organization of the United Nations (FAO), http://www.fao.org/nr/water/aquastat/data/query/index.html?lang=en (accessed June 12, 2018).

Figure 3.3).[3] As these regions contain richer countries with more advanced economies, agriculture is significantly less important. Nevertheless, even in these regions, water withdrawals remain high. For example, in the Americas, nearly 50 percent of water use is for agriculture, and around 25 percent in Europe.

Even the most affluent country in the world—the United States—still uses a lot of its freshwater for agriculture. The biggest water demand comes from power generation, to operate steam-driven turbines and cool discharge, which accounts for about 45 percent of the country's total water withdrawals annually. But irrigated agriculture is the next biggest use, at 33 percent of total withdrawals. The remaining 22 percent is mainly for public supply (i.e., municipal) and industrial use.[4]

Moreover, the amount of water used for irrigation in the United States rose steadily from around 340 million m^3 per day in 1950 to a peak of 570 million m^3 per day in 1980. In recent decades, water withdrawals for irrigation use have fallen, but not significantly. In 2005, the US was still using around 510 million m^3 of water per day to irrigate its farmland, which is approximately the same amount used in the 1970s.[5]

However, the figures for average irrigation use across the United States are misleading. Take California, which produces the most food and agricultural exports of any US state. In 2012, for example, California generated more than $18 billion in agricultural exports, which was around 13 percent of all exports from the United States. California's $25 billion farming sector accounts for over one-third of the country's vegetables and nearly two-thirds of fruits and nuts; and, for these products, California's exports are three-fifths of the US total. In addition, nearly all of the almonds, olives, broccoli and celery in the US are produced in California.[6]

California's prolific agricultural production and exports have been made possible only through heavy reliance on freshwater. Because of its large urban populations, industrial development and power generation, California does employ significant amounts of water for these other uses. But around 80 percent of California's freshwater use is still for agriculture, which is a pattern of allocation more associated with a developing country rather than with one of the most prosperous US states.

Given the continuing dependence of global agriculture on new supplies of water, there is growing concern that there will be insufficient water resources to meet the needs of future food production. Population growth, increasing climatic and hydrological variability, and changing food preferences are likely to aggravate water scarcity further, with potential implications for food security for millions of people, especially in developing countries. On the other hand, since World War II, there have been dramatic increases in agricultural productivity and techniques which have decreased the water requirements for producing food, boosted yields, and improved the food production potential of agricultural land. Is water scarcity starting to impact food security, or are agricultural improvements preventing this constraint from occurring?

To answer this question, Miina Porkka and colleagues examined the potential impacts of water availability worldwide and in specific regions on the ability to produce a minimum diet that guarantees food security for the average inhabitant—a food supply of 3,000 kilocalories per day that consists of at least 20 percent animal products.[7] They conducted this analysis for the past hundred years, from 1905 to 2005.

Although technological advances in agriculture have ensured that a given food supply today can be produced with half of the water it took a century ago, water scarcity as a potential constraint on food security has increased. In 1905, there were 360 million people living in food-producing zones limited by water availability, or 21 percent of the world population at that time. By 2005, this number had increased to 2.2 billion— over a third of the global population. In south Asia, three-quarters of the population are now affected by water scarcity in food production, in the Middle East 42 percent, across Africa almost 40 percent, and in east Asia 35 percent.

Projecting future water demand for agriculture is not easy, as it will depend on net irrigated area, irrigated area of water-intensive crops, efficiency of irrigation water use and crop yields.[8] If developing countries continue to expand agricultural production based on utilizing more water supplies, and crops in the agricultural regions of wealthier nations—such as California—continue to dominate freshwater use, then global water demand for irrigated crops, livestock and aquaculture will continue to increase.

In addition, the challenges of growing water scarcity for agriculture are likely to be exacerbated by the increasing costs of developing new sources of water, groundwater depletion, increasing water pollution, the degradation of freshwater ecosystems, and wasteful use of existing water supplies.[9] Rapidly increasing nonagricultural demands for water, changing food preferences, global climate change and new demands for biofuel production will also place increasing pressure on scarce water resources. Given these competing demands and challenges, it is not surprising that many experts conclude that "growing water scarcity will increasingly constrain food production growth, causing adverse impacts on the goals of food security and human well-being."[10]

Trade and Water

The alternative to producing more food with less land and water resources is to increase agricultural trade among countries. As some experts have pointed out, this could be a "win-win" by both alleviating water scarcity and improving food security.[11] When the trade occurs from a region that has abundant water supplies and high productivity in agriculture to a region with low supplies and productivity, then the latter region both saves on water and gains more food. That is, if agricultural exporters are more efficient in water use than importers, then global water saving will increase. Further savings will occur if water originally intended for agriculture in the importing country or region is then allocated to more efficient and productive uses, such as industry or cities.

Overall, the evidence suggests that, over the past two decades, the volume of water associated with the global food trade has doubled.[12] And, on the whole, more water-abundant countries tend to export more water-intensive products, and less water-abundant countries less water-intensive goods.[13] Thus, the expanding international food trade may have led to more efficient water use and increased conservation of water resources worldwide. This effect appears to be especially important for water-scarce regions like the Middle East and north Africa, where importing water-intensive commodities allows for consumption that would otherwise be limited by the shortage of water. For example, through food trade, Jordan imports the equivalent of around 5–7 billion m³ of water each year, which compares to the 1 billion m³ of water available for agriculture from its domestic sources.[14]

But there are also concerns about the growing trade in water and food.

For one, some regions and countries may be fostering water-intensive exports despite lower efficiency in their use of water. The inefficiencies can be so pronounced that the trade actually worsens water scarcity rather than alleviates it. This appears to occur in Australia and the United States, where the export of water-intensive commodities may be contributing to the water shortage and scarcity problems of some regions.[15] For example, Indonesia, New Zealand and Papua New Guinea import a considerable amount of water from water-scarce regions in Australia, in the form of wheat, cotton, livestock and meat, and prepared foods. The United States exports water from regions with frequent water shortages, such as California and other western states, through agricultural trade with Canada and Mexico.

A disturbing trend is that a growing number of water-scarce developing countries are major exporters of water through agricultural and other trade.[16] India, Pakistan and China are the largest exporters of scarce water globally. The top ten exporters of scarce water also include Syria, Thailand, Egypt and Morocco. For example, Egypt exports its scarce water through cotton and cotton products, vegetables and fruit to Saudi Arabia, Japan, the United States, Germany and Italy.

As many scholars have observed, the problem lies not in trade per se, but in policy distortions and mismanagement that facilitate the export of water-intensive commodities increasingly from water-scarce regions and countries.[17] That is, trade has the potential to improve water efficiency and alleviate water scarcity, but, instead, the current global policy environment for water is increasingly encouraging trade patterns that exacerbate scarcity. As one scholar puts it, "This policy environment is characterized by water prices that are oftentimes regulated, subsidized, and distorted, which tends to encourage wasteful use of water."[18] As long as water continues to be *underpriced* in this way, then exports of water-intensive commodities will continue from a growing number of countries and regions, despite their relative disadvantages in terms of water availability.

A further problem of the growing food trade is its dependence on depletable groundwater supplies. Approximately 11 percent of non-renewable groundwater use for irrigation is embedded in international food trade, of which two-thirds are exported by Pakistan, the United States and India alone.[19] Global groundwater depletion has increased by 22 percent in ten years, from 240km^3 annually in 2000 to 292km^3 in 2010. Over this same period, the amount of global groundwater depletion accounted for by food exports increased from 17.7km^3 to 25.6km^3 annually, or by 45 percent. These trends suggest that the dependence of the global food trade on groundwater depletion is likely to continue in the near future. For one, groundwater depletion is increasingly concentrated in a few regions that grow most of the world's crops, such as India, Pakistan, China, the United States, Mexico, the Middle East and north Africa. In addition, a large and growing share of the global population live in countries that depend on food imports from regions that are increasingly relying on groundwater depletion for crop production.

Urbanization and Water

Since 1900, the world has seen an unprecedented growth in cities and their populations. In 1800, only 3 percent of the world's population lived in urban areas. By 1900, this share rose to 14 percent, although only twelve cities contained 1 million or more inhabitants. In 1950, 30 percent of the world's population lived in urban areas, and the number of cities with over 1 million people had grown to eighty-three.[20]

The urban population of the world has grown even more rapidly since 1950, from 746 million to 3.9 billion in 2014. By 2008, for the first time ever, more people lived in urban areas than in rural areas, and, today, 54 percent of the world's population reside in cities. The urban population is expected to increase to 5.4 billion inhabitants by 2050, around two-thirds of the world population. Nearly 90 percent of the increase in urban populations will likely occur in Asia and Africa. In fact, three countries—India, China and Nigeria—will account for over one-third of the projected growth in the world's urban population from 2014 to 2050. The urban population of India is expected to increase by 404 million, that of China by 292 million, and that of Nigeria by 212 million.[21]

Cities are also getting bigger. In 2014, there were 488 cities of 1 million or more inhabitants, including 43 that have over 5 million people and 28 with over 10 million. By 2030, there are expected to be 662 cities with 1 million or more people, with 63 cities containing over 5 million inhabitants and 41 with more than 10 million.[22]

The rapid expansion of urban areas and their populations is putting considerable pressure on available freshwater resources. As cities grow in size and population, the total water needed for adequate municipal supply rises as well. This increase in demand has been driven not only by growing urban populations but also by the expansion of large-scale and publicly provided municipal water systems delivering larger and larger volumes of water to these urban areas and their inhabitants. In addition, the increased municipal supply that accompanies urbanization leads to increases in per-capita water use, especially when it facilitates the adoption of modern household appliances, such as bathrooms with running water, showers, washing machines and dishwashers. For example, between 1995 and 2010, per-capita municipal use of water worldwide increased by 44 percent, from 54m^3 per person to 78m^3. By 2025, municipal water use could reach 102m^3 per person.[23]

To cope with these growing demands, most cities have developed extensive public infrastructure and water supply systems, often drawing on multiple freshwater sources across vast distances. Today, four out of every five residents of large cities globally obtain their water from reservoirs, lakes, rivers and other surface sources of freshwater—many of which are increasingly located far away. On average, large cities transport over 500 billion liters of surface water daily for use over a distance of nearly 30,000km. Most of the remaining urban residents (just under 20 percent) of large cities rely on groundwater, and a few (2 percent) depend on desalination. Across the globe, the water infrastructure supporting large cities supplies 668 million liters of water daily, and, although these cities occupy only 1 percent of the earth's land surface, their total sources of water cover 41 percent of the land surface of the whole earth.[24]

A worrying trend is the number of large cities that are facing water stress. Table 3.2 indicates that the twenty largest cities under water stress currently contain about 300 million people. Six of these cities are in China, five are in India and several more are in other developing countries. As we saw earlier, urbanization and the emergence of large cities are proceeding at a fast pace in low and middle economies, with China and India expected to account for most of the urban growth over the coming decades. In addition, five of the major water-stressed cities rely heavily on cross-basin transfers, which is the transportation of water from one river basin to another. These five cities—Tokyo, Karachi, Los Angeles, Tianjin and Chennai—currently transfer nearly 17 billion liters of water daily across river basins to supply their populations. Another seven large cities also rely on cross-basin transfers of about 65 billion liters of water daily. Globally, about one-quarter of the population in large cities, or nearly 400 million people, may be dependent on water supplies that are already stressed.[25]

As cities and their populations grew throughout the modern era they were faced with another problem: how to treat the vast volumes of water-borne sewage generated by expanding urban areas and their concentrated populations, and how to prevent contamination and decline in the lakes, rivers, streams and other water bodies around cities. This led to an important innovation, which was the development of modern sewage treatment capable of handling water-borne human waste on an extremely large scale.[26] The essence of this system was, first, to develop methods to treat the urban wastewater flowing from the industries and households concentrated in cities, and, second, to design pipe and drainage networks to release the large volumes of treated water safely

Table 3.2 The 20 Largest Cities Facing Water Stress

City	Population (thousands), 2010	Water sources	Cross-basin transfer (million liters per day)
Tokyo, Japan	36,933	Surface	2,170
Delhi, India	21,935	Surface, ground	
Mexico City, Mexico	20,142	Surface, ground	
Shanghai, China	19,554	Surface, ground	
Beijing, China	15,000	Surface, ground	
Kolkata, India	14,283	Surface, ground	
Karachi, Pakistan	13,500	Surface, ground	2,529
Los Angeles, United States	13,223	Surface, ground	8,895
Rio de Janeiro, Brazil	11,867	Surface	
Moscow, Russia	11,472	Surface, ground	
Istanbul, Turkey	10,953	Surface, ground	
Shenzhen, China	10,222	Surface	
Chongqing, China	9,732	Surface, ground	
Lima, Peru	8,950	Surface, ground	
London, United Kingdom	8,923	Surface, ground	
Wuhan, China	8,904	Surface	
Tianjin, China	8,535	Surface, ground	2,179
Chennai, India	8,523	Surface, ground	1,130
Bangalore, India	8,275	Surface, ground	
Hyderabad, India	7,578	Surface, ground	
Total	**268,504**		**16,903**

Source: Robert I. McDonald, Katherine Weber, Julie Padowski, Martina Flörke, Christof Schneider, et al. (2014), "Water on an Urban Planet: Urbanization and the Reach of Urban Water Infrastructure," *Global Environmental Change* 27: 96–105.

into the surrounding environment. In addition, the entire system had to be designed to handle the age-old problem of managing the large increases in water that occur when it rains heavily, which are often ten to twenty times higher than during periods of little or no rain. Initially, the approach was to develop a combined sewer system, which channels both rainwater and sewage to treatment plants, and only allows the release of the mixture to surface water after extreme storms when the volume of water exceeds the capacity of the system. However, in more recent times, the tendency has been to separate the drainage and treatment of sewage from rainwater outflows. In the United States, combined sewer systems still predominate in the old industrial and urban areas of the northeast and Great Lakes, and around 40 million urban residents continue to depend on them.[27]

The "Hydraulic Mission" of the Modern Era

Overall, then, the hallmark of the modern era has been to try to meet every new demand for water—whether it is for agricultural or municipal and industrial use, for domestic food production or expanding exports to other countries—by finding and harnessing new supplies of freshwater. This has been the "hydraulic mission" of the modern era, and it was made possible by the considerable technological advances, economic wealth and energy resources generated by the Industrial Revolution that began in the late eighteenth century. The global spread of industrialization from the 1900s onward further cemented the association between economic progress and increased water appropriation, control and use. As a consequence, in today's economies, water use management, and its accompanying innovations, institutions and incentives, is dominated by this "hydraulic mission" of finding and exploiting more freshwater resources.[28]

Water developments in the modern economy therefore became tied both to energy use and to investments to increase supply capacity through large-scale engineering applications (e.g., dams, pumping stations, pipelines, diversions, etc.).[29] However, as discussed in the previous chapter, almost all abstraction regimes that were developed during the modern era evolved during periods of relative water abundance and where rapid changes in technology were not common.[30]

One outcome is that water is still predominantly used for agriculture, which, as we noted previously, still accounts for 70 percent of water withdrawals globally. In most countries, water allocation does not go to its highest-valued use, and there is much wasteful water consumption. For example, water use in agriculture is often inefficient, which has led to the overexploitation of groundwater resources as well as the depletion of the natural flow of major rivers. As we have also seen, the food trade may have improved more efficient and less wasteful use of water, but there are growing concerns that policy distortions and mismanagement are promoting the export of water-intensive commodities increasingly from water-scarce regions and countries with high opportunity costs for water as well as from depletable groundwater sources.

At the same time, the predominant expansion of water demand is through urban population growth served by public water supply systems. For example, about 46 percent of the population in the United States is served by very large public water supply systems (serving more than 100,000 persons), and a further 36 percent are served by large systems (serving 10,000–100,000 persons).[31] Globally, public water supply systems are under increasing pressure to replace aging infrastructure and accommodate the demands of growing urban populations. Developing economies have not only to find water supplies to meet agricultural development and urban expansion but also to meet the basic water needs of 663 million people who lack access to safe water and 2.4 billion people with inadequate sanitation.[32]

This means that the "hydraulic mission" of the modern era, which relies on the expansion of large-scale public water supply infrastructure and systems to provide for the growing demand for multiple uses of water—whether for agriculture, municipal and industrial use, flood control or absorbing pollution—is still dominant today. As we have seen, it has a long history, with its roots in the aftermath of the Industrial Revolution. For example, publicly funding large-scale dams to generate multiple water services to growing populations, agriculture and industries began in the United States in the late nineteenth century, and then was adopted throughout the twentieth century by other frontier economies with major river basins and watersheds—such as Canada, temperate Latin America, Australia, New Zealand and South Africa. After World War II, large dams and water infrastructure projects quickly spread to low- and middle-income economies. These publicly funded investments in developing countries were often supported by substantial foreign aid, and include such infamous projects as the Aswan Dam in Egypt, the Three Gorges Dam in China, the Narmada Sardar Sarovar Dam in India and the Belo Monte Dam in Brazil. Today, there are over 55,000 dams worldwide, built almost exclusively through public investment and operation.[33] Although around 70 percent are for single purpose, with most built for irrigation, followed by hydropower, water supply and flood control, the demand for multipurpose dams is increasing, especially in developing countries. More importantly, they represent the dominance of public provision in the planning, funding and implementation of the expansion of water supplies and services worldwide.

Perhaps the most extreme manifestation of the global hydraulic mission has been the development of water "megaprojects" in semi-arid and arid environments worldwide.[34] These schemes are large-scale and costly infrastructure investments, usually involving dams, diversions, canals and pipelines, for water transfer schemes that aim to attract large numbers of people to desert areas by encouraging agricultural, industrial and urban development. Although such projects have been magnificent engineering achievements, and have frequently succeeded in their objectives of transforming deserts with cities, people and economic activity, too often they have been huge economic and financial failures.

A classic example is the Central Arizona Project (CAP), which was the largest and most expensive water transfer project in US history.[35] Completed in 1992, the CAP invested over $5 billion to divert water from the Colorado River and transport it by canals to support irrigated agriculture in Phoenix, Tucson and surrounding areas of the southwestern state of Arizona in the United States. Although farmers received the water, irrigation fees were unable to cover the investment. Several agricultural water districts went bankrupt, the substantial loan burden was shifted to urban residents and taxpayers, and the remaining debt will not be paid off until 2046.

Developing similar megaprojects for economic development and population expansion in water-scarce areas of the world still remains a dominant paradigm. For example, six of the largest cities facing water stress listed in Table 3.2—Delhi,

Mexico City, Karachi, Beijing, Los Angeles and Lima—are located in desert environments and depend on megaprojects for their water. This trend is likely to continue. As noted by the geographer Troy Sternberg, "As ever-greater water is needed for agriculture, industry and domestic use in drylands, megaprojects give short-term solutions, satisfy current demand and offer political expediency."[36] Unfortunately, this approach of finding and delivering more freshwater supplies to meet growing and competing demands, even in the most water-scarce and inhospitable environments, illustrates how pervasive and monolithic the hydraulic mission has become worldwide.

If widespread water scarcity and its economic and social consequences are to be averted, we must urgently take a different path to managing water resources. The hydraulic mission of the modern era, and more importantly the pattern of institutions, incentives and innovations accompanying it, evolved during a time of water abundance. Consequently, today's approach to water management is inappropriate for coping with the emerging global water crisis. In an age of rising water scarcity, the world can no longer afford innovations, institutions and incentives perpetually geared toward finding and exploiting more freshwater resources. Instead, we must look to an alternative strategy of managing and reducing water demands, minimizing the economic, social and environmental costs of water use, and improving the efficiency of water delivery, consumption and treatment systems. The next chapters explore the institutions, incentives and innovations that are needed for such a transformation in water management.

4

A GLOBAL CRISIS IN WATER MANAGEMENT

The global water crisis is predominantly a crisis of inadequate and poor water management. In the near future, many countries, regions and populations may face rising costs of exploiting additional water resources that could constrain growth as well as make it increasingly difficult to meet the needs of those poor populations and countries that face chronic water insecurity. If unchecked, water scarcity could increase the likelihood of civil unrest and conflicts. There is also a risk of disputes over the management of transboundary water sources and "water grabbing" acquisitions. Yet this crisis could be avoided. Inadequate policies, governance and institutions, coupled with incorrect market signals and insufficient innovations to improve efficiency, underlie most chronic water problems.

Subsequent chapters will explore these themes in more detail. The aim of this chapter is to discuss the social and economic implications of rising global water use and scarcity.

Several manifestations of this problem will be explored: the additional threat posed by climate change on meeting increasing future demands for water; the implications of water scarcity for economic growth, especially in developing countries; the growing dependence on transboundary water resources and its potential for disputes and conflicts; the worsening groundwater crisis; and the recent emergence of "water grabbing" to secure long-term sources of fertile agricultural land and water resources.

Climate Change and Water Scarcity

In the coming decades, increasing water demands and population growth will put more pressure on the world's available water resources. Climate change is likely to exacerbate further any resulting water scarcity.

Currently, between 1.6 and 2.4 billion people are estimated to be living within watersheds exposed to water scarcity. Most are located in east Asia (around 0.7 billion) and south Asia (0.5 to 1.0 billion). In the absence of any climate change, by 2050 there will be 3.1 to 4.3 billion people affected by water scarcity, including 1.5 to 1.7 billion in south Asia and 0.7 to 1.2 billion in east Asia. However, scenario predictions from Global Climate Models suggest that climate change between now and 2050 will likely increase substantially the number of people impacted by scarcity. Under the most likely scenario, global warming will increase the number of people exposed to water scarcity by an additional 0.5 to 3.1 billion. This could include as many as 1.5 billion extra people in south Asia and 0.5 billion more in east Asia.[1]

Climate change could have its most dramatic impact on the freshwater available for irrigated agriculture. As we saw in the previous chapter, agriculture accounts for 70–80 percent of freshwater use in much of the world. The lack of water available for agriculture, and especially food production, is likely to increase in coming decades, because of increasing population, higher demand for meat and other water-intensive products, and growing competition in water use for industries and cities. The increasing temperatures and changing precipitation patterns associated with climate change will further exacerbate the impacts of water scarcity on agriculture.

Existing climate models suggest, for example, that the global losses to basic food crops, such as maize, soybeans, wheat and rice could result in declines of between 8 and 24 percent in food production potential, compared to present-day totals.[2] Growing freshwater scarcity in the western United States, China and west, central and south Asia could lead to between 20 and 60 million hectares of cropland reverting from irrigation to rainfed farming. If this occurs, the losses in global food production could double. It is possible that some regions, such as the northern and eastern United States, southeast Asia, Europe and parts of South America, may have extra freshwater to supply additional irrigated cropland. However, this would require substantial investments in irrigation infrastructure and supply in these regions.

The previous chapter also noted that the fastest growth in water use is for rapidly expanding cities and their populations. Not only is urbanization accelerating around the world, but urban dwellers are expanding how much water they use each year. The result is that the world's urban areas are using more freshwater, and extending their "water footprint" to secure water supplies from more distant rivers and reservoirs. Climate change will put further stress on available hydrological supplies for cities, and make it even harder for them to access the water needed for their rapidly expanding populations.

From 2000 to 2050, for example, the number of urban residents worldwide is expected to increase by 3 billion. Already, in 2000, there were 150 million people living in cities that faced chronic water shortage, which is annual water availability that averages to less than 100 liters of water per person per day. By 2050, urban population growth alone will expand this number to nearly 1 billion people. Climate change is projected to increase the number of urban dwellers facing chronic water shortages by another 100 million.[3] More significant may be the impact of climate change on the costs of providing more water to cities, as water must be conveyed over greater distances and more expensive sources are appropriated. In addition, there may be substantial ecological costs to overcoming urban water shortages, both chronic and seasonal, as more freshwater ecosystems, river basins and other water bodies are tapped and diverted for urban populations.

Economic Growth and Water Scarcity

Global water demand is anticipated to rise from about 3,500km^3 in 2000 to nearly 5,500km^3 in 2050, primarily due to increased use for agriculture, manufacturing, electricity and domestic purposes in developing economies.[4] As noted previously, there are potentially billions of people who could be affected by water scarcity in coming decades, and many will be located in poorer regions. Climate change will put additional water supplies at risk. This raises the question as to whether increasing water use and scarcity may impose constraints on economic growth, especially for today's low and middle-income countries that are anticipated to need more water as their economies develop and populations grow.

There are two ways in which water scarcity may affect economic growth. First, as water becomes increasingly scarce, a country must appropriate less accessible sources of freshwater through allocating a greater share of aggregate economic output, in terms of dams, pumping stations, supply infrastructure, etc. That is, there are likely to be rising economic costs as the country tries to secure more supplies of freshwater. But there will also be a positive impact on growth. Increased water use benefits the economy by boosting agricultural and industrial productivity. However, if the increasing costs of appropriating more and more scarce supplies exceed the gains in productivity, then rising water use and scarcity will begin to constrain economic growth.

Second, it is also possible that water utilization in an economy may be restricted by the absolute availability of water. In such extreme cases, it may be difficult and costly for a physically water-constrained economy to meet all its growing demands for increased use. As discussed in the previous chapter, countries in the Middle East are highly dependent on agricultural imports to overcome the constraints imposed by the extreme water shortages found throughout the region. For example, through food trade, Jordan imports the equivalent of about 5 to 7 billion m^3 of water each year, which compares to the 1 billion m^3 of water available for agriculture from its domestic sources.[5]

One study examined these two mechanisms by which water scarcity might affect economic growth across 163 high-income and developing countries.[6] The results suggest that current rates of freshwater utilization in the majority of countries are not yet constraining economic growth. Most countries may be able to increase growth further by utilizing more of their freshwater resources, although there are obvious limits on how much additional growth can be generated in this way. However, countries that are "water stressed," that is, they have limited freshwater supplies relative to current and future populations, may find it especially difficult to generate additional growth through more water use. Many countries in the Middle East appear to be already facing this problem.

Even if water scarcity is yet to act as a constraint on overall economic growth in most countries, there may be other concerns. For example, urbanization and industrialization place additional stress on freshwater resources not only through increased abstraction but also through more water pollution. An analysis of 177 countries over the period 1960–2009 confirms that water utilization impacts economic growth, but water quality also proves to be highly significant and to have an even greater impact on growth.[7] This suggests that increasing water pollution may be another avenue through which scarcity of available supplies affects economic growth.

For many countries, freshwater supplies and use rates vary considerably across specific regions and water basins within a country. Thus, a country as a whole may appear to have sufficient freshwater supplies relative to demand, but specific regions may not. This is especially the case for large countries, such as the United States and China. For example, the western United Sates is generally arid and semi-arid, and is already experiencing constraints on agriculture and increased urban use because of water shortages, whereas the eastern United States has plentiful water supplies. In China, the Yellow and Yangtze river basins are facing increasing water shortage and scarcities, but the river basins in south and west China are less affected by water stress.[8]

In addition, water scarcity may be an important constraint on specific sectors within an economy, such as agriculture. As an example, Box 4.1 summarizes a study of the impacts of water use on agricultural growth in the western state of Wyoming in the United States. Water availability varies considerably across Wyoming's counties, and drought occurs periodically. In counties where water is relatively abundant, agricultural uses of water can increase, and long-run agricultural yields per capita are higher. However, in counties facing chronic water shortages, prior claims on water for agriculture are frequently fully used, and this water scarcity constrains agricultural growth. Drought further limits water use, thus additionally lowering agricultural growth.

As noted above, most of the increase in global water demand and use is expected to occur in developing countries. Already, many developing economies are facing increasing environmental and social costs as they devote more infrastructure and investments to achieving greater water security through expanding access to available freshwater supplies. However, there is also evidence that poor water policies, governance and institutions may be fostering inefficient and expensive increases in publicly provided water supplies, and thus artificially increasing the economic costs of obtaining additional water in many developing countries.[9] For example, irrigation accounts for 70 percent of water use in developing economies, yet many

Box 4.1 Water and Agricultural Growth in Wyoming

Wyoming is an arid, predominantly rural state in the western United States where water development has contributed significantly to agricultural expansion. About 60 percent of ranches and farms use surface water to irrigate, with the rest relying on rainwater. Groundwater is not a primary source of irrigation, and irrigated agriculture accounts for 95 percent of Wyoming's water resources. Water availability varies considerably across Wyoming's counties, with abundant supplies in some counties whereas others face chronic shortages. Drought is a persistent threat faced by ranchers and farmers.

As in all western US states, water is allocated by prior appropriation. This allows the right holder to divert and use water based on priority of claim, and thus a farmer or rancher must demonstrate that the amount claimed is necessary for some "approved" application, such as irrigation for crops, watering livestock, and so forth. The prior water claim is effectively an upper limit on how much water the holder can use for agricultural purposes.

Chaudhry and Barbier analyze the impacts of water use on agricultural growth for twenty-three Wyoming counties from 1980 to 2004. They find that increased water use leads to higher growth in agricultural yield per capita, but, if prior claims constrain water use, there are significant losses in long-run agricultural growth. That is, if long-term water use is well within the prior water rights allocated to agriculture, then increased water use can lead to higher growth in agricultural yields. However, in counties facing chronic water shortages, prior claims on water for agriculture are frequently fully used, and thus there are constraints on using more water to boost agricultural yields. For example, the average agricultural growth rates are about 21 percent lower in the water scarce

Platte River basin counties of southeast Wyoming than in counties that are not water constrained. Finally, the study shows that if periodic drought exacerbates any water-rights constraint on water use, it will lead to lower longer-run agricultural growth.

Source: Anita M. Chaudhry and Edward B. Barbier (2013), "Water and Growth in an Agricultural Economy," *Agricultural Economics* 44:2, 175–189.

of their irrigation systems lose between one-half and two-thirds of the water in transit between source and crops, mainly because water is subsidized so that the price does not reflect the costs of delivery to farmers, let alone its value in use.[10]

If water appropriation incurs rising costs and is socially inefficient across many developing economies, then a higher rate of water utilization could be associated with a decline in economic growth. That is, growth initially declines with a higher rate of water utilization and only increases if higher rates of water utilization force the economy to become more efficient in its water policies and use. Such outcomes might occur if the negative growth impacts of government's appropriation of output to supply water overwhelm the positive contribution of increased water use to productivity.

This possible impact of increasing water use on growth has been examined for 112 developing economies over the period 1970–2012.[11] The analysis found evidence that increased water use first leads to declining economic growth, but eventually growth may rise with higher rates of water utilization relative to freshwater supplies. The most likely explanation for the initial negative impact of increased water use on growth is inefficient water policies and institutions. However, once developing economies have reached a relatively high rate of withdrawal relative to freshwater supplies, the increasing economic costs of inefficient policies and institutions may lead to reform. This could explain why, for some countries, as the rate of water utilization exceeds two-thirds, further increases lead to higher growth. That is, as water becomes increasingly scarce, countries may be realizing that they can no longer afford inefficient and wasteful policies and institutions, and start instigating water reforms.

Transboundary Water Resources

Increasingly, countries are sharing water. There are 286 surface water basins that cross international boundaries, and there are nearly 600 transboundary aquifers. International water basins alone cover nearly half of the world's land area and contain 40 percent of the global population.[12] As we have discussed previously, rising populations, increased economic activity and climate change will mean that more and more people will be living within watersheds exposed to water scarcity. Thus, as water scarcity increases, and transboundary water sources become more important for global supply, the potential for disputes and conflicts over shared surface and groundwater resources could be significant.

Sometimes transboundary water resources are equally distributed across countries, making it reasonably easy for the countries to agree on sharing arrangements. But this might change as water scarcity increases and countries become more dependent on external sources of water. Already, twenty-five countries receive 50–75 percent of their water from outside their borders, and fifteen countries rely on external sources for over 75 percent of their water.[13] All but two of the countries are developing economies. The freshwater impacts of climate change are especially likely to pose a challenge for such economies.[14] Also, many of the countries are in regions that are already prone to longstanding conflicts as well as water shortages, such as the Middle East.

As the number of countries sharing water resources increases, it becomes more difficult to negotiate joint management of transboundary supplies. Three or more countries share the water of fifty-three river basins worldwide; the Amazon River has seven countries sharing it, the Nile ten countries, and the Danube seventeen.[15] When multiple countries facing both climate change and chromic water shortages share a river or other water body, the competition over available water resources will be acute, and meeting the freshwater demand for agriculture and other vital uses could be a major challenge for policy makers.[16]

Equally problematic is when a country shares multiple water resources with a number of different countries. This occurs frequently in sub-Saharan Africa, which has many small countries and numerous rivers. Of seventy-seven pairs of countries worldwide that share three or more rivers, twenty-five are in Africa. China and Russia also face considerable challenges, as they share multiple rivers with multiple countries. For example, China shares three or more rivers with India, Kazakhstan, North Korea, Mongolia, Myanmar, Russia and Vietnam. Russia shares three or more rivers with Azerbaijan, Belarus, China, Finland, Georgia, Kazakhstan, Latvia, Mongolia and Ukraine.[17]

While most countries have institutional mechanisms and policies for allocating internal water resources and resolving water disputes, negotiating and implementing workable agreements to manage and share international water resources has proved more difficult. Currently, there are more than 300 international freshwater agreements.[18] Yet many international river basins and other shared water resources still lack any type of joint management structure, and some existing international agreements need to be updated or improved. Although the potential for armed conflict between countries over shared water resources remains low, cooperation to resolve disputes over water is often lacking.[19] Countries in Asia and Africa appear less likely to conclude international treaties over transboundary water than countries in Europe.[20] In some cases, such as the shrinkage of Lake Chad in sub-Saharan Africa, the lack of cooperation is having a detrimental effect on the shared water system.[21] In south Asia, the 1996 Ganges River Treaty between India and Bangladesh may unravel unless the treaty is extended to allow river flow to be supplemented by water transfers from Nepal.[22]

An assessment of the risk of political conflict over shared river basins found that the greatest threat occurs in basins in which countries are planning major infrastructure projects to meet future water needs without any formal agreements with neighbors on managing transboundary water resources.[23] As indicated in Table 4.1, the vulnerable basins are largely in developing countries—several in southeast Asia, south Asia, Central America, the northern part of South America, the southern Balkans and across Africa. These basins are already areas of considerable political tension as well as having suffered past conflicts, which does not bode well for future cooperation on transboundary water management.

Table 4.1 River Basins at Risk of Future Conflict over Water

River basin	Riparian countries	Region	Population (thousands)
Bei Jiang/Hsi	China, Vietnam	East Asia	77,098
Benito/Ntem	Cameroon, Equatorial Guinea, Gabon	Sub-Saharan Africa	657
Ca/Song-Koi	Laos, Vietnam	East Asia	2,741
Chiriqui	Costa Rica, Panama	Latin America	90
Drin	Albania, Macedonia, Montenegro, Serbia	Eastern Europe	1,766
Irrawaddy	China, India, Myanmar	East & South Asia	28,583
Krka	Bosnia & Herzegovina, Croatia	Eastern Europe	59
Lake Turkana	Ethiopia, Kenya, South Sudan, Uganda	Sub-Saharan Africa	11,733
Ma	Laos, Vietnam	East Asia	2,985
Mira	Colombia, Ecuador	Latin America	625
Mono	Benin, Togo	Sub-Saharan Africa	2,159
Neretva	Bosnia & Herzegovina, Croatia	Eastern Europe	633
Ogooue	Cameroon, Congo, Gabon, Equatorial Guinea	Sub-Saharan Africa	768
Red/Song Hong	China, Laos, Vietnam	East Asia	17, 864
Sabi	Mozambique, Zimbabwe	Sub-Saharan Africa	3,428
Saigon	Cambodia, Vietnam	East Asia	10,911
Salween	China, Myanmar, Thailand	East Asia	7,851

Table 4.1 River Basins at Risk of Future Conflict over
Water (cont.)

River basin	Riparian countries	Region	Population (thousands)
Sanaga	Cameroon, Central African Republic, Nigeria	Sub-Saharan Africa	3,443
San Juan	Costa Rica, Nicaragua	Latin America	5,057
Tarim	Afghanistan, China, Kazakhstan, Kyrgyzstan, Tajikistan	Central Asia	10,323
Thukela	Lesotho, South Africa	Sub-Saharan Africa	1,975
Vardar	Bulgaria, Greece, Macedonia, Serbia	Eastern Europe	2,126

Source: L. De Stefano, Jacob D. Petersen-Perlman, Eric A. Sproles, Jim Eynard and Aaron T. Wolf (2017), "Assessment of Transboundary River Basins for Potential Hydro-Political Tensions," *Global Environmental Change* 45, 35–46.

The Global Groundwater Crisis

The growing stress on surface water supplies and freshwater ecosystems is also leading to increased depletion of underground aquifers, which some suggest has produced a "global groundwater crisis."[24] Groundwater already accounts for one-third of total water withdrawals worldwide, and over 2 billion people rely on aquifers for their primary water source.[25] The volume of groundwater abstraction worldwide is currently increasing by 1–3 percent, and contamination of remaining groundwater supplies by pollution and saltwater intrusion is becoming a more widespread problem.[26]

In addition, as we discussed in the previous chapter, the global food trade is becoming more dependent on using groundwater. From 2000 to 2010, groundwater depletion attributed to food exports increased from 17.7km^3 to 25.6km^3 annually, or by 45 percent.[27] One in five urban residents currently rely on groundwater as the principal source of water, and, as cities and their populations continue to grow, the pressures on aquifers from urbanization are expected to mount.[28]

Unlike most surface water, however, groundwater is not easily replenished. Aquifers are often fixed or isolated stocks that are consumed far faster than their slow rate of recharge. Thus, groundwater is often referred to as *fossilized water*, as it has characteristics more in common with non-renewable and exhaustible resources such as fossil fuels than it does with freshwater from rivers, lakes and other bodies of surface water. Yet, in many of the most drought-prone and driest regions of the world, groundwater depletion is the "backstop" resource to which farmers, ranchers and herders, and expanding cities and industries rely on when there are inadequate or failing surface supplies of freshwater.

As a result, the rapid rates of annual depletion in the major aquifers of arid and semi-arid regions far exceed natural replenishment (see Table 4.2). Most of these regions are important sources of global agricultural production, especially food. In addition, some of the aquifers are so large that they are shared by two or more countries. Some of these countries are already in conflict with their neighbors, and sharing rapidly depleting aquifers may worsen further existing political tensions in regions such as north Africa, the Middle East and south Asia.

Table 4.2 Groundwater Depletion in the Major Arid and Semi-Arid Aquifers

Aquifer	Countries Affected	Depletion Rate (km³/year)
Northwestern India	India, Pakistan	17.7
Arabian	Iraq, Jordan, Oman, Qatar, Saudi Arabia, United Arab Emirates, Yemen	15.5
Northern Middle East	Iran, Iraq, Syria, Turkey	13.0
High Plains (Ogallala)	United States	12.5
North China Plain	China	8.3
Canning Basin	Australia	3.6
California Central Valley	United States	3.1
Northwest Sahara	Algeria, Libya, Tunisia	2.7
Guarani	Argentina, Brazil, Paraguay, Uruguay	1.0

Source: J. S. Famiglietti (2014), "The Global Groundwater Crisis," *Nature Climate Change* 4:11, 946–948.

Water Grabbing

As countries with large populations and sufficient wealth face rising water scarcity, they are increasingly investing in other countries to acquire additional fertile land and water resources. These extra agricultural resources are then used to grow crops that can be exported back to feed expanding populations or provide raw materials for growing industries in the water-scarce countries. This global phenomenon is often referred to as "water grabbing."[29]

As we saw in the previous chapter, more and more regions and populations globally are increasingly affected by water scarcity for food production. By acquiring land in regions that have more abundant freshwater resources, countries in which freshwater is scarce can ease the demand on their water supplies for growing food. This could be a "win-win" by both alleviating water scarcity and improving food security.[30] If the country with less freshwater saves on water and obtains food more cheaply, acquiring land in water-abundant regions can lead to more efficient use of water and land for agricultural production globally.

As indicated in Table 4.3, twenty-four countries account for almost all the agricultural land associated with water grabbing. This includes both surface and groundwater used for irrigated crop production ("blue water") and rainwater used for rainfed agricultural production ("green water"). Almost all the countries that are targets for water grabbing are low- and middle-income economies. Consequently, there are concerns that there can be adverse impacts on food security and even malnourishment in these poor target countries and regions.[31] If future land and water acquisitions continue to occur mainly in poor economies, they could generate considerable conflict through increasing disputes about the legality of the expropriation, the basis of compensation, meeting the needs of local people for water, protecting the environmental integrity of ecosystems, and ensuring food security in targeted countries.[32]

Table 4.4 indicates that the majority of countries behind water grabbing are mainly wealthy economies in North America, Europe and the Middle East, as well as large newly emerging market economies in Asia, Latin America and

Table 4.3 Top Water-Grabbed Countries

Water-Grabbed Country	Grabbed water (billion m³)			Grabbed water per unit area (m³/ha)		
	Green	Blue	Total	Green	Blue	Total
Indonesia	117.4	7.0	124.4	16,000	1,000	17,000
Sudan	24.5	19.8	44.4	5,000	4,000	9,000
Tanzania	15.6	25.5	41.0	8,000	13,000	21,000
Philippines	36.7	1.4	38.1	7,000	0	7,000
Democratic Republic of Congo	24.9	10.4	35.3	3,000	1,000	4,000
Brazil	20.2	8.4	28.7	9,000	4,000	13,000
Mozambique	8.0	12.2	20.2	5,000	8,000	13,000
Russia	3.4	13.7	17.1	1,000	5,000	6,000
Ethiopia	5.5	7.9	13.4	6,000	8,000	14,000
Liberia	10.9	0.8	11.6	17,000	1,000	18,000
Republic of Congo	5.5	4.5	10.0	8,000	7,000	15,000
Ukraine	5.6	4.1	9.7	5,000	3,000	8,000
Cameroon	2.6	6.8	9.4	9,000	18,000	26,000
Sierra Leone	4.9	2.5	7.3	10,000	5,000	15,000
Papua New Guinea	5.4	1.4	6.8	17,000	4,000	21,000
Gabon	3.3	3.3	6.6	8,000	8,000	16,000
Morocco	3.7	2.8	6.5	5,000	4,000	9,000
Uganda	3.1	2.4	5.5	4,000	3,000	7,000
Pakistan	1.0	3.8	4.7	3,000	11,000	14,000
Australia	1.0	3.6	4.6	0	1,000	1,000
Nigeria	1.4	2.8	4.2	4,000	8,000	12,000
Madagascar	1.7	0.7	2.4	5,000	2,000	7,000
Uruguay	1.5	0.1	1.6	4,000	0	4,000
Argentina	0.5	0.3	0.8	1,000	0	1,000
Total	308.2	146.0	454.2	160,000	119,000	278,000

These twenty-four countries account for 90 percent of grabbed land globally. "Green water" refers to rainwater used for rainfed agricultural production. "Blue water" refers to surface and groundwater used for irrigated agricultural production.
Source: Maria Cristina Rulli, Antonio Saviori and Paolo D'Odorico (2013), "Global Land and Water Grabbing," *Proceedings of the National Academy of Sciences* 110:3, 892–897.

Africa. Some of these countries that engage in water grabbing and trade do not face water scarcity or agricultural production constraints, and there is increasing concern that the large-scale investors and companies behind water grabbing are simply looking to make substantial profits from acquiring cheap water resources to grow exportable crops.[33]

In addition, there are indications that water grabbing may not be reducing the pressure on scarce water supplies in the countries that participate in this activity. For example, as discussed in Chapter 3, India, Pakistan and China are the largest exporters of scarce water globally, and the United States exports water from regions with frequent water shortages, such as California and other western states.[34] Yet, Pakistan is also a target for water grabbing, and China, India and the US are among the leading countries that acquire land and water overseas (see Tables 4.3 and 4.4). This suggests that countries engage in water grabbing to obtain food more cheaply, but not necessarily to save on freshwater. In fact, it is possible that wealthier countries may be acquiring cheaper land and water resources for agriculture overseas to avoid the consequences, and possibly rising costs, of inefficient water management at home.

Water grabbing is not the only symptom of the global water crisis that has its roots in mismanagement. As we have seen in this chapter, every manifestation of the problem—the

Table 4.4 Top Water-Grabbing Countries

	Grabbed land		Grabbed water per (billion m³)		
	Grabbed area (million ha)	% of total global land	Green	Blue	Total
United States	3.70	7.9	28.2	15.2	43.5
United Kingdom	4.41	9.4	26.9	7.5	34.4
United Arab Emirates	2.68	5.7	16.8	11.9	28.8
Israel	2.0	4.3	20.1	3.8	23.8
India	1.21	2.6	8.6	10.3	18.9
Egypt	1.45	3.1	7.9	6.1	14.0
Singapore	0.93	2.0	8.9	3.7	12.6
South Africa	1.11	2.4	7.2	5.2	12.5
South Korea	1.26	2.7	8.4	3.2	11.6
Malaysia	0.97	2.1	7.4	3.1	10.5
France	0.77	1.6	6.0	3.9	9.9
China	3.41	7.3	5.8	2.3	8.0
Argentina	0.7	1.5	6.0	1.6	7.6
Saudi Arabia	0.76	1.6	3.9	3.2	7.1
Sweden	0.83	1.8	3.0	3.2	6.2
Qatar	0.85	1.8	2.8	2.1	4.9
Kazakhstan	0.66	1.4	0.9	2.2	3.0
Italy	0.16	0.3	1.0	1.6	2.6
Sudan	0.15	0.3	0.8	1.8	2.5
Canada	0.35	0.7	2.0	0.2	2.2
Germany	0.33	0.7	0.8	1.1	1.9
Russia	0.25	0.5	1.0	0.7	1.7
Portugal	0.21	0.4	0.4	1.3	1.7
Brazil	0.11	0.2	1.2	0.4	1.6
Total	29.0	62.3	176.0	95.6	271.5

These twenty-four countries account for 62 percent of grabbed land globally. "Green water" refers to rainwater used for rainfed agricultural production. "Blue water" refers to surface and groundwater used for irrigated agricultural production.
Source: Maria Cristina Rulli, Antonio Saviori and Paolo D'Odorico (2013), "Global Land and Water Grabbing," *Proceedings of the National Academy of Sciences* 110:3, 892–897.

threat posed by climate change, water scarcity constraining economic growth, disputes and conflicts over transboundary water resources, and the worsening groundwater crisis—can be traced to inadequate institutions, incentives and innovation for managing freshwater. As we shall explore in the next chapters, resolving these shortcomings is the key to overcoming the looming global water crisis.

5

REFORMING GOVERNANCE AND INSTITUTIONS

In the coming decades, the demand for freshwater will continue to grow as population and incomes increase worldwide. Moreover, most freshwater resources are fully allocated for one principal use—agriculture—yet there are competing demands for municipal, industrial and, increasingly, recreational and environmental uses. All supplies of water are likely to become more variable and uncertain as climate change intensifies.

Unfortunately, the existing governance and institutional regimes of most countries are incapable of meeting these water management challenges. As we saw in previous chapters, the main reason for this institutional inertia is that most of the world's current abstraction regimes evolved during periods of relative water abundance.[1] As a consequence, water management today, and its accompanying innovations, institutions and incentives, are not equipped to handle rising water scarcity. Instead, they are still driven by the "hydraulic mission" of finding and exploiting more freshwater resources to meet growing demands.[2] All too often, policy distortions and institutional and governance failures compound water scarcity by encouraging wasteful use of water and ecosystem degradation. That is, just as the world is facing a water crisis and increasing scarcity, countries are not responding with the correct institutions, policies and technological innovations to avert this crisis.

Reforming governance and institutions to meet the challenge of growing water scarcity and competing demands is at the heart of the solution to this water paradox. Water *governance* consists of the processes and institutions by which decisions that affect water are made.[3] *Institutions* are the informal and formal rules, arising from well-established social arrangements and structures, which provide incentives and determine outcomes in both individual and collective decisions related to water development, allocation, use and management.[4] Important influences on water governance include legal and social institutions that protect property rights, enforce contracts and encourage collective action for the physical and organizational infrastructure needed to manage the resource. Thus, water institutions and governance are the bedrock upon which water management is built. If the foundation of governance and institutions is strong, then good water management ensues; if it is weak, then management will collapse.

Currently, there is a mismatch between water governance and institutions and our management needs. Because they evolved during periods of relative water abundance that did not require novel innovations to address scarcity, today's governance regimes and institutions have been inadequate or slow to adapt to the rapidly changing conditions of water availability and competing demands, including the threat posed by climate change.[5] Of particular concern is the lack of sufficient regulations or institutions in most countries governing use of groundwater resources.[6] The continued treatment of freshwater in most countries and regions as a "freely available" resource or an unpriced commodity that should be publicly provided regardless of cost is another pervasive problem.[7] A further challenge is that governance regimes are often based on arbitrary political and administrative boundaries, whereas effective and efficient management of water resources, especially in response to environmental and human impacts, requires governance across geographical boundaries, such as river basins and watersheds.[8] Correcting such inefficiencies through institutional and governance reforms should be a priority to meet the water management challenges faced by many countries and regions. The purpose of this chapter is to explore some of these options for reform of water institutions and governance.

River Basin Management

Managing river basins and watershed catchments is important to resolving the growing water crisis.[9] For the past several decades, this has been increasingly recognized in the growing calls for integrated water resource management, with its focus on the management of river and other bodies of surface water as the appropriate governance unit in deciding how the water should be allocated to various competing uses.

Although this seems sound in principle, river basin management along hydrological boundaries has been very difficult to implement in practice. A survey of 134 countries by the United Nations found that, since 1992, 80 percent had undertaken some steps to improve integrated water resource management. However, only half indicated that they had made significant progress toward developing and implementing widespread institutional reforms.[10] Others have also raised concerns about how such reforms have been put into practice, and whether they have led to improved river basin management.[11]

Historically, governance of river basins has followed political and administrative, rather than hydrological, boundaries.[12] Governments function through legal and jurisdictional subnational units, such as provinces or states, districts and counties, and municipalities and cities. The jurisdiction of these administrative units often does not conform to the natural boundaries of river basins, which often cross multiple jurisdictions and political boundaries. Rivers and watersheds typically meander across different provinces, states, districts and countries, and contain many different cities and municipalities.

To overcome these complications, river basin management and planning is often instigated "top down" from the national level. Such efforts have proven difficult to implement and coordinate across different national agencies and bureaucracies. For one, different uses of water and sectors come under different jurisdictions. Irrigation, industrial and municipal uses of water are typically administered through separate government agencies and bureaucracies. Jurisdiction over environmental uses of water may also be spread across different administrative units. For example, in the United States, water pollution is regulated by the Environmental

Protection Agency, water-based recreation and tourism by the Department of the Interior, and inland freshwater fisheries by the Wildlife Service. These sectoral and administrative divisions over water use and sectors further complicate institutional arrangements for integrated river basin management and basin-wide planning.

Yet some progress is being made and important lessons learned. For example, Canada has attempted over several decades to implement integrated river basin management. Starting with Ontario, all Canadian provinces and territories now have established watershed management agencies and river basin planning. Despite significant progress, however, there still remain substantial challenges for integrated river basin management: "In common with practice in much of the world, the responsibility for implementing integrated watershed management in Canada is fragmented, and there is a need for water management agencies to foster partnerships, coordinate planning and management activities, engage stakeholders, secure funding, monitor and report on progress, and update and adapt plans when necessary."[13]

To overcome these challenges and spur further progress, water agencies across Canada have been assessing and comparing their experiences from implementing integrated river basin management. Box 5.1 outlines the key lessons learned from this shared experience in Canada. The fundamental features and major challenges listed are important starting points for all countries developing institutional arrangements for river basin management and planning to manage increasing water scarcity and competing demands. However, it is equally important to recognize that there is no single best practice in formulating such institutional

Box 5.1 Integrated River Basin Management: Key Features and Challenges

Key features*

The catchment or river basin rather than an administrative or political unit is the management unit.

Attention is directed to upstream–downstream, surface–groundwater, and water quantity–quality interactions.

Interconnections of water with other natural resources and the environment are considered.

Environmental, economic and social aspects receive attention.

Stakeholders are actively engaged in planning, management and implementation to achieve an explicit vision, objectives and outcomes.

Key challenges†

Determining the appropriate boundary for the catchment or river basin unit.

Ensuring the accountability of catchment-scale or basin-scale decisions and decision-making bodies.

Appropriate "scaling up" from local administrative or political units (e.g., municipalities, districts, counties, etc.), and "scaling down" from national-level units (e.g., nations, states and provinces).

Accounting and controlling for all of the physical, social or economic factors outside of the catchment or river basin unit that may impact upon the area within its borders, and vice versa.

Accounting and controlling for all of the policy decisions outside of the catchment or river basin unit that may impact upon the area within its borders, and vice versa.

Notes:
* From Dan Shrubsole, Dan Walters, Barbara Veale and Bruce Mitchell (2017), "Integrated Water Resources Management in Canada: The Experience of Watershed Agencies," *International Journal of Water Resources Development* 33:3, 349–359.
† Based on Alice Cohen and Seanna Davidson (2011), "An Examination of the Watershed Approach: Challenges, Antecedents, and the Transition from Technical Tool to Governance Unit," *Water Alternatives* 4:1, 1–14.

arrangements; instead, as the Canadians have learned, "All the provinces and territories in Canada have developed unique approaches or governance models."[14]

A key initial decision is to determine whether establishing governance regimes and new institutional arrangements at the river basin level is worth it, given the difficult challenges faced (see Box 5.1). Some have argued that it may not always be necessary to implement integrated basin-wide management as a solution in order to overcome specific water management problems that are not necessarily at the basin scale.[15] Consequently, an important issue is: when is it useful and appropriate to adopt a basin-wide governance approach to managing water problems, and when is it not?

In answer to this question, water management experts Alice Cohen and Seanna Davidson cite the lessons learned from Canada.[16] One example occurred in Ontario when flood mapping revealed that the adverse impacts of downstream flooding and sedimentation on farm property values and agricultural production could be better controlled if a watershed-based approach to managing these impacts was implemented. In this case, the nature of the hydrological problem—flooding and damages throughout the watershed—dictated that a basin-wide approach was appropriate for tackling the problem. In a number of river basins throughout Canada, rescaling management of the river basin has also improved governance over some critical water problems. These include implementing national directives on drinking water standards and control of eutrophication due to phosphorus loading.

Although the Canadian experience with integrated river basin management may be instructive, some might argue that it is not representative. After all, Canada is a rich country with a relatively small population and sufficiently abundant water to meet its competing water demands. Climate change may affect its freshwater availability somewhat, but Canada hardly comes to mind when thinking of countries that are facing the brunt of the global water crisis.

However, there have been attempts to improve river basin management and planning in countries and regions that are facing more pressing water problems, including the threats posed by climate. One study has assessed the strengths and weaknesses of governance efforts to address water scarcity and improvement integrated in four critical and large river basins: the Colorado in the United States and Mexico, the Yellow (Huang He) in China, the Murray–Darling in Australia and the Orange–Senqu in southern Africa (Botswana, Lesotho, Namibia and South Africa).[17] Table 5.1 summarizes the key findings.

As the table indicates, governance across the four river basins varies considerably. Nevertheless, the authors of the comparative study conclude that there are five important insights on river basin governance and management that could be useful to all countries:

- Crises can provide a catalyst for reform.
- There is a need for economic valuation of freshwater ecosystem services to evaluate the trade-offs between consumptive and instream uses.
- Water management plans should take into account the inherent variability of rivers and streams shared between water users and instream uses for environmental benefits.
- Water markets and trades are needed to help reduce the

Table 5.1 Comparison of Governance of Four Major River Basins

River basin	River length (km)	Basin area (thousand km²)	Catalyst for reform	Key governance features
Colorado, United States and Mexico	2,100	622	Environmental	Multiple jurisdictions that coordinate actions across the basin; limited use of water markets to allocate water between and within states.
Yellow (Huang He), China	5,464	752	Severe drought	Single basin authorities plan and manage water across jurisdictions; top-down water allocations by central government.
Murray–Darling, Australia	2,589	1,061	Severe drought	Single basin authorities plan and manage water across jurisdictions; decentralized administration and extensive use of water markets to allocate flows.
Orange–Senqu, Botswana, Lesotho, Namibia, South Africa	2,300	973	End of Apartheid in South Africa	Multiple jurisdictions that coordinate actions across the basin; limited use of water markets to allocate flows.

Source: R. Quentin Grafton, Jamie Pittock, Richard Davis, John Williams, Guobin Fu et al. (2013), "Global Insights into Water Resources, Climate Change and Governance," *Nature Climate Change* 3:4, 315–321.

costs of reallocating water to environmental benefits, especially during times of low instream flows.

- There should be a greater contribution from centralized and nested water governance structures within basin-wide management institutions to revise water allocations as environmental conditions, scientific knowledge and societal values change.

To illustrate further the implications for integrated river basin management of water scarcity and competing uses, we will explore in more detail one of the more successful cases, which is the development of basin-wide management in the Murray–Darling river basin in Australia. We will then explore other examples of river basin management—some less successful than others—elsewhere in the world.

Management of the Murray–Darling River Basin[18]

The Murray–Darling river basin covers an area of just over 1 million square kilometers in Australia. Around 80 percent of this area is used for agriculture, but only 2 percent is irrigated. Yet, irrigation accounts for 90 percent of the freshwater diverted in the river basin. In addition, there are very large annual fluctuations in precipitation and frequent droughts, which, coupled with climate change, make future water flows highly uncertain.

In recent decades, a major challenge has been to manage the river basin for competing demands, due to growing populations, economic activity and urbanization. The pressure for increased abstraction for all these water uses has also raised concern that there are insufficient instream flows to maintain essential freshwater ecosystems and biodiversity. The threats posed by climate change, variable rainfall and periodic drought have further exacerbated the impending water scarcity afflicting the basin.

In response to these challenges, Australia has been transitioning over several decades from a traditional regulatory and administrative water abstraction regime for the Murray–Darling river basin to a more bottom-up and market-driven process, overseen by a basin-wide management authority. This transformation in governance involved three novel institutional arrangements:

- The development of a robust water-sharing regime at the basin level.
- The conversion of licenses to take water into entitlements, and the separation of these licenses from land titles.
- The establishment of water accounting, entitlement registration and administrative protocols that lowered the transaction costs of water trading.[19]

The reform process began in the 1960s with a few pilot water trading programs, and gradually expanded during the 1970s and 1980s as irrigators and administrators became more familiar with making trades and the benefits were more apparent. However, trading really took off in 1996, when a maximum limit was established on how much water could be diverted each year throughout the entire river basin. A further catalyst for reform was the prolonged drought in the region, from 2002 to 2012, which led to the creation in 2007 of the independent basin-wide management regime, the Murray–Darling Basin Authority (MDBA). Since then, continuing expansion of trading schemes is credited with ameliorating the worst effects of the drought, as well as demonstrating that reallocations from water diversion to protect instream flows are not only feasible but also can be achieved at minimal cost to farmers and their communities who depend on irrigation. There have also been substantial benefits associated with the improved ecosystem services from increased instream flows arising from healthier floodplain vegetation, waterfowl breeding, resurgence of native fish populations, and the rehabilitation of Coorong, Lower Lakes and Murray Mouth.

The next phase in management of the Murray–Darling river basin was the launch of the Basin Plan in 2012, which will be implemented in stages through 2024. The plan establishes, for the first time, a limit on annual groundwater extraction across the basin. In addition, it proposes "sustainable diversion limits" (SDLs) for total surface water diversion in the basin, which not only cap the overall amount of water diverted each year but also aim to reduce this annual limit by around 20 percent from 2019 to 2024. The aim of these SDLs for surface water and groundwater is to increase further efficiency in use and promote additional water trading to higher-valued uses throughout the basin.

Despite its continuing success and ambitious aims, continuing progress in improving integrated management of the Murray–Darling river basin has some challenges. For one, there is concern that the current SDLs for surface water and groundwater abstraction do not adequately take into account the potential hydrological impacts of climate change on the basin.[20] In addition, continuing political conflict between local government and the MDBA indicates that not all parties are cooperating fully with the current Basin Plan and that there are still important jurisdictional challenges to overcome.[21]

Finally, as pointed out by the Australian economist and water planner Michael Young, although other countries and governments may gain important and valuable insights from the transformation of governance and institutional arrangements in managing the Murray–Darling river basin, they should also be aware of two important caveats.[22] First, the reforms were costly. Australia's federal government invested billions of dollars in making the institutional transformation in the Murray–Darling river basin, which amounted to around A\$750,000 per irrigator. Second, the sequencing of the reform process was not ideal. Water trading was initiated and expanded rapidly before efforts were made to control the overallocation of water in the basin. Although the introduction of SDLs in the 2012 Basin Plan to reduce overuse is an attempt to correct this oversight, control of water abstraction should have been introduced simultaneously with water trading in the late 1990s.

River Basin Management in Other Regions

As indicated in Table 5.1, management reforms have also been introduced in the Orange–Senqu river basin, notably in South Africa. Recent assessments indicate that the governance transformation has been prolonged and the results mixed.[23]

In 1999, the South African government initiated the establishment of nineteen catchment management agencies (CMAs), which were later reduced to nine in 2012. To date, only two CMAs are functioning, with the remaining seven in process. The boundaries of these agencies are based on watershed catchments and overlap traditional state and local government administrative jurisdictions.

The reduction in the number of planned CMAs was due to the concern over the viability of the new governance regime, conflicts with state and local government over management of municipal and agricultural water use, insufficient financial resources, and lack of sufficient management skills and leadership. So far, the functioning CMAs are showing signs of overcoming these obstacles, but the process of institutional reform to improve basin-wide management has been slow. Water trading has been introduced, but is highly restricted and localized. Jurisdictional issues between the CMAs and local and state governments remain a concern.

An important challenge is how the CMAs will reconcile their goals of managing water and controlling overuse in their individual river basins with the overall national goals of providing clean water and improved sanitation for all South Africans. Access to basic water and sanitation services improved from 59 percent of the population in 1994 to 83 percent in 2005, which occurred through considerable investments in public infrastructure and supplies to increase municipal and domestic water use.[24] As South Africa's economy and population grow, there will be increasing demand for water across agricultural, municipal and industrial uses, as well as a need to maintain instream flows for preserving freshwater ecosystems and biodiversity. It is unclear yet what role or overall authority the CMAs will have in managing these competing demands in their respective catchment areas.

Interest in managing river basins has been growing in Latin America and the Caribbean. However, in Latin America, only Brazil and Mexico have developed legal and institutional frameworks to establish river basin organizations as the basis for water resource management.[25] So far, it is difficult to determine how effective these organizations have been in addressing key water scarcity issues and problems, compared to existing federal, state and local jurisdictions. In contrast, attempts to implement river basin management in the Caribbean have yet to be successful.[26] The most promising initiatives have addressed specific issues of concern to the main stakeholders at national and community levels, which has led to renewed interest in management of watersheds and coastal areas. Sufficient financing appears to be the most critical obstacle in the way of transforming institutions and governance to basin-wide management.

Adopted in 2000, the European Union's Water Framework Directive (WFD) is one of the most ambitious efforts worldwide to implement basin-wide water management.[27] However, rescaling water governance across Europe, involving multiple stakeholders, has proven to be difficult. On the one hand, the WFD required water management and planning to be conducted at basin-level scales, with greater participation of the public in decision making; on the other, the WFD also endorsed a top-down regulatory strategy of pursuing strict adherence to European-wide standards for improving water quality and environmental improvement.

Unfortunately, the inherent conflict between these two principal goals of the WFD has hindered the adoption of effective basin-wide management in Europe. The enforcement of water quality regulations was imposed from the start of the WFD, before river basin management plans were fully implemented and yielding benefits. This led to considerable alienation of stakeholders—from farmers to local officials—in many river basins across Europe, and the general perception that the WFD was yet another example of the European Commission exceeding its administrative authority. Some European countries opted to conduct catchment management through traditional administrative units and centralized decision making. As one study has concluded, this has led "to missed opportunities for efficient policy implementation gains at the local level, as more centralized institutional arrangements only focus on shallow integration of water management. Even in Member States that had previous arrangements for catchment management, the policy shift toward the WFD's integrative and participatory requirements has proven to be difficult."[28] Attainment of the ambitious water quality goals has also proven elusive. During the first phase of the WFD, from 2009 to 2015, the number of European surface water bodies achieving the benchmark "good" ecological status increased only by 10 percent, leaving 47 percent of European surface water still falling below this "good" status.[29]

Despite these difficulties with the WFD, for some river basins in Europe progress is being made in transforming governance. For example, in the Wupper sub-basin of the Rhine River in Germany, there is evidence that "public authorities at all scales—from local to national—are not simply reacting defensively to shore up the authority of 'their' territorial jurisdictions against a new hydro-technical scalar regime, but are actively engaged in working collaboratively across scales and are developing new avenues of influence—as well as new modes of cross-scalar governance—as a result."[30] Hopefully, this and other examples of more successful transition to basin-wide governance of water management will provide valuable insights for further development of river basin management across Europe and elsewhere.

Groundwater Governance

An important institutional challenge is the reform of groundwater governance worldwide (see Box 5.2). Given that this freshwater resource is found well below the surface—often very deep below ground and requiring extensive drilling to reach—it is not easy to determine how much is available, how fast we are using it up or how quickly the water is naturally recharged. Equally, it is unclear what we are dumping or leaking into the resource to pollute it.

Yet the world's dependence on groundwater is growing. Global abstraction of groundwater has increased fourfold in the past fifty years, and today it provides 36 percent of potable water, 42 percent of irrigation for agriculture, and 24 percent of water for industry. Groundwater now supplies over a billion urban residents, and many rural households throughout the world.[31] Unfortunately, the technological advances that have made it easier to abstract and use more groundwater than ever before have also undermined governance of the resource.

Groundwater governance in most countries developed from the customary principle of "rule of capture." According to this principle, the owner of the land under which groundwater is found has an exclusive right to abstract and use it for whatever purpose the water is needed. As long as wells were dug by hand or by limited mechanical methods, there was little need to change private ownership and user rights to

Box 5.2 Groundwater Governance: Key Features and Challenges

Key features*

Monitoring and assessment required of the state of the resource and its use.

Requires establishing clear ownership and user rights over abstraction and protection, whether private or public.

Should not be managed in isolation but in conjunction with other water sources.

Both the quantity and quality of groundwater should be co-managed, and thus be harmonized with uses of the surrounding landscape and watershed.

Requires coordination of groundwater planning and management between national and local levels.

Groundwater planning and management should be in conjunction with other sectors, such as agriculture, energy, health, urban and industrial development, and the environment.

Key challenges†

The extent of the resource and rate of recharge are often unknown, and monitoring and assessment costs are high.

Water quality is affected by diffuse sources of pollution, e.g., agricultural runoff, storm water from urban areas, saltwater intrusion, waste dumps, underground storage of toxic substances.

Use and ownership rights often poorly defined.

Lack of an effective regulatory and legal framework for controlling use or quality.

Lack of coordination across sectors on policies toward groundwater use; e.g., agricultural versus environmental policies, crop production versus groundwater protection, industrial uses and toxic waste disposal, etc.

Notes:
* Marguerite de Chaisemartin, Robert G. Varady, Sharon B. Megdal, Kirstin I. Conti, Jac van der Gun, et al. (2017), "Addressing the Groundwater Governance Challenge," in Eiman Karar, ed., *Freshwater Governance for the 21st Century* (London: Springer Open), pp. 205–227.
† Groundwater Governance (2016), Global Diagnostic on Groundwater Governance, March, available at http://www.ground watergovernance.org/ fileadmin/user_upload/groundwatergovernance/ docs/GWG_DIAGNOSTIC.pdf (accessed June 22, 2018).

groundwater. However, the "hydrological mission" of the modern era, and especially the improvements in drilling technology, tubewells and pumping, has severed the link between land ownership and the right to abstract groundwater. As development needs require more water use and employ more advanced drilling and pumping methods, individual and community control and use of groundwater become obsolete. For example, in developing countries, customary "rule of capture" is still widespread in rural areas for domestic use, small-scale agriculture and livestock rearing, but it does not apply when public infrastructure projects tap groundwater for large-scale municipal, industrial or agricultural use.

As a consequence, in most countries of the world, including throughout much of Europe, Latin America, Africa, Asia and Australia, groundwater is now legally owned by the state and not private landowners or communities. Responsibility for groundwater management is then assigned to public agencies at the national or subnational level, and, often, water quality is subject to a separate regulatory framework and agency.[32]

In some countries, however, notably Japan, Sri Lanka and the United States, private groundwater ownership or user rights still predominate. In the US, the degree of control of the private landowner varies from state to state, with four different types of doctrines: the rule of capture (unlimited abstraction); the reasonable use rule (abstraction rights restricted by liability conditions), the correlation rights doctrine (in cases of scarcity, abstraction rights are restricted to size of land owned), and prior appropriation (senior rights prevail over junior abstraction rights). Authority for groundwater monitoring and enforcement is largely the responsibility of state agencies, which is sometimes shared with local agencies.[33]

Establishing effective groundwater ownership regimes— whether public or private—is necessary for improved management, but it is only the start (see Box 5.2). Monitoring the quality and quantity of groundwater levels is an important task for determining the state of the resource. In addition, legal frameworks for groundwater can differ widely in recognizing the hydrologic connection between surface water and groundwater and the protection of water quality. Finally, there needs to be coordination of groundwater planning and management between the national and local levels, and with other sectors of the economy, such as agriculture, energy and industry.

Overall, there appear to be three common priorities for groundwater governance worldwide: water quality and contamination, conflicts between users, and increasing groundwater depletion.[34] Designing governance regimes and institutions to overcome these challenges requires well-funded, transparent monitoring and information systems combined with broad, multilevel participatory processes that support learning. Institutional arrangements should be strong enough to establish clear lines of authority and rules, yet allow sufficient flexibility to adapt as environmental, economic and social conditions change. There also need to be sufficient resources for integrated planning and allocation of responsibilities across jurisdictions and sectors.

Effective governance begins with establishing reliable monitoring and assessment of the resource. In the Netherlands, the national government is responsible for maintaining a national groundwater quality and abstraction monitoring network, but provinces are in charge of groundwater management at the regional and local level.[35] Thus, the provinces conduct primary monitoring that keeps track of groundwater levels in the principal freshwater aquifers. The national network is not extensive enough to monitor small, highly variable and shallower groundwater levels and quality, and thus the provinces also use additional wells for this purpose. The provinces also maintain a register of groundwater abstraction rates from all licensed groundwater wells.

Municipalities, which have the responsibility of managing groundwater levels in urban areas, have implemented secondary networks to monitor abstraction and quality in the most at-risk shallow aquifers. Groundwater users and environmental organizations are encouraged to develop their own monitoring networks, and all the stakeholders input their findings into the national groundwater database, which is made publicly available. Currently, the database contains observations over time for around 70,000 monitoring wells and over 136,000 groundwater samples. The monitoring data are then used by all stakeholders involved in groundwater governance and management at the national, provincial and local level.

Public ownership of groundwater is not necessary to implement governance reforms. Two very different US states, Texas and Maryland, have made significant progress in recent years without changing private groundwater ownership and user rights.[36] In both states, periodic drought and competing pressures on groundwater supplies were the spur to improving groundwater governance and institutions.

In Texas, surface water is allocated under prior appropriation, whereas groundwater is subject to absolution dominion (i.e., rule of capture). The state legislature provides the authority and financial resources to the Texas Water Development Board (TWDB) to monitor water resources and develop surface and groundwater models to plan allocations across the state. Texas's ongoing water planning effort was further modified, following a series of droughts as well as concerns over the impact on water resources of hydraulic fracturing—commonly known as "fracking"—for oil and gas extraction. From 2007 to 2012, the state legislature instigated new institutions for groundwater management and planning, authorized the TWDB to collect more water use data, and created a five-year water planning process for available resources and demands out to 2050. The adaptive water planning framework also encourages the participation of local water managers and stakeholders, which has in turn led to the improvement of long-term management and planning at the local level. In addition, Texas state funding for local water projects is now linked to how consistent they are with statewide plan objectives and recommendations. However, the biggest hurdles remaining for improved groundwater governance in Texas are the need to overcome the resistance to further groundwater regulation of private use and conflicts, and the need to account adequately for the environmental impacts of abstraction on ecosystem-dependent groundwater.

In Maryland, counties are responsible for water planning in the state, although state agencies collect data and monitoring information from drilled wells across Maryland that the counties use in their planning efforts. These data also help inform intensive modeling directed toward areas with high water use and stress in the state. The main regulatory tool available to regulate private groundwater use is the permit process, which is informed by the monitoring process. Groundwater abstraction permits are issued with a renewal date, and thus renewals offer the opportunity to adjust permits to meet overall groundwater management plans. For example, Maryland's monitoring and modeling of its coastal plain aquifer was used to inform decisions over new groundwater permit requests and to review existing permits to improve overall management of the aquifer. Ongoing monitoring data and reporting via the permitting program helped the state track groundwater conditions during the 2007 drought. Since then, Maryland has introduced a "drought factor of safety" that effectively sets a more stringent cap on total groundwater abstraction allowed through new permits and renewals.

Lessons Learned

Reforming governance and institutions to meet the challenge of growing water scarcity and competing demands is essential to combating the global water crisis. Yet, as we have seen in this chapter, institutional reform can be difficult to implement, is costly and takes time. To meet all water challenges, it may not be necessary—as in the case of management of the Murray–Darling river basin—to instigate complete transformation from a traditional administrative water abstraction regime to a more bottom-up basin-wide management authority. Nor is it necessary, as the examples of Texas and Maryland in the United States indicate, for groundwater to be fully publicly owned to foster improved planning and management of the resources. To be effective, governance and institutions must be adapted to best meet the unique scarcity and demand problems at the local, regional and national level. And they must also be flexible, especially given the increasing pressure on managing resources from growing and competing demands, climate change and the need to protect freshwater-based ecosystems.[37]

As we shall see in the next chapter, perhaps the most important challenge for improved governance and institutions is that they overcome the chronic underpricing of water resources. In a world of inadequate water supplies to meet growing demands, managing these demands must become a priority. Thus, good water governance and institutions must invariably encourage more efficient and sustainable water use to reduce pressure on available supplies. This can only come about through more effective pricing of water.

6

ENDING THE UNDERPRICING OF WATER

In a world of rising water scarcity, the chronic underpricing of water is anathema to good water management. This failure lies at the heart of the water paradox as to why a scarce and valuable resource remains so poorly managed.

There is growing recognition that this needs to change. Nearly all countries are embarking on pricing reforms and encouraging water markets to emerge. But most of these efforts are still not confronting the main management paradigm of the modern era's "hydraulic mission," which is that lack of water can be always be met by new sources of supply. As long as this view persists, water pricing and markets will remain peripheral and will have little impact on reducing water scarcity.[1] In short, the lack of appropriate water markets, pricing and policies is a key symptom of the global crisis in water management.

Nevertheless, the pricing of water is contentious, and designing and implementing a marketing mechanism for a resource that has long been underpriced is a major challenge. But rising scarcity and the growing threat of water crises mean that it is time to grapple with this challenge and view pricing and markets as the basis for a new paradigm in water management.

As we saw in previous chapters, the "hydraulic mission" of the modern era was born out of the drive to meet water-related needs on a massive scale, usually through huge, government-funded capital projects, to provide navigation, control floods, irrigate agriculture, provide hydroelectricity, and supply water and sanitation services to cities.[2] The capital intensity and high fixed costs of water services infrastructure, and the predominance of economies of scale, require considerable financing and investment. It is becoming increasingly difficult and expensive to extend this supply infrastructure to meet new water demands.[3] To reduce water use and encourage conservation, administrative water pricing and tariffs are sometimes introduced. Too often, however, these prices and tariffs fall well below the cost of supply, and this underpricing of irrigation, water and sanitation, and other water-related services, leads to large inefficiencies, unsustainable use and even inequity.[4] The cost of supply should also account for the social and environmental damages associated with water infrastructure investments and use, including those arising from human threats to freshwater ecosystems, pollution impacts on water quality, and the depletion of groundwater resources. Yet, these additional impacts are rarely considered.

This chapter explores how water markets and pricing reforms can make a difference in ending the underpricing of water. Water markets have long been promoted as one of the most efficient ways of reallocating water, especially under growing scarcity and rising demands. As water scarcity worsens worldwide, there is growing interest in finding ways to reduce water consumption and to allocate the saved water to higher-valued uses. Well-functioning water markets and trades can facilitate water conservation and reallocation, as many examples from around the world show.[5] In this chapter, we will explore some of these case studies, to illustrate the lessons learned about how best to use water markets to facilitate better management and allocation of scarce water supplies. Other pricing reforms are also required to improve water management, control excessive use and conserve resources. These include more efficient pricing of water and sanitation services, improving the cost-effective delivery of clean water and sanitation in developing countries, using economic instruments to manage water quality and pollution, and reducing or eliminating irrigation and other agricultural subsidies that lead to overuse of water.

Creating Water Markets

The case for employing water markets as a means to conserve water use and, more importantly, to transfer water from lower-value uses (e.g., irrigation) to higher-value uses (e.g., municipalities and industries) is illustrated in Figure 6.1.

In many parts of the world, historical water rights usually mean that farmers have first claim on water in a region for irrigation. The main costs to farmers are the pumping, conveying and energy expenses of irrigating their fields. They typically do not pay for how much water they use. Thus, as indicated in Figure 6.1, the cost of irrigation to farmers is

Figure 6.1 The Mutual Gains from Trading Water

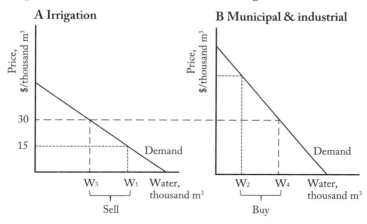

Because of historical water rights, irrigation farmers have first claim on water and have abundant supplies. They consume W_1 amount of water but pay only \$15 per thousand cubic meters. Municipal and industrial users of water in a nearby city consume W_2 amount of water, but pay \$60 per thousand cubic meters. If farmers sold just 1,000 cubic meters of water to urban users, then there would be a net gain of \$60–\$15, or \$45. Farmers would keep on selling water, and reducing their use for irrigation, until the prices of water for irrigation and for municipal and industrial uses were equal, at \$30 per thousand cubic metres. At this price, irrigation farmers would have sold W_1-W_3 water, and urban users would have bought this water and increased consumption from W_2 to W_4 amount of water. The municipal and industrial users gain, as they are consuming more water at a lower price. The farmers appear to be consuming less water at a higher price, but they would also gain substantial revenues by selling W_1-W_3 water to the city. The higher price for irrigation also provides an incentive to farmers to be more efficient in their use of water in irrigated agriculture.

often much lower than the cost of water used for industrial and municipal purposes in a nearby city. Supplying water to the city requires expensive investments in piping and distribution networks, and there are also the costs of hooking up and supplying varying amounts of water to each residence, business or firm. This cost difference between irrigation versus municipal and industrial use is the basis for trade.[6] Farmers can sell some of their excess water to urban areas, which is much cheaper for the city to buy. Municipal and industrial users gain from purchasing the water, because they are able to pay lower prices and can increase consumption. Farmers receive revenues for selling their excess water, and they will most likely be more efficient in the use of irrigation water, as it now has a higher opportunity cost—any water wasted could instead be sold at higher prices to the city.

If creating markets to sell water from low-value users (e.g., irrigation) to high-value users (e.g., municipalities and industry) is such a "win-win" for both parties, why do we not see such markets popping up everywhere?

Many economists and water policy experts have been asking this question for decades. The general consensus is that there are widespread problems of institutional, market and policy failures that inhibit the creation of such water markets. Tackling these failures is critical both to promoting water markets and, ultimately, to ending the underpricing of water. According to economist and water policy expert Frank Convery, a pervasive institutional failure is the current system of water rights worldwide, which still tends to tie those rights to land ownership.[7] This is done directly through riparian rights, whereby all landowners whose property adjoins a body of water, or in the case of groundwater are above the resource, have the right to make "reasonable" use of it. Consequently, this right to water cannot be transferred other than with the transfer of the adjoining land.

But even under prior appropriation, where water rights appear to be separated from land ownership, there is a disincentive to trade water from one sector (e.g., agriculture) to other sectors (e.g., industry and municipalities).[8] Recall that, under prior appropriation, those with the earliest water claims have the highest priority, or "senior rights," and those with subsequent claims have lower-priority claims, or "junior rights." The problem with this system of property rights is that it tends to favor the historical "first users" of a scarce water resource, which in most countries and regions tend to be irrigated agriculture. Although water is not tied to the land, and therefore can be sold or leased separately from it, rights to water are often traded more among existing senior and junior property right owners for the same purpose—irrigation agriculture—and not to new users, such as nearby cities, new industries or to maintain instream flows for recreation and protecting the environment. Thus, new users are effectively locked out of these trades. In effect, prior appropriation may legally separate water and land rights, but in practice farmers and ranchers have little incentive to sell or lease their water to outside users unless they plan to cease their agricultural operations. Instead, farmers and ranchers have an incentive to use as much of their water rights as possible or risk "losing" these rights. This not only leads to inefficient and excessive water use, but also a reluctance to parcel water rights to sell any excess. Drought, climate change and other hydrological uncertainties reinforce this reluctance.

Facilitating more water markets and correcting the artificially low prices for some uses depends crucially on ensuring that water rights are fully separated from land ownership and land use decisions. As Convery argues, "Prices that reflect scarcity can be introduced either by government asserting de facto ownership and charging for use on behalf of the public, or by facilitating the creation of property rights that allow water to be separated from land and bought and sold; the price ensuing from such transactions corrects in part for market failure."

Transaction Costs

Overcoming property rights that tie water to land and other obstacles to creating markets are part of the many additional administrative and other costs incurred in organizing and participating in a market or implementing a new government policy or regulation. Economists refer to these additional expenses as *transaction costs*.[9]

As indicated in Box 6.1, there are considerable transaction cost barriers to establishing water markets and trading. For example, after surveying the literature, natural resource economist Sheila Olmstead suggests that three types of transaction costs for creating water markets can be especially large: the search costs of identifying and matching willing buyers and sellers, the investments in physical infrastructure necessary for transporting water from sellers to buyers, and the legal costs of creating and enforcing contracts and obtaining regulatory permission.[10]

Moreover, as noted by economists Laura McCann and William Easter, the full transaction costs associated with creating water markets are embedded in a hierarchy of increasing costs: "Market transactions depend on the development of market institutions, which in turn depend on the existing legal system."[11] Not only does creating markets incur transaction costs in establishing trading schemes, but also for such schemes to function there are complementary—and increasingly expensive—market-enabling as well as legal

---

Box 6.1 Transaction Cost Barriers to Establishing Water Markets and Trading

- Water rights or water usage rights are not well established, quantified and separated from the land.
- Water rights are not registered, and people are not well informed about water trading.
- Organizational or management mechanisms are not in place to ensure that the traded water reaches the owner or owners.
- The infrastructure for conveying water is insufficiently flexible for water to be rerouted to the new owner.
- Mechanisms are not in place to provide "reasonable" protection against damages caused by water sale for parties not directly involved in the sale.
- Mechanisms are not in place to resolve conflicts over water rights and changes in water use.

Source: Edward B. Barbier (2011b), "Transaction Costs and the Transition to Environmentally Sustainable Development," *Environmental Innovation and Societal Transitions* 1:1, 58–69, Table 1.

---

and regulatory actions that must be taken. As a result, the aggregate transaction costs of establishing markets could be extremely large.

For example, overcoming the search costs of linking and matching buyers with sellers to create a market for water is one important and large transaction cost. But, to make this market work, there is likely to be an even larger investment expense for creating new supply infrastructure to convey water from sellers to buyers. Finally, the largest costs may be incurred from creating and enforcing contracts, separating land rights from water rights, and obtaining regulatory permission through the legal system. Overcoming all these barriers is necessary for water markets and trades to function successfully; consequently, the full transaction costs associated with creating such markets will involve a combination of search costs, investment expenses and getting through numerous regulatory and legal hurdles.

Because of the high transaction costs associated with setting them up, markets for water have been used even less frequently for allocating water to new public uses that benefit many individuals and businesses, such as maintaining instream flows for protecting the environment and water-based recreation and tourism activities.[12] Especially in rich countries, the latter "nonconsumptive uses" of water are rivaling abstraction for irrigation, drinking supplies, industry and other "consumptive uses." Increasingly, nonconsumptive uses of water support many higher-valued activities, such as recreation, tourism and associated businesses, and there are a growing number of environmental organizations that raise significant amounts of money to protect instream water flows. Yet, in the past, the high transaction costs of creating and facilitating water markets have meant that other allocative mechanisms have been employed instead to transfer water to nonconsumptive uses or to preserve instream flows. For example, in the United States, this reallocation has been typically done through administrative transfers, pursuing water rights forfeiture and abandonment proceedings under state law, public agency exercise of eminent domain, legal challenges to existing water rights allocation, legislative settlements of conflicting claims, and redesign of large-scale water projects.[13]

Despite these difficulties in establishing successful water markets, in a number of countries and regions the development of water markets has shown the potential to help mitigate problems of overuse and scarcity. However, even among successful cases, some important obstacles and challenges remain. It is therefore instructive to examine some of the lessons learned from the efforts to create water markets in Australia (the Murray–Darling river basin), Chile, the western United States and other countries and regions.

The Murray–Darling River Basin, Australia[14]

As discussed in the previous chapter, the Murray–Darling river basin in Australia—which covers an area of approximately 1 million square kilometers—has been transitioning over several decades from a traditional regulatory and administrative water abstraction regime to a more bottom-up and market-driven process, overseen by a basin-wide management authority. A major aim of the governance reforms has been to foster water markets, through separating water abstraction entitlements from land titles and lowering other transaction costs that inhibit trading.

The buying and selling of permanent and temporary water entitlements has now been in place since the mid-1980s. Overall, these water markets have been considered a success in ensuring that water is allocated to its highest-value use, in assisting farmers in overcoming prolonged drought and other hydrological risks, and in delivering improved environmental outcomes and other social objectives. Trading has also encouraged greater on-farm water conservation and innovations to reduce use.

The principal buyers and sellers of water rights in the Murray–Darling river basin are irrigators, who account for 90 percent of the freshwater diverted in the basin. Two types of water trading occur: water allocation markets and water entitlement markets. The first are trades in physical volumes of water allocated each irrigation season to holders of water entitlements, and the second is the buying and selling of the entire water entitlement. Both types of trades first took off after 1994, when water entitlements were formally separated from land ownership. More recently, the imposition of a basin-wide cap on aggregate surface water use to control shortages and scarcity has also spurred trades.

Farmers who grow mainly trees, vines and orchards tend to be buyers of water allocations and entitlements as they require a minimum amount of water for growing their crops. As a consequence, farmers who grow mainly higher-valued perennials tend to pay the most for water, and only sell if water prices are very high. In comparison, if water prices are low, dairy farmers will generally retain their own water allocation to irrigate pasture, but as prices rise it becomes more profitable for them to sell water, forgo irrigation and purchase feed for their livestock. Rice and cotton farmers will also retain their own water or even buy more if prices are low, but, as they rise, they forgo production and sell water. For horticultural farmers, purchasing water allocations in the market has been mainly a risk-reducing strategy, which is used to reduce variability in profits and suscepti-bility to drought due to having insufficient water supplies on hand.

Thus, the emergence of markets and trades among irriga-tion users has increased the efficiency of water use, encouraged reallocations from lower- to higher-value farming, and improved the resilience of farming to periodic drought. Most farmers who depend on irrigation in the Murray–Darling river basin now actively engage in water trading, and many believe that the markets are beneficial to their businesses, reduce risks and promote water conservation.

However, less trade in water has occurred between farmers with water entitlements and nonagricultural users, such as mining, manufacturing, electricity production or even urban areas. There have been substantial purchases of water entitlements held for irrigation by the federal government, mainly to preserve instream flows for environmental protection as well as to limit overall abstraction in the river basin. This occurs through the voluntary sale of water entitlements from farmers back to the government via reverse tenders: the government bids to purchase the entitlements held by farmers that they tend otherwise to use for irrigation. Not only have these water entitlement purchases by governments been effective at reducing basin-wide water extractions, but they also appear to have successfully mitigated the worst environmental impacts of the recent severe drought in the region. The majority of surveyed farmers report that such sales had no impact on their profits, and most state that they are happy with the decision to sell their entitlements and would not change it.

Based on their extensive studies on the water markets in the Murray–Darling river basin, the economists Quentin Grafton and James Horne suggest that there are twelve key lessons that can be learned, which could assist the establishment or improvement in such markets elsewhere. This list is summarized in Table 6.1.

Table 6.1 Lessons Learned from Water Markets in Murray–Darling River Basin, Australia

Key lesson	Description
Crises may facilitate reform	Severe drought, economy-wide interest in pricing reforms, and realization that water use is limited spurred the creation of water markets.
Water markets support regional resilience	The resilience of agriculture and the environment throughout the river basin has improved through water trading.
Political and administrative leadership is crucial	The Australian government has been a driver of water market reform in the basin, including working with state governments to change the rules that govern water entitlement and allocations.
Capping extractions promotes effective use and sustainability	An overall cap or limit on surface water extraction was imposed in 1995, supported by monitoring and enforcement, which has been key to the development and expansion of water trading.
Regulated water framework facilitates water trading	Storing water, with regulated and controlled releases in the basin, has facilitated trading between upstream buyers and downstream sellers and allowed downstream purchasers to use water bought from upstream sellers at ideal times.
Reliable, accessible and timely market information promotes effective decision making	The Australian government has invested substantially in improved water information and regulations, which have improved market effectiveness and assisted monitoring.
Statutory rights offer flexibility	Water entitlements are separated from land ownership and are statutory rights that can be modified without recourse to the courts.

Table 6.1 Lessons Learned from Water Markets in Murray–Darling River Basin, Australia (cont.)

Key lesson	Description
Markets can promote environmental outcomes	Government purchases of water entitlements from farmers have increased end-of-system flows from upstream tributaries and instream flow generally, which has been especially important to mitigate the environmental impacts of droughts.
Acquiring water for the environment through buybacks has proved effective	Government purchases of water entitlements for environmental protection have proven less costly than subsidies to farmers, and appear to foster rather than inhibit the regional economy.
Prices provide good indicators of water scarcity and risk	The prices for water allocations appear to reflect drought and shortage conditions, rising when water is seasonally scarce and falling when it is abundant. Water entitlement prices have also reflected changes in demand and perceptions of expected risk.
Basin-wide and local perspectives have important roles	Developing a robust water market that crosses state borders requires that planning be managed basin-wide and takes into account state and local concerns.
Effective monitoring and control of extractions are critical to sustainability	The introduction of the cap on overall surface water extraction had the unintended initial impact of encouraging users to switch to groundwater extraction, which has since been corrected through greater monitoring and control of groundwater use.

Source: R. Quentin Grafton and James Horne (2014), "Water Markets in the Murray-Darling Basin," *Agricultural Water Management* 145, 61–71.

Chile[15]

Chile is often lauded as one of the first countries to create markets for trading water on a large scale. In 1981, the country adopted a National Water Code, which established freely traded water rights separate from land ownership, and these rights were allowed to be bought, sold, leased and mortgaged—just like private property—across Chile. However, most exchanges take place in Chile's central valley, where trading occurs between municipalities, industry and agriculture. Water use rights are also designated based on consumptive versus nonconsumptive uses. For example, nonconsumptive rights were designated to facilitate hydroelectric generation and required users to return flows to rivers, whereas consumptive use rights for agriculture, municipalities and industry allow complete use of all water without any obligation to return water to the source. An additional challenge is that all water rights are governed by private civil law—they are fully privately owned—and owners have no legal obligation to use their water rights nor do they face any legal or financial penalty for not doing so.

Much of the direct management of rivers and canals in Chile is the responsibility of individual water use associations, which number over 4,000 across the country. Although these associations can play an important role in facilitating water transactions, they mostly provide information, they often do not have sufficient technical capacity, and they may not always communicate effectively with their members. In some regions, such as the Limarí valley, the associations have been active in promoting trade among irrigation farmers. However, in general, their role in initiating and fostering markets across Chile has been limited. In addition, there are no water use associations that manage groundwater.

Due to the lack of oversight and monitoring of the water markets in Chile, problems emerged with the speculative hoarding of water use rights. This occurred especially with nonconsumptive water rights for hydroelectricity. Reforms introduced in 2005 reduced the incentive for such hoarding by establishing a fee for accumulating water rights without using the water. Other efforts to reduce distortions and transaction costs in water trading include the establishment of consulting services for water trading and the launch of internet platforms for electronic transactions. However, there remains little central government support to promote and improve water markets, such as facilitating basic information, monitoring and enforcement services.

Despite the legal separation of land and water rights, many farmers are still reluctant to trade their water rights unless they sell their land as well. In addition, Chile's booming agricultural economy has kept the value of water for irrigation high, and reduced the incentives for many farmers to sell water to non-agricultural users. In addition, even if they have excess water rights, many agricultural users are reluctant to sell these rights, which they view as a hedge against possible drought. These factors help to explain why Chile's water markets are also dominated by trades within the agricultural sector, although trades with urban areas are limited by the lack of sufficient infrastructure to convey water long distances and the general abundance of water supplies in cities.

As observed by Carl Bauer, the mixed success of Chile's water markets is due mainly to the limited role of the government in facilitating, planning and managing water resources.

In effect, Chile created a decentralized and legal system to facilitate private water trading without providing the corresponding administrative and governance structure to use markets more effectively as a water management tool to control competing demands and scarcity. According to Bauer, Chile's approach has had two main economic benefits:

> First, the legal security of private property rights has encouraged private investment in water use, for both agricultural and non-agricultural uses; and second, the freedom to buy and sell water rights has led to the reallocation of water resources in certain areas and under certain circumstances ... However, those benefits are directly linked to a legal, regulatory, and constitutional framework that has proven not only rigid and resistant to change but also incapable of handling the complex problems of river basin management, water conflicts, and environmental protection.[16]

The Western United States[17]

The western United States is predominantly an arid and semi-arid region, and most of its rivers and water sources are fully appropriated. In most western states, this water use is still predominantly for agriculture, with irrigation accounting for up to 80 percent of total freshwater withdrawals. In turn, agriculture in the region has become vital to the nation's economy. California on its own produces nearly $45 billion in agricultural products, including half of the vegetables, fruits and nuts in the United States.

But, in recent decades, scarce freshwater resources in the western United States have come under further pressure from the rise in other demands for water. Some of the driest areas of the region contain the nation's largest and fastest growing metropolitan areas and industries. Hydroelectricity from dams accounts for approximately 25 percent of the energy produced in thirteen western states. Recent droughts and continued pressure from consumptive uses of water has led to many western rivers, including the Colorado, Gila, Green, Klamath and San Joaquin rivers, declared the "most endangered" in the country because of their poor environmental condition. For example, projected demand from all water uses is expected to continue to outstrip supply in the Colorado River Basin for the foreseeable future. The Colorado currently supports more than 40 million people, over 16,000 square kilometers of irrigated agriculture, and at least one-quarter of US gross domestic production.[18]

The only way to meet the growing municipal, industrial, recreational and environmental water demands in the western United States will be through reallocating water out of agriculture. There are some encouraging signs that water markets are starting to play a role in this reallocation of water. A study of water marketing in twelve western states between 1987 and 2005 found that prices are higher, on average, for agricultural-to-urban transfers than for transfers between agricultural producers, and that this difference is growing over time.[19] As a result, water right sales and agricultural-to-urban transfers are increasingly more common than short- and long-term leases. What is more, states with the highest rates of metropolitan growth appear to be undertaking the most water transactions.

Yet, it is also widely recognized that existing institutional and legal conditions and the dominance of agriculture as the main "first user" of water are inhibiting the spread and effectiveness of water markets in the western United States and the transfer of water to higher-value uses, such as urban and industrial consumption as well as environmental protection and recreation. For example, the economists Christopher Goemans and James Pritchett note that three layers of laws constrain the reallocation of water in the western United States.[20] For the many rivers that cross western states, inter-compacts largely determine how much water each state is allocated from each river. Water use within a state's boundary is then primarily allocated through prior appropriation, which as discussed previously, discourages the selling of "senior" water rights for irrigation to other uses, such as for industrial, municipal or environmental purposes. In addition, given the preponderance of federal water projects throughout the West, irrigation districts associated with these large-scale projects are responsible for constructing, delivering and maintaining networks that allocate water to farmers for irrigation. In many cases, it is the district and not individual farmers that has legal title to the water rights and how they are used. If irrigation districts do not allow farmers the flexibility to lease or sell the water allocated to them, then this restriction is binding. Consequently, as argued by the economist Gary Libecap, the combination of these two institutions across western states—prior appropriation and irrigation districts—is "much less effective today for market transactions of water out of agriculture in light of new demands and greater supply uncertainty associated with climate change. Indeed, by exacerbating return-flow externalities and by diluting property rights and decision making over water use and distribution, they raise the costs of exchange."[21]

In addition to these two institutional constraints, water markets in western states are impeded by a number of other complicated procedural and regulatory requirements. Table 6.2 summarizes some of the key transactions costs emerging from these legal doctrines.

Despite the difficulties in establishing water markets, their use in many western states is growing. As noted previously, the main incentive appears to be the growing gap in prices between water used for irrigation as opposed to higher-value uses for municipal, industrial and urban purposes. A number of different states and regions are experimenting with a wide range of transaction mechanisms, which include both direct and indirect transfers of ownership. Direct transfers involve buying the actual water right, whereas indirect transfers occur when a water user buys shares of an irrigation district or its network to gain water resources and the district retains the overall right. In addition, when sellers lease rights to other users, they still retain the right for future use. This is often done through water supply agreements, single- or multiple-year leases, and water banks.

Water banks function similarly to regular banks, acting as a centralized exchange by holding water rights to pool supplies from many sellers and then finding and making the water available to potential customers. They effectively hold deposits of water rights until the depositor decides to use them, or to lend, give or sell them to another user. Water banks may post a fixed price that is intended to clear the market between buyers and sellers, or the water may be auctioned. They can also pool water saved through conservation, retain excess

Table 6.2 Legal Doctrines and Transaction Costs Impeding Water Markets in Western United States

Doctrine	Description	Transaction cost
Appurtenancy doctrine	Legally links the ownership of water rights to the ownership of particular lands.	Special procedures must be followed to sever and transfer from one place of use to another.
No-harm-to-juniors rule	Permits surface water transfers only if the owner of the right shows that the transfer will not harm those with more junior water rights.	Generates a disincentive to market water by prolonging the transfer process and creating uncertainty about the scope of the transferred rights.
Anti-speculation doctrine	Requires the applicant for a transfer to demonstrate precisely the new location, purpose and use of the water.	Increases the costs of transactions and therefore discourages transfers.
Beneficial use doctrine	Requires that all water be used for a beneficial purpose; any water deemed not used in this way may be considered abandoned or forfeited.	Creates incentives by water owners to ensure its use every year, regardless of efficiency or the potential consequences, in order to avoid the permanent loss of the water right.
Salvaged water doctrine	Prohibits water users from obtaining the benefits of water that they conserve because it will be used instead by other water rights holders.	Encourages overuse of water, as it does not allow farmers and other parties who reduce their water use to lease or sell conserved water.
Open access rule	Failure to regulate or restrict private use, mostly for groundwater, means that access and use are unrestricted.	Substantially impedes the development of water markets because a prospective water user has access to free groundwater compared to purchasing or leasing water.

Source: Peter W. Culp, Robert Glennon and Gary Libecap (2014), *Shopping for Water: How the Market Can Mitigate Water Scarcity in the American West,* Hamilton Project, October.

water that can be made available later during droughts, and administer state or local programs that control water use during droughts and other periods of shortage.

Two of the more promising uses of water banks are by the city of Santa Fe, New Mexico, and the state of Arizona.[22] In 2005, the Santa Fe City Council required developers to tender sufficient water rights to cover the amount of water required by any development project in the metropolitan area for commercial, residential, industrial or other purpose. Developers began purchasing rights from farmers, and depositing them in a city-operated water bank. When the developer initiated the construction of the project, then sufficient water rights would have to be withdrawn to cover the water use associated with the project. The costs of acquiring the water needed for additional urban development would therefore be absorbed into the cost of new projects. If the project was stalled or cancelled, the banked water rights could be sold to another developer or water user. Santa Fe also enacted an aggressive water conservation program and adopted tiered water rates that rise on a per-unit basis as city residents consume additional water. The combination of the water banks, conservation program and tiered water rates has reduced water use per person in Santa Fe by 42 percent since 1995.

The western state of Arizona has also been experimenting with water banks, especially to control groundwater use. Arizona allows municipal, industrial and other water users to store water in exchange for credits that they can transfer to other users. A unique feature of the Arizona approach is that it counts water stored underground naturally in aquifers as part of this credit scheme. This approach is facilitated by

Arizona laws that restrict the use of groundwater in several of the state's most important aquifers which, combined with additional statutory and regulatory provisions, allow for the creation and recovery of credits for trade in stored groundwater. Arizona's water banking of groundwater credits and control of use also facilitates trading of surface water, as water users no longer can resort to "free" groundwater as an alternative to buying and selling water.[23] As a result, numerous transactions of surface water and groundwater have occurred between various municipal interests, water providers and private parties.

Other Regions and Countries

Compared to the Australian, Chilean and US experience, water markets remain relatively undeveloped in Europe. The exception is Spain, where water trading began in 1999, modeled on the markets developed in California, partly because Spain and California share similar geographies and climate.[24] However, water markets in Spain have had only limited success, and are widely criticized for failing to mitigate the shortages caused by the 2006–2008 droughts. Much of this failure is attributed to the lack of sufficient support from the government in performing key roles to facilitate the markets. In other words, the Spanish water markets may have been inspired by the California model, but in reality, they resemble the "laissez-faire" approach adopted by Chile discussed earlier. In particular, government inaction and failure to regulate, monitor and facilitate water markets may explain the low number of transactions and why they are only a peripheral tool used to manage water use and allocation in Spain.

Although there are many other examples of experiments of water markets in other regions and countries throughout the world, the examples discussed so far are probably the most well developed and well known to date. As William Easter and Qiuqiong Huang emphasize: "Water markets tend to be established in countries where water is scarce and the government organization is fairly effective and operates under a sound legal system. This may help explain why formal water markets have developed in Australia, the western US, Spain and Chile. The big question is can these and other countries facing growing water scarcity use water markets to reallocate water and minimize the negative impacts of water scarcity?"[25]

This question is especially relevant for developing countries, which must grapple with managing the global water crisis as their water demands rise rapidly with economic development and growing populations. As suggested by Henning Bjornlund and Jennifer McKay, there are important lessons to be learned from the Australian, Chilean and US experiences, in particular for the introduction of water markets in developing countries. These lessons are summarized in Box 6.2.

In tackling the issues raised in Box 6.2, developing countries have many different approaches that they could adopt. For example, two contrasting approaches have been taken by India and China, with India developing a more "bottom-up" approach to creating water markets and China a more "top-down" method.

In India, water markets are emerging spontaneously from local trading.[26] Informal water markets have existed within irrigation districts for decades, sometimes illegally. In the most common form of trading, larger and wealthier

Box 6.2 Lessons Learned for Developing Countries in Creating Water Markets

Lesson 1. Developing countries introducing water markets must develop methods of communicating market information to irrigators at the outset and design the practicalities of market operations.
Action: The methods of communicating information should be adapted to local circumstances, and preferably use existing channels of information used by irrigators, such as farmers' or water users' associations.

Lesson 2. Remove obstacles to the spatial transfer of water, especially the movement between different classes of water rights (e.g., from agricultural to municipal, industrial or instream flow protection for environmental purposes).
Action: Government intervention is likely to be necessary and beneficial, by financing the necessary infrastructure to spatially transfer temporary or permanent water uses and rights.

Lesson 3. The issues of total water use, unused entitlements, and environmental and instream needs should be addressed prior to the introduction of trade.
Action: Local communities need to understand fully these issues and the process needed to address them, the gainers and losers need to be identified and accept the outcome, and compensation issues have to be addressed.

Lesson 4. The issue of unused water must be considered and addressed.
Action: Failure to address this issue with adequate regulatory mechanisms can lead to inefficient and unsustainable water uses, speculation, and monopolistic behavior, which can result in harmful economic, environmental and social impacts.

Lesson 5. When developing water market policies and evaluating their potential benefits, it is important to thoroughly understand the legacy of past policies.
Action: To be effective, water markets need a complementary regulatory and policy framework, and it is important to understand whether such a legacy exists or needs to be created before introducing trading.

Box 6.2 Lessons Learned for Developing Countries in Creating Water Markets (cont.)

Lesson 6. A balance must be found between private market forces and government regulation to protect third-party interests, including environmental concerns.

Action: For example, government regulation is essential for ensuring security of supply specified in transactions, reliability of delivery, the period in which the water can be used, constraints on trade and duration of the water right, and the expected quality of water.

Lesson 7. Water rights must be clearly specified and formally registered, so that the buyers have full information about water purchases, and ownership is secured. Such registers will also enable third parties to register and participate fully in water markets.

Action: It is important to overcome problems of inadequate water registers, water use based on customary rights, and poor monitoring and enforcement of laws prior to introducing water trades and markets.

Lesson 8. It is important that procedures and conditions for water trade be explicit, and designed to accommodate transfers quickly and at low cost.

Action: Conditions for trade are clearly specified, procedures for settling disputes are in place, and key transaction costs for creating markets are identified and overcome.

Lesson 9. It is important to identify cultural and religious values associated with water use, and how these can be equitably incorporated into the market.

Action: Recognizing and incorporating key cultural and religious values at the onset of the creation of markets is likely to be essential to their social acceptance.

Source: Henning Bjornlund and Jennifer McKay (2002), "Aspects of Water Markets for Developing Countries: Experiences from Australia, Chile, and the US," *Environment and Development Economics* 7:4, 769–795

farmers, with access to groundwater through tubewells and pumps or surface water through lift irrigation systems, extract and sell water to poorer and smaller farmers without such equipment. Payment can be made in cash, labor or shares of crops. Although most water sales are for irrigation, sales for nonagricultural uses, such as brick making and urban domestic use, also occur. These informal water markets are highly localized and vary across regions. With poor regulations for water use, monitoring and enforcement, the markets can lead to problems with overabstraction and sustainability, as well as concerns over monopoly and excessive pricing.

As explained by the water economist R. Maria Saleth, the problems with efficiency, sustainability and equity in the spread of informal water markets across India are largely the result of the current "legal and institutional vacuum" surrounding these markets, that is, "the absence of mechanisms to quantitatively fix, enforce, and monitor individual and collective withdrawals."[27] In this regard, India needs to take many of the steps outlined in Box 6.2, not necessarily to create new markets but to develop the necessary institutional and regulatory framework to support the functioning and development of the many existing local water markets. In particular, there are three urgent areas of support for these markets that should be provided by federal, state and local governments in India:

- Establishing legally instituted and locally managed water quota systems defined within an ecologically consistent overall withdrawal limit.
- Monitoring groundwater and surface water supplies, and sharing this information with local water use stakeholders and market participants.

- Assisting local irrigation districts and other community farming groups in the monitoring of market functioning and controlling any abuses of market power and influence.

If India is able to make the institutional and regulatory changes needed to make informal water markets an efficient and more equitable option for water management, it could provide important lessons for many other developing countries where such markets are emerging spontaneously and growing rapidly.

At the opposite end of the spectrum, China is experimenting with the development of water markets within a governance and political legacy of centralized administrative control and decision making over the allocation of water resources.[28] Similar to India, groundwater markets are emerging in which owners of tubewells are selling extracted water, mostly to fellow villagers but in some cases to farmers elsewhere. However, in recent years, the Chinese government has also begun promoting the legal framework for formal establishment of a tradable water rights system, in which usage rights are initially allocated to both regions and enterprises that could then sell any excess water saved from these allocations. Several water-trading projects funded by the state have also been developed.

Despite the emergence of these informal and formal water markets, water resource allocation in China is still subject to strong administrative control. As pointed out by Scott Moore, "the hierarchical model by which state-owned water resources are allocated by the central government to various provinces, and then by the provinces to local government persists"; consequently, water-rights trading in China "represents a transfer of water usage, entitlements allocated to administrative entities, rather than constituting true trading between individual rights-holders."[29]

Clearly, what is needed in China is a more flexible policy and an institutional environment that encourages decentralized trading in water rights and uses among individuals and enterprises to flourish. This will require more interagency cooperation as well as coordinated efforts between national, provincial and local governments. In addition, China needs to take similar steps as outlined for India to foster and encourage the informal groundwater markets that are emerging in many rural areas.

Efficient Pricing of Water and Sanitation Services

Many of the water and sanitation services supplied to municipalities, industries and large-scale irrigation developments are through large-scale and expensive publicly funded infrastructure projects and utilities. Although prices and tariffs may be charged for these services, they are largely administrative and rarely cover the full costs of operating and managing the water supply and sanitation infrastructure—let alone the construction costs and possible environmental impacts of the investment.

As Table 6.3 indicates, even in wealthy countries, governments typically pay a large share of the investment costs, and also often subsidize the operating costs, for water and sanitation services delivered to municipal and industrial users. Among the countries included in the table, only in France and Japan do consumers fully cover the operating costs of these services. However, in Japan the government pays the

Table 6.3 Distribution of Investment and Operational Costs for Water and Sanitation Services, Selected Countries

Country	Share (%) of investment costs		Share (%) of operational costs	
	Government	Consumers	Government	Consumers
Canada	75	25	50–70	30–50
France	50	50	0	100
Japan	100	0	0	100
Spain	70	30	50	50
United States	70	30	50	50

Source: Organisation for Economic Cooperation and Development (OECD) (2012a), *Meeting the Water Reform Challenge* (Paris: OECD), Table 2.3.

entire investment costs for water development infrastructure, whereas the French government funds half these costs.

As many economists have argued, there is clearly greater scope in many countries to end the chronic underpricing of water and sanitation services to improve cost recovery and lead to greater water conservation by users. If designed correctly, the pricing scheme could reduce the burden of higher prices on low-income families paying for water and sanitation services.[30]

A water pricing scheme can achieve these three objectives if it includes:

- a *fixed service charge* per month for any residence or business connected to the water and sanitation service system, to cover the costs of operating and maintaining the water system; and

- a *two-tier block rate charge* per unit of water used per month, which means that the costs borne by any residence or business would vary with the amount of water and sanitation services delivered and used each month.[31]

The purpose of the flat rate charge would be to cover the fixed costs of operating and maintaining the water and sanitation system. Any residence or business that is connected to the system would pay the fixed service charge, regardless of how much water is used. The amount of the charge should be set to ensure that consumers pay a greater share for the operation of the entire system and, where appropriate, a larger contribution of the investment costs of improving or extending the system (see Table 6.3). The variable block rate charge would provide an incentive for residences and businesses to conserve water, and the two-tier block rate would address the concern about the impacts of water pricing on low-income families.

A two-tier price for water services for households would increase water conservation while protecting low-income households from the burden of higher water prices. The first price for these services would be set low, with an upper limit equating to the amount low-income households typically consume each month through water and sanitation services. However, a higher charge would be placed on monthly use that was above the limit, ensuring that all households had an incentive to conserve their water use. For example, suppose a typical low-income household consumed on average each month up to 20m³ of water for domestic use. Then a low price of \$2/m³ could be charged for the first 20m³ of water consumed each month, and the household's monthly water bill would be only $40. However, if a household consumed more than 20m³ of water, it would pay $4/m³ for the additional water used. Consequently, if a household consumed 40m³ of water each month, its monthly water bill would rise to $120.

Although the second block price is a fixed (or flat-rate) charge, it could also be an increasing block rate. For example, for monthly consumption above 20m³, the block rate price could be $4/m³, but if monthly consumption increased above 40m³, the price could rise to $6/m³ and then continue to rise as monthly water use went even higher. Such an increasing or variable block rate for the second-tier price is especially important for large-scale consumers of water and sanitation services, such as business, industries and large, wealthy residences. As argued by Easter, "To maintain efficient water allocation and conserve water, the variable rate can be set at the long-run marginal cost to the water utility of obtaining new water supplies (or the opportunity cost of water). If an increasing block rate price is used, then the highest block price used would be set at the long-run marginal cost of obtaining new water supplies."[32]

Finally, if water pricing schemes generate sufficient revenues for local utilities and governments, then some of these funds could be used for complementary investment programs and subsidies for the adoption of selected water-saving technologies by consumers, such as low-flow toilets, drip irrigation and more water-efficient appliances (e.g., dishwashers, washing machines and bathrooms). The subsidy program could also be targeted specifically to low-income households, who would otherwise find it difficult to pay for water-saving appliances and innovations.

Because of the rising costs of supply and the concerns over water scarcity, several metropolitan areas and cities in the United States have begun experimenting and implementing more efficient price schemes for water and sanitation services. After reviewing many of these schemes, the economists Sheila Olmstead and Robert Stavins have concluded that efficient pricing of water-related services appears to be more cost-effective in managing demand and conserving water than reliance on regulations, water rationing or mandatory installation of water-saving technologies. Improved pricing schemes also were more effective than regulatory approaches and quantitative restrictions in terms of monitoring water use and enforcing conservation goals.[33]

In Italy, the Po River basin district initiated a series of water pricing reforms for residential water and sanitation services from the 1990s onward. The reforms have helped to reduce the problems in quality of service and coverage in the region, and the rising water tariffs have noticeably curtailed water pipeline leakage and have improved household water consumption. However, even with the increased tariffs, the prices are still low compared to those for similar water and sanitation services in other wealthy economies. In addition, the tariffs do not appear to cover investment costs in the supply system and, as a result, planned infrastructure investments are too low to guarantee sustainable and reliable services for the region. Current efforts at reform are attempting to address some of these issues.[34]

Since the 1980s, China has introduced an urban water supply tariff to control water use in its rapidly growing cities.[35] The recommended pricing structure was further modified in 1998 and now conforms more closely with the efficient pricing framework outlined above. The basic formulation is a two-part tariff for non-residential use, where a capacity charge covers fixed costs of the supply infrastructure and a volumetric charge covers operational costs. For residential use, a three-tier block tariff is recommended, where the lower-price block covers basic water usage, the middle-price block is for water use that is 1.5 times basic water use, and the high-price block is for 2 times basic use. However, the implementation of the urban water supply tariff has been mixed. The two-part non-residential tariff has achieved some cost recovery in most cities, and is essentially viewed by most enterprises as a mandatory service charge. It is unclear whether the tariff has achieved significant water savings. Implementing the three-tier block tariff for residential use has proven more difficult, especially since the widespread lack of household meters has inhibited monitoring water use. The introduction of the "one household, one meter" regulation in the 2000s has facilitated monitoring, but issues concerning the design of the block tariff still remain. For example, the costs of the metering requirement are borne fully by households, which increases the burden on low-income families. On the other hand, concern for the impacts of water pricing on poorer households has led to a high limit set on the first-tier block price, which may be good for equity but is unlikely to lead to much water conservation.

Balancing the objectives of cost recovery, conservation and equity has also been an issue for Colombia, which has attempted to implement water pricing reforms for urban water and sanitation services since the 1980s.[36] Initially, the reforms were too cautious and overly concerned about the financial impacts on water users, especially poor households and small enterprises. Prices were set too low to meet essential operation and investment costs, even as these costs increased rapidly as the supply infrastructure was expanded to provide water services and sanitation to more households, businesses and industries in urban areas. The utilities providing the infrastructure and services became overly dependent on government funding. By the 1990s, the water and sanitation service sector was in a major crisis, with low coverage and poor quality of basic services, insufficient investment and financial insolvency for most utilities. Beginning in the mid-1990s, a series of reforms were enacted that revised the pricing structure to recover the costs associated with investment, operation and delivery of water and sewage services. Implementation of the reforms began in 2006, and, after several years, they appeared to have improved cost recovery significantly and restored the financial viability of the utilities. The reforms include a subsidy program for basic water consumption to cushion the financial impact on poorer urban households. Although this may improve the equity of the new tariff structure, the subsidies may reduce the effectiveness of water pricing for conservation. There is also concern over the long-term financing of the subsidy program.

Clean Water and Sanitation

A major and urgent challenge for developing countries is extending water and sanitation services to the millions of people in these countries that currently do not have any access. An estimated 663 million people—one in ten worldwide—lack access to safe water and 2.4 billion people—one in three—do not have use of a toilet.[37] As urbanization proceeds at a rapid pace in developing countries, and poor people flock to unplanned urban slum settlements from rural areas, the problem of providing clean water and sanitation could be the most important management crisis facing low- and middle-income economies.

Ephias Makaudze and Gregory Gelles discuss the challenges of providing water and sanitation to urban slum settlements in South Africa.[38] Around 14 percent of South Africa's 50 million inhabitants currently live in such settlements, and the number is growing rapidly due to rural–urban migration and the influx of immigrants—many illegal—from neighboring countries. Since Apartheid ended in 1991, the government has significantly extended water and sanitation to urban slums and other regions across South Africa. On aggregate, these efforts appear to be successful: since 1993, the share of the population with access to clean water has increased from 56 percent to nearly 90 percent and the share with access to sanitation has increased from 43 percent to 78 percent. But this expansion in water and sanitation services has been almost entirely funded by the government, and there are now substantial problems with a continued rise in water and sanitation backlogs in slum settlements, poor cost recovery, pervasive nonpayment of services, and huge and unsustainable water shortages. These challenges are not only hindering the ability of municipalities to invest in and provide water and sanitation services but are also contributing to the growing social unrest in urban slum settlements.

As the South Africa example suggests, ensuring successful water and sanitation investments to meet the clean water and sanitation needs of developing countries will depend critically on implementing forms of service and payment mechanisms that will provide adequate and affordable services to households who must pay for them. In many developing countries, expecting the government to invest in, maintain and operate a large-scale supply infrastructure and network to deliver clean water and sanitation to every resident for free or with little payment is no longer an option. And the international community does not have sufficient financial resources or the will to aid every developing country's government in achieving such a goal. As water economist Dale Whittington and his colleagues explain:

> The plain truth is that international donors are simply not willing to pay the high capital costs of conventional water and sewer networks for the hundreds of millions of people in developing countries without these services, nor to assume the ongoing financial obligation to keep them operational. People in developing countries will have to pay the vast majority of these costs themselves, and careful cost–benefit and financial analyses are needed to accurately characterize the magnitude of this challenge.[39]

Whittington and his colleagues suggest a two-pronged strategy for targeting and sequencing water-related services in developing countries, based on the needs and income levels of the intended beneficiaries, their ability to pay for improved clean water and sanitation, and the overall costs of providing clean water and sanitation services.

First, the main reason why a large number of households in developing countries lack access to clean water and basic sanitation is because they are poor. Extending water services to poor households through expensive, large-scale infrastructure and supply networks will mean that these households are rarely able to afford to pay for these services, despite the benefits. The result is that this financial burden will be borne solely by governments and public utilities, and, as we saw in the case of Colombia discussed above, this can quickly result in a financial disaster, and, as in the case of South Africa, the service network itself can fall into a vicious cycle of unreliable and inadequate water services, poor cost recovery, pervasive nonpayment of services and growing water shortages.

Thus, the first step would be to find methods of improving access to clean water and sanitation for poor households that are sufficiently cost-effective and cheap that the households can afford to pay for them. Small-scale interventions that do not involve large-scale infrastructure and supply networks for delivering clean water and sanitation include rural water supply programs that provide communities with deep boreholes and public hand pumps, community-led total sanitation campaigns (CLTS), and biosand filters for household water treatment. These interventions are not only affordable even by extremely poor households and communities but also generate essential health and economic benefits. Both boreholes and biosand filters can be scalable to large numbers of communities in developing countries, and the filters can be used by households in both rural and low-density urban areas.

In cities with rapidly growing economies, the high costs of investing in and operating conventional water and sanitation network infrastructure may be worthwhile, but only if the financial challenge of constructing and extending such networks can be met through pricing schemes that are affordable to the residents and industries that benefit from these services. As the case studies of Colombia and China have shown, it is essential that pricing mechanisms be designed to achieve greater cost recovery, equity and conservation. This will mean that poor households will have to be protected and possibly even subsidized to avoid unfair financial burdens, but, as economic growth proceeds and incomes grow, more households should be expected to contribute to cost recovery and conserve water use. This is for several reasons. First, there is a strong association between household income and the provision of both piped water and sewer services from a modern and large-scale supply network, especially among urban households in developing countries. As the incomes of households rise, they not only want these modern services but also can afford to pay toward the operating costs and invest-ments of the supply networks providing such services.

Paying for Improved Water Quality

Pricing and other economic instruments can also help to reduce the growing impact of pollution on the quality of rivers, aquifers, lakes and other freshwater sources. As long as the environmental damages to water quality remain "unpriced," too much pollution will occur, and the use of freshwater as a sink for pollutants will be excessive.

There are two principal ways to improve the pricing of pollution impacts on water quality. The first approach is through charging households and industries for their waste-water and sewage discharges. This can be either in the form of a flat-rate fee or a tax that rises with the amount of pollu-tion discharge. The second approach is tradable permits for water pollution. The first step is to set a cap or limit on the total allowable amount of effluent, such as nitrates, phosphates, raw sewage or chemicals, that can be discharged into the water source over a given period of time. Once the cap is established, permits can be issued and then allocated or sold to those discharging the pollutants, such as firms in an industry or farmers who have pollution runoff from irrigating their crops. The total number of permits issued must be equal to the maximum amount of pollution allowed under the cap. However, if it is too expensive to reduce pollution levels, a firm or farmer may choose instead to buy more permits from another firm or farmer who finds it cheaper to abate pollution and thus has excess permits to sell. Thus, the market for trading pollution permits determines a price for the permits which is essentially equivalent to the cost of discharge.

Wastewater and sewage charges are more common than tradable permits, and a growing number of different taxes are being used for pollution control at national, regional and local level worldwide. Some examples include the heavy metals and organic discharge tax in the Netherlands, water pollution charges in France, effluent taxes in Germany and Colombia, the Chinese pollution levy system, and effluent charges for the palm oil industry in Malaysia.[40]

If properly implemented, water pollution taxes will motivate those responsible for the discharges to reduce wastewater and sewage, reuse or recycle water, and switch to cleaner production processes. Although some charges have been successful in reducing pollution, most instruments are not set high enough to cover the additional damages from discharges, which limits their effectiveness in controlling pollution and improving water quality. Too often wastewater fees for industries and households are included in water bills, appear as fixed charges per dwelling, or are included in property taxes. Such charging mechanisms dilute the effectiveness of the fees as a tax on water pollution, and thus provide less incentive for reducing effluents. Sewage and pollution charges are increasingly imposed on industries, but often these fees are included in the overall cost of water and sanitation services to firms, and frequently as a flat fee. As the costs of these services apportioned to sewage have little to do with environmental damages and are not related to the amount of sewage released, such fees are less effective in controlling pollution.

Germany introduced an effluent tax in 1976 as part of its overall policy strategy to control pollution of its rivers.[41] In addition to the tax, Germany has for some time employed discharge limits, technical standards and permits. Although it is difficult to identify the impacts attributable just to the tax from this policy mix, since it was introduced the overall quantity and harmfulness of discharged effluents have decreased substantially, and water quality has improved considerably. All discharges of effluents by industries and municipalities require a permit, and then the effluents are taxed. Pollutants subject to the tax include phosphorus, nitrogen, organic halogens, mercury, cadmium, chromate, nickel, lead, copper and a variety of toxic or oxygen-demanding chemical substances. If abatement measures are introduced or sewage treatment plants are constructed or improved, effluent taxes can be reduced by 50 percent. In addition, the costs of pollution control equipment can be offset against overall pollution charges. On the other hand, if effluent levels exceed the permitted discharge, rising taxes may be imposed. Multiple violations can lead to noncompliance penalties.

Despite the apparent success of the effluent tax in reducing pollution and improving water quality, there is concern that the tax rate is too low and has not been adjusted sufficiently for inflation since its introduction. Thus, the effectiveness of the pollution tax is likely to have diminished over time. Political lobbying may have been an important reason for this outcome. In addition, private industries and public municipalities appear to have responded differently to the imposition of the tax. Industries were more likely to respond to the incentives to offset pollution control costs and introduce other innovations and processes to reduce the overall pollution charge, whereas municipalities largely complied with the standards and paid the full costs of pollution allowed by permits. An important challenge will be for the effluent tax system to be updated to address these issues and to reduce water pollution from sources other than municipalities and industries.

China currently employs both a wastewater collection and treatment tariff and a pollution discharge fee.[42] The tariff is essentially a service charge from wastewater and sewage treatment companies for their collection and treatment services. As discussed previously, it is unlikely that this type of tariff is very effective in controlling pollution, although it does help recover the costs of wastewater treatment. The pollution discharge fee more closely resembles an effluent tax. The fee is paid if pollution is released directly into the environment, but is waived if wastewater is discharged into urban treatment facilities and the wastewater collection and treatment tariff is paid. The pollution discharge fee is based on the volume and concentration of key pollutants, and a uniform fee system is applied across China. If the discharge standard is exceeded, additional charges are imposed.

One implication of China's pollution tax system is that it clearly provides an incentive for industries and municipalities to switch from releasing effluents directly into the environment and instead to use urban wastewater treatment facilities to avoid pollution discharge fees. On the other hand, if the wastewater collection and treatment tariff is a significant cost, then polluters have an incentive to dump effluents directly into the environment, especially if they are not properly monitored or pollution discharge fees are not enforced effectively. A worrisome indication of this problem is that, despite changes in the fee structure and rising charges, water pollution continues to increase significantly. An additional problem is that the wastewater collection and treatment tariff was initially set too low to cover operational and maintenance costs of urban treatment facilities. Since 2000, the fee has been raised significantly to improve cost recovery, but less than one-third of China's 663 cities have collected fees.

One of the difficulties in establishing successful water quality tradable permit schemes has been accounting for the mix of water pollutants that come from a variety of different sources. Consequently, successful trading schemes have generally been for single pollutants from one type of source, although some programs and pilot projects for effluents from multiple sources are showing potential.[43]

A particularly difficult problem has been reducing nutrient pollution water. Most of the progress in reducing the "wicked mix" of effluents contributing to this growing global problem occurs through regulating or taxing single sources of these effluents, such as from industries or municipalities.[44]

Nevertheless, one of the most successful applications of tradable permits to control nutrient pollution is in the Tar–Pamlico River basin of North Carolina in the United States.[45] Municipalities and other single sources purchase agricultural nutrient reduction credits for nitrogen and phosphorus from the Tar–Pamlico Basin Association, which acts as an intermediary between the farmers who were issued the credits and the municipalities and other sources. The latter were willing to buy the credits since their purchase price was lower than the potential costs for abating pollution. The farmers, in turn, found it cheaper to reduce their nitrogen and phosphorus effluent and sell excess credits. The result has been significant reduction in nitrogen and phosphorus concentrations in the basin.

A unique program is the salinity offset and trading scheme in Australia.[46] Environmental effects of salinity are substantial in Australia, estimated to cost around US$230 million each year. The salinity offset program is designed to compensate for salinity impacts from agricultural activity by providing a commensurate reduction of salinity impact elsewhere. The aim is to ensure that there is no net increase in environmental impacts from salinity. The trading aspect of the offset program is that it allows an irrigator with relatively low cost of abatement, or one located in an area where the environmental impact is low, to provide an offset for the effects of another, higher-cost enterprise located in an area where environmental effects are high. For example, an irrigated farm might offset its salinity impact by establishing new perennial pastures or by revegetation, both of which might be low-cost options for reducing salt loads in a nearby location. These offsets have proven to be a cost-effective way to mitigate salinity and its environmental impacts across Australia. Where the program has had more limited success, such as in South Australia, the problem is related to lack of state government support for aiding potential participants in the program through providing a register of offsets or a clearinghouse to facilitate trading.

A separate initiative is the Hunter River Salinity Trading Program in New South Wales, which was initiated as a pilot project in 1995 and was made fully operational in 2002.[47] Under this program, the river is monitored to determine whether the flow is low, high or at flood levels. Tradable permits are issued to coal mines and power plants to allow each enterprise to emit a share of the total allowable discharge of saline water. However, the permits allow discharge of saline water into the river only during periods of high flow, when dilution is greatest. These permits are tradable among polluters, and an online trading platform was developed for exchanging credits, with prices and credit transactions negotiated by buyers and sellers. Since trading began, the salinity targets for the entire river have not been exceeded, and, for many enterprises with large discharges, purchasing permits from smaller polluters who can control discharges more cheaply is a more cost-effective alternative than constructing and maintaining saline water reservoirs.

As indicated in Box 6.3, the Hunter River Salinity Trading Program is one of several water quality trading programs and pilot projects that are showing progress. As explained in the table, some important lessons can be learned from such schemes, which hopefully will lead to further use of this important mechanism for improving water quality in river basins and other water sources.

Box 6.3 Lessons Learned from Water Quality Trading

The economists James Shortle and Richard Horan have studied water quality trading schemes worldwide. Seven programs and projects appear to be either successful or promising.

Program	Pollutant	Sources
Hunter River Salinity Trading Scheme, Australia	Salinity	Coal mines, power plants
South Nation River Total Phosphorus Management Program, Canada	Phosphorus	Industries, municipalities, agriculture
Lake Taupo, New Zealand	Nutrients	Grazing-based agriculture
California Grasslands Area, United States	Selenium	Agriculture
Connecticut Nitrogen Credit Exchange, United States	Nitrogen	Wastewater treatment plants
Greater Miami Watershed Trading Pilot, United States	Nutrients	Industries, municipalities, agriculture
Pennsylvania Nutrient Credit Exchange, United States	Nutrients	Industries, municipalities, agriculture

Shortle and Horan suggest that several important lessons can be learned from these schemes, and others that have been less successful:

• Leadership in water quality trading has come from "bottom-up" innovations at the state, provincial or local level.

• Current programs provide a range of different mechanisms and schemes; there is no one successful method of water quality trading that applies to all local circumstances and contexts.

• Water quality trading does not replace traditional pollution regulations but improves the effectiveness and efficiency of these regulations.

• Successful design of water quality trading scheme benefits requires interaction with experienced practitioners and representatives of consulting firms, nongovernmental organizations that serve or advocate for the trading business, and regulators.

• Regulators have three important tasks to assist water quality trading:

  ◦ defining the sources of the pollution that should be involved in the trading;

  ◦ setting caps on overall pollution levels; and

  ◦ defining, monitoring and enforcing the rules of trading.

• Water quality trading remains largely an experiment that can benefit from additional research and outreach.

Source: James Shortle (2013), "Economics and Environmental Markets: Lessons from Water-Quality Trading," *Agricultural and Resource Economics Review* 42:1, 57–74; Richard D. Horan and James S. Shortle (2011), "Economic and Ecological Rules for Water Quality Trading," *Journal of the American Water Resources Association* 47:1, 59–69.

Removal of Irrigation and Agricultural Subsidies

As discussed previously, farmers worldwide generally pay too little for the water they use for irrigation, as they often do not have to contribute to the capital, operation and maintenance costs of the irrigation infrastructure that delivers water to the farm. In addition, almost all governments subsidize agricultural production, either directly or through supporting the incomes of farmers. These agricultural subsidies lead to more production than necessary, and thus contribute to further overuse of agricultural inputs, including irrigation water.

Although removal of irrigation and agricultural subsidies is politically difficult, there is increasing evidence that such subsidies are perpetuating agricultural overuse of water, which is worsening problems of water allocation and scarcity. Water pricing reforms in agriculture must therefore begin with ending the underpricing of irrigation and of agricultural subsidies that lead to overproduction and excessive water use by farmers.

Increasing the price of water may actually benefit farmers, as it may encourage them to adopt more efficient irrigation technologies that raise water productivity. By comparing water pricing, subsidizing efficient irrigation technology and water rationing, a simulation study of farmers in the Tulare River basin of California's Central Valley found that charging more for water was the most effective method of increasing agricultural water productivity.[48] Water pricing encouraged investment in more efficient irrigation technology and reduced water consumption from reduction in percolation to groundwater or return flow. Thus, the study found that a 20 percent increase in water price raises agricultural water productivity by 43 percent.

Ideally, pricing for irrigation should be similar to the efficient pricing for water and sanitation services discussed previously. An irrigation pricing scheme that improves cost recovery, encourages water conservation and reduces the burden of higher prices on poor farming smallholders would have the following elements:

- a *fixed service charge* per irrigation season that contributes to the costs of capital, operation and maintenance of the irrigation infrastructure that delivers water to the farm;
- a *volumetric charge* that varies with the amount of water used on the farm per irrigation season; and
- a *lower initial-tier block rate* for the volumetric charge that would set a reduced price for irrigation, with an upper limit that corresponds to how much water poor small-holders typically use during an irrigation season.

Although there is considerable interest in irrigation pricing reform in many countries, instigating more efficient water pricing—even to improve cost recovery—has proven to be a challenge.

The Organisation for Economic Co-operation and Development (OECD) reviewed progress on agricultural water pricing to enhance cost recovery in irrigation across a number of countries.[49] Most of the countries employ a mix of a fixed charge and a volumetric price above a certain threshold for surface water used for irrigation. The result is that the countries have recovered at least some or all operation and maintenance costs, but they have generally fallen short of full cost recovery (see Table 6.4). Only a handful—Australia, France and the United Kingdom—have water charges to recover some of the environmental impacts of irrigation use. But there is also evidence that the rate of cost recovery for irrigation in agriculture is increasing across the European Union and in Australia, Mexico, Turkey and the United States.

Since the 1990s, for example, policy reforms in Mexico have removed government subsidies for irrigation operation and maintenance, which has led to increases in water prices of between 45 and 180 percent. The result is that the rate of recovery of operation and maintenance costs has increased from a low point of around 15 percent in 1983 to around 75 percent currently. However, there is concern that water prices are still too low to achieve full cost recovery.

In Turkey, the operation and maintenance costs of irrigation networks are being progressively transferred from the government to self-financed local water user associations, which means that farmers are paying for a higher share of these costs. As a result, irrigation operation and maintenance charges paid by farmers have nearly doubled since 1999, and

Table 6.4 Cost Recovery for Irrigation in Selected Countries

Cost recovery	Countries
100% recovery of operation, maintenance and capital costs	Austria, Denmark, Finland, Sweden, United Kingdom
100% recovery of operation and maintenance costs, but less than 100% recovery of capital costs	Australia, Canada, France, Japan, United States
Less than 100% recovery of operation, maintenance and capital costs	Greece, Hungary, Ireland, Italy, Mexico, Netherlands, Poland, Portugal, Spain, Switzerland
Less than 100% recovery of operation and maintenance costs, with capital costs supported	South Korea
Recovery of some additional environmental costs	Australia, France, United Kingdom

Source: Organisation for Economic Co-operation and Development (OECD) (2010), *Sustainable Management of Water Resources in Agriculture* (Paris: OECD).

cost recovery has improved significantly. However, farmers pay for these costs through annual crop- and area-based charges, and there is concern that the lack of volumetric prices on water use will continue to lead to overuse of irrigation for many crops.

The need to use irrigation pricing to improve cost recovery, conserve water and reduce inequity is especially important in developing countries, where agricultural area is still expanding through the investment and development of large-scale irrigation supply projects. In India, government subsidies account for 14 percent of the country's gross domestic product, and a significant share is allocated to irrigation.[50] One of the leading states in India for irrigated agriculture is Andhra Pradesh, which is still expanding its infrastructure development. For example, current plans are to create another 4.5 million hectares of irrigated land at cost of around $37 billion. However, irrigation is heavily subsidized in Andhra Pradesh, which is becoming an increasing financial burden as the supply infrastructure and network expands. The level of irrigation subsidies increased from just under $10 million in 1980/81 to $188 million in 1999/2000. Current estimates suggest that the subsidies of the three newest major water irrigation projects in Andhra Pradesh amount to $282 million. These subsidies and the failure to recover costs, especially for operation and maintenance of irrigation networks, have contributed to problems in the state and across India with underutilization of the irrigation potential, inequity in irrigation, indifferent quality of irrigation, wastage of irrigation water, waterlogging, soil salinity and alkalinity, unsustainability of irrigated farming, and substantial financial losses due to low pricing of water. Even where water charges exist, they are extremely low and many farmers fail to pay them.

To assist in cost recovery of its irrigation investments and networks, China imposes an agricultural water supply tariff to contribute to capital costs as well as operation and maintenance expenditures.[51] Since 2014, tariffs have been imposed on large and medium-sized irrigation projects, with the aim of covering at least the operational and management expenditures associated with the projects, and, if possible, capital costs and any environmental impacts. Smaller irrigation projects have tariffs on the extension of canal systems, which aim to contribute to operation and maintenance costs. Additionally, a fee is imposed on agricultural users of groundwater who exceed quota limits. This fee is also higher for regions with groundwater depletion problems.

Agricultural production is heavily subsidized around the world. Support to agricultural producers amounts to $258 billion annually in the countries of the OECD, which amounts to around 18 percent of gross farm receipts.[52] In 2012, seven other major agricultural producers—Brazil, China, Indonesia, Kazakhstan, Russia, South Africa and Ukraine—had farm subsidies totaling $227 billion, with China alone accounting for $165 billion in subsidies.[53] As these six countries plus the OECD members produce almost 80 percent of global agricultural value added, this suggests that agricultural output worldwide is heavily subsidized—with payments totaling around $485 billion annually.[54]

Removal of such subsidies would improve the efficiency of agricultural production, boost the competitiveness of smaller producers and poor economies, reduce environmental degradation, and, most importantly from the standpoint of this book, significantly reduce water use by global agriculture. As we shall see in the next chapter, phasing out these subsidies could have another important benefit. It would provide many governments with the funds to finance public support, policies and investments to spur private research and development (R&D), which is necessary for the "new wave" of water-saving and efficient technologies that are critical to meeting future water demands and rising scarcity.

7

SUPPORTING INNOVATIONS

Reforming institutions and ending the underpricing of water are essential to averting the global water crisis. Equally important is the role of innovation.

Recent technical advances, such as desalinization of saltwater, geographical information systems (GIS) and remote sensing, have the potential for managing and increasing freshwater supplies. There is also a new generation of urban water supply systems that can improve efficiency and sustainable use. Water use in agriculture, too, can benefit from a range of innovations in irrigation technologies and delivery systems.

To some extent, better governance and institutions for managing water, more efficient water pricing, and well-functioning markets to allocate water among competing and growing demands will spur the development of new water-saving technologies and distribution systems. If our decisions concerning how water is allocated and used begin to reflect the actual economic, social and environmental costs of these decisions, then there will be increasing incentives to research, develop and adopt new technologies that increase the productivity of water, reduce inefficient and wasteful use, and improve the additional value gained from consumptive and nonconsumptive allocations.

But even if we overcome the problems of underpricing of water and the lack of good governance and appropriate institutions, fostering the new wave of water technologies will require additional policies to support and spread these innovations. The purpose of this chapter is to explore the key policies and other initiatives that are necessary for prompting more economy-wide innovation in water technologies: public policies and investments that facilitate private research and development (R&D) activities of firms; overcoming the water efficiency paradox; privatization of some activities currently undertaken by public supply utilities; and initiatives by the private sector and corporations to account for water costs and risks.

The Innovation Challenge

As we noted in Chapter 3, annual global water withdrawals are expected to rise to 4,300 billion m^3 by 2050, and average water use will be around 400m^3 per person. Imagine instead a world in which global water withdrawals decline significantly by 2050, despite the continuing rise in population. The result is average water use reduced to 350m^3 per person in 2025, and to just 250m^3 by 2050. This more optimistic outcome for global water use is what a new wave of water technologies could offer over the next several decades (see Box 7.1).

Box 7.1 Innovation and Global Water Use

Figure 3.1 depicted trends and projections for global population and water withdrawals from 1900 to 2050. The figure below replicates these trends and projections for 1990 to 2050. It also shows (with a dotted line) what could happen over the next several decades to 2050, if the world embarks on extensive research and development leading to the widespread adoption of water-saving technologies in agricultural, industrial and domestic uses. For example, suppose these innovations significantly reduce global water withdrawals from now until 2050, even though the global population continues to rise. The result could be a substantial drop in per-capita water use. As an illustration, if global water use is 2,800 billion cubic meters (m^3) in 2025 and declines further to 2,345 billion cubic meters by 2050, then per-capita withdrawals will fall to 350m^3 in 2025 and 250m^3 in 2050.

Global population and water withdrawals, 1990–2050

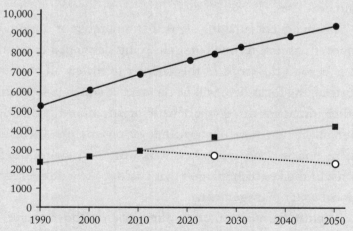

—●— Total population millions
  ■   Total water withdrawal (billion m^3/year)
  ○   Total water withdrawal with innovation (billion m^3/year)

Source: Total population from 1990 to 2050 from World Population—Total Midyear Population for the World: 1950–2050, U.S. Census Bureau, updated August 2016. Available at https://www.census.gov/population/international/data/worldpop/table_population.php
Total water withdrawal from 1990 to 2010 from AQUASTAT Main Database, Food and Agriculture Organization of the United Nations (FAO), http://www.fao.org/nr/water/aquastat/data/query/index.html?lang=en (accessed June 12, 2018).
Total water withdrawal projections for 2025 and 2050 (most plausible) from Upali A. Amarasinghe and Vladimir Smakhtin (2014), *Global Water Demand Projections: Past, Present and Future* (Colombo, Sri Lanka: International Water Management Institute).

Although the projections depicted in Box 7.1 are only for illustrative purposes, they do show the importance of innovations in managing the global water crisis. Curbing the growing demand for water will require that the world embarks on extensive R&D leading to the widespread adoption of water-saving technologies in agricultural, industrial and domestic uses.

There are encouraging signs that a number of important innovations and technologies are being developed currently. It is beyond the scope of this chapter to review all of them. Instead, the focus here will be on ways in which policies and other initiatives can support widespread, more rapid adoption of the new wave of water innovations. Before discussing these policies and initiatives, it is worth reviewing briefly some of the key technologies that could make a difference to global water management.

Continuously monitoring the state of the resource is extremely important to managing it. In the case of water, this is especially important, given its unique characteristics. As discussed in Chapter 1, water is a unique resource, because it is highly mobile, fluctuates in supply, varies from season to season, and is highly solvent, thus absorbing many substances. A difficulty with groundwater is that it is often difficult to know how much is contained in underground aquifers or how fast they are naturally recharging.

Advances in the use of remote sensing, GIS and the internet have the potential to improve how we monitor and assess the state of water resources, as well as assist in the design and implementation of better water management practices and policies.[1] Remote sensing and GIS are helpful in planning for the regions and populations affected by drought, prolonged water shortages and climate change.[2] These technologies are also assisting in the monitoring of water quality and the protection of instream flows and inland waters for environmental purposes.[3]

But perhaps the most promising application of the new remote sensing and GIS technologies is for improving the water use and efficiency of agriculture. They can identify regions in which a combination of decreased water availability and increased demand may reduce water available for irrigation, as well as regions with potential for climate change adaptation via intensified irrigation.[4] One important irrigated crop that may benefit is rice, which is the staple food of more than half of the world's population—mainly in developing countries—and which accounts for around one fourth to one-third of the world's developed freshwater resources.[5] Remote sensing technologies have the capability of mapping, monitoring and assessing water use and productivity in fields and how hydrological processes affect crop yield.

Overall, remote sensing and GIS have an unlimited potential for fostering "precision agriculture" worldwide, which uses intensive data and information collection and processing in time and space to make more efficient use of farm inputs, leading to improved crop production and environmental quality.[6] As argued by David Mulla, an expert on the application of remote sensing in agriculture, "the farms of the future are likely to be managed with much greater spatial and temporal resolution than they are with present approaches to precision agriculture."[7] This will have two important benefits. First, more efficient use of irrigation water will help avoid crop water stress, nutrient leaching and runoff, water shortages and overuse of water. Second, more efficient use of fertilizer, pesticides and other agricultural inputs will reduce phosphate, nitrogen, chemical-contaminant and other pollution that impact water quality in freshwater resources.

Research and development into other water-saving agricultural technologies is emerging. For example, the combination of crop rotation and residue management practices is enhancing yields of conservation agriculture in sub-Saharan Africa and south Asia, improving the potential adoption of these systems by farmers.[8] The introduction of increasingly cheap tubewell and mechanical pump technology and its wide availability has facilitated a "social revolution" in the use of groundwater, allowing for more precise and efficient applications of the new technology.[9] Improvements in drip irrigation and sprinkler systems have the potential for applying water more efficiently to high-valued row crops and increasingly perennials, as they lose practically no water to runoff, evaporation or deep percolation in silty soils, yielding additional benefits in terms of increased yield, improved crop quality, and reduced agronomic costs for weed control, fertilization and tillage.[10] However, as with any technology that improves the delivery of water, adoption of drip irrigation must not inadvertently lead to increased water use rather than conservation.

Urban water supply and sanitation systems also have the prospect of a major technological revolution. For example, the hydrological engineer David Sedlak argues that the rising costs of increased investments in, and maintenance and operation of, existing large-scale urban water service systems will lead to the need for more aggressive water reuse, including "toilet to tap" recycling, and a return to the decentralized systems of the past: household wells, rooftop water harvesting and local groundwater use.[11] More research and development is required not only for developing these specific technologies but also into how these technologies can be combined and designed so that more decentralized systems for water use and sanitation may become available to urban communities, residences and businesses worldwide.

Perhaps the most ambitious technological advance is the potential for creating new freshwater resources from desalinization—the removal of salt from seawater to make it potable for human use and consumption.[12] Currently, desalinization is a reliable and efficient water supply option only in countries and regions with severe constraints on water availability and chronic shortages. High infrastructure and energy costs translate into high prices for desalinated water—twice or three times higher than those from traditional water sources—and have been hindering an uptake in the development of desalination in many countries. Yet, recent developments in the technology are changing the perception that desalinization is only a last resort for addressing water scarcity. For example, in one of the few studies of its kind, a comparative cost analysis of desalinization versus large-scale diversion and conveyance of water over long distances for north coastal China found that removing salt from seawater was the more cost-effective option.[13] This suggests that further breakthroughs in desalinization technologies could soon make this source of freshwater a promising alternative to large-scale supply from traditional sources.

Given the promise of these and other water-saving innovations in impacting the global water crisis, the key challenge will be overcoming some of the obstacles to the widespread development and adoption of the new wave of technologies. The rest of this chapter discusses the important policy and other initiatives that could make this happen.

Innovation and Technology Spillovers

An important impetus for rapid economy-wide innovation in water technologies is *technology spillovers*, which occur when the inventions, designs and technologies resulting from the R&D activities by one firm or industry spread relatively cheaply and quickly to other firms and industries. However, such technology spillovers also undermine the incentives for a private firm or industry to invest in R&D activities. The private investor bears the full costs of financing R&D, and may improve its own technologies and products as a result, but it receives no returns from the subsequent spread of these innovations throughout the economy. The consequence is that private firms and industries routinely underinvest in R&D, and the result is less economy-wide innovation overall. Overcoming this persistent market failure is a chronic problem limiting such innovations, as recent literature on green and clean energy innovation has pointed out.[14]

Consequently, underinvestment by the private sector in R&D is a significant obstacle to more widespread and rapid innovation, adoption and spread of water-saving technologies. Overcoming this obstacle requires two types of policies.

First, as we saw in the previous chapter, ending the under-pricing of water and other market barriers to using water more efficiently is an important policy for signaling that water should be used more productively and allocated to its higher-valued uses. Such market-based incentives for efficient pricing of water are inducements to innovation in water-saving technologies, because they indicate that there are greater returns from investing in such technologies. Such incentives for innovation can be referred to as *pricing and market-based policies*.[15]

These policies may be essential for ending the underpricing of water, thus boosting the returns to water-saving technologies, but on their own they do not directly address the tendency of firms and industries to underinvest in the development and dissemination of these innovations. Instead, a second set of *technology-push policies* are needed to support private R&D in innovations and to encourage learning-by-doing as firms gain familiarity with new water-saving technologies, products and processes.[16]

Such policies generally include some form of subsidies and other public support for technological R&D that is developed by one set of firms but might spill over to create wider benefits if all firms adopt and use the technologies. In addition, agencies responsible for overall water planning and management should be responsible for identifying the new wave of water technologies that are essential for managing demand and scarcity in all key sectors—municipalities, industries and agriculture. Further, there should be public support and investments in the key government agencies, private entities and public, private and academic research institutions that are currently at the forefront of R&D efforts to develop these technologies. In urban areas, city planners, utilities and local government need to plan and invest in ways in which new water-saving technologies can be combined and designed so that more decentralized systems for water use and sanitation can be made available to urban communities, residences and businesses. Government-financed technology competitions, strengthened patent rules and other public programs to support R&D should also be considered.

Both sets of policies are important for spurring greater economy-wide innovation and adoption of water-saving technologies. Technology-push policies induce private-sector innovations and learning-by-doing that spill over quickly across all industries and sectors, whereas pricing and market-based policies increase the returns to adopting such innovations and thus encourage investment by all users of water in these technologies.

Overcoming the Water Efficiency Paradox

Studies of the incentives for consumers and firms to adopt energy-saving technologies and products have noted an *energy efficiency paradox*. This is the tendency to reject investing in such products because market and other barriers make them appear more expensive in the short term than they actually are.[17] For example, car purchasers may not fully account for the possible future costs of rising gasoline prices, and thus choose cars that have poor fuel efficiency. Firms that purchase energy-saving equipment and machines may face higher maintenance and operating costs, because of lack of familiarity with the new technologies or poor after-sales servicing information and support. Households choosing domestic appliances do not have enough product information on the energy-saving potential of different options.

A similar *water efficiency paradox* may exist for many water-saving products and technologies. Market and other barriers may make them more expensive, or at least appear to be, than they actually are to water users. For example, in Spain, improved irrigation technology with greater water efficiency has not been adopted as quickly by farmers, because the expenses of operating and maintaining the systems have quadrupled due to the higher energy costs of the new pumping pressurized systems.[18] Surveys of households with automatic sprinkler systems show that they consume more water than households that use manually operated irrigation systems, and other households that install other water-saving appliances, such as high-efficiency toilets, actually increase their overall water use. In the case of sprinklers, the convenience of the automatic system may actually encourage overwatering, even though it is designed to conserve use; in the case of toilets, there may be a "rebound effect," where, after installing the water-saving devices, households adapt their water use practices and behavior in such a way that the overall effect is an increase in water consumption.[19] In developing countries, the lack of knowledge and information about improved water-saving irrigation technology has hampered its adoption by poorer farmers, especially female-headed households that face shortages of labor, which make the new systems more expensive to install, operate and maintain.[20]

A number of information, market and technological barriers may be responsible for the water efficiency paradox. As Table 7.1 indicates, the barriers that impede the adoption of water-saving technologies are highly diverse and require different policy interventions. Although inefficient pricing of water, subsidies and other price distortions may be one of the most important barriers—as emphasized in Chapter 6— there are many other information, market and technological barriers that can also prevent water users from investing in or purchasing new technologies that could improve water conservation and efficient use. The first step in overcoming the water efficiency paradox is to identify in each specific case the key barriers that are preventing the adoption of water-saving technologies. This will ensure that the correct mix of policies is identified and enacted to enhance the spread of new technologies, equipment and products.

For example, programs to retrofit water-saving devices in urban residences, such as water-efficient washing machines, low-volume or dual-flush toilets, water-flow restrictor taps or low-flow shower heads, can be mandated by regulations or incentivized through subsidized purchases. When these regulations or incentives are combined with public information programs that convey messages about the importance of these appliances for water conservation, adoption rates are much higher.[21] Labeling schemes that provide a rating level for the water efficiency of appliances also assist conservation. Australia's mandatory system of labeling water-saving

Table 7.1 Barriers to Adoption of Water-Saving Technologies

Category	Barrier	Key problem associated with barrier	Policy actions
Information and behavioral barriers	Price distortion	Costs associated with less efficient water-using technologies may not be included in their prices; the inefficient technologies may be subsidized	Remove price distortions and subsidies; apply appropriate market-based instruments
	Information	Information on availability and nature of water-saving technology is not easily available or accessible at time of investment	Improve accessibility and availability of information on water-saving technology
	Transaction costs	Perceived costs involved in making a decision to purchase water-saving technology outweigh perceived benefits	Reduce transaction costs
	Bounded rationality	Constraints on time, attention and the ability to process information lead consumers to make less efficient and suboptimal decisions	Reduce the constraints on consumers' decisions
Market organization barriers	Finance	The initial cost of investing in or purchasing a water-saving technology may be too high; poor or	Enhance access to finance

Table 7.1 Barriers to Adoption of Water-Saving Technologies (cont.)

Category	Barrier	Key problem associated with barrier	Policy actions
		constrained access to funds	
	Inefficient market organization	Principal agent problems; sellers of less efficient water-using technologies may have market power to guard their positions	Enhance access to finance; better market organization; better-designed policies
	Poor regulation at national or international level	Regulations and codes not keeping pace with development or leading to inefficient outcomes	Improve regulatory framework, standards and implementation
Technological barriers	Capital stock turnover rates	Sunk costs; tax rules or regulations that encourage long depreciation; inertia	Improve incentives to invest in new capital embodied with water-saving technology
	Uncompetitive market pricing and practices	Failure to benefit from scale economies, learning-by-doing, technological diffusion	Regulate and reform uncompetitive pricing practices; improve scale economies, learning-by-doing and technological diffusion.
	Technology and skill-specific barriers	Lack of familiarity with water-saving technology or insufficient human skills for that technology	Enhance skills and technical know-how

200

products and appliances has become the inspiration for similar schemes in other countries, including systems adopted in Europe and New Zealand. In comparison, the voluntary WaterSense product-labeling scheme in the United States has proved less effective.[22]

In developing countries, a variety of methods have been adopted by the International Water Management Institute (IWMI) to overcome nonprice information, market and technological barriers to adoption of water-saving irrigation systems by farmers. The IWMI is collaborating with farming collectives in India and Nepal, including those led by female-headed households, to disseminate information of the new technologies and training in their installation, operation and maintenance. In west India and Pakistan, the IWMI is using laser-guided land-leveling technology as a cost-effective method of smoothing soil surfaces and making changes to field layouts, which improves the efficiency of water use in rice paddies irrigated with groundwater.[23]

A Comprehensive Innovation Strategy

In sum, a comprehensive strategy for promoting and disseminating water-saving innovations requires a combination of *technology-push policies* that induce greater private R&D and learning-by-doing, *pricing and market-based policies* that increase the returns on investments in water-efficient technologies, and *policies targeting barriers to adoption* of these technologies. Not only are these policies complementary in achieving greater water conservation and management of demand but also the revenues gained or saved from the pricing and market-based policies can be allocated to financing technology-push policies and any programs aimed at removing the barriers to water efficiency.

Figure 7.1 illustrates the comprehensive strategy for water-saving innovation. Subsidy removal and cost recovery along with water pricing and markets will generate additional revenue and cost savings. These financial savings and revenues could be used to fund the specific technology-push policies necessary to spur water-saving technological innovations, such as subsidies for the private and public R&D necessary for these innovations, fostering decentralized water-saving systems, and so forth. There should also be funding for the policy actions outlined in Table 7.1 that target specific market, information and technological barriers to adoption of water-saving technologies.

For example, as noted in Chapter 6, agricultural subsidies among major global producing countries amount to approximately $485 billion annually. Phasing out some or all of these subsidies would not only significantly reduce water use in agriculture and lead farmers to invest in more water-saving technologies: the savings would provide countries with additional funds to invest in the technology-push and adoption policies indicated in Figure 7.1.

For some countries, irrigation subsidies themselves are extremely high and should be rationalized. For example, Chapter 6 also discussed the case of the state of Andhra Pradesh in India, where irrigation subsidies associated with three major water projects were estimated to be just over $282 million. If these subsidies were phased out through improved recovery of capital, operation and maintenance costs, then the savings could be redirected to expanding some of the IWMI programs and pilot projects in India aimed at

Figure 7.1 A Comprehensive Water-Saving Innovation Strategy

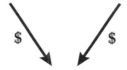

Subsidy removal and cost recovery

Removing irrigation and agricultural subsidies

Cost recovery of water supply and sanitation

Water pricing and markets

Efficient water pricing

Creating water markets

Water quality trading and prices, permit auctions, effluent taxes

$

$

Technology-push and adoption policies

Subsidies to R&D in water-saving technologies

Public sector R&D in water-saving technologies

Fostering decentralized water-saving systems

Dissemination of information on water-saving technologies

Strengthened patent rules, government-financed technology competitions

Investments and policies for overcoming market, information and technological barriers to adoption

removing barriers to the adoption of water-saving irrigation systems by farmers.

As countries move to more efficient water pricing, create markets and trading schemes for reallocating water among competing uses, and develop auctions, effluent taxes and trading systems to reduce water pollution and improve quality, additional revenues will be raised. The first priority of these funds should be to ensure the long-run sustainability and functioning of these market and trading systems, especially as they expand in coverage. However, any additional funds generated could also be used to support the technology-push and adoption policies outlined in Figure 7.1 that would induce greater economy-wide innovation and implementation of water-saving technologies.

Privatization

The comprehensive strategy for water-saving innovation suggests that the private sector has a large role to play in researching, developing and disseminating many of the technologies that will be critical to improving water efficiency and reducing overall use in economies. Yet, as previous chapters have noted, existing water supply infrastructure and delivery networks are largely invested in, managed and operated, and even owned by the public sector, such as government agencies and publicly owned utilities.

This leads to an important policy question: would privatization of some of the infrastructure, delivery networks and water services currently undertaken by the public sector lead to greater economy-wide innovation in water-saving technologies and improvements in the efficiency of water use and management?

This is a difficult question to answer conclusively. For one, privatization in most countries has been limited to taking over the water supply services previously undertaken by a publicly owned utility. Only in a few cases has there been private acquisition of entire water supply networks or full funding from private sources of the capital investments in large-scale water or wastewater infrastructure.[24] In most cases, public water utilities still remain the least-cost alternative to expand water services to large areas of coverage, given the economies of scale that are inherent in water storage, treatment and delivery.

However, lack of access to capital by many governments, which leads to low investment in storage and delivery infrastructure, causing low coverage rates and in turn low cost recovery, poor maintenance and expansion in water services, has led to a rethink of this model in many countries. For example, in the United States, over 80 percent of the population is served by large public water supply systems that serve 10,000 people or more; over half the population is served by very large systems that serve 100,000 people or more. However, these public water supply systems are under increasing pressure to replace aging infrastructure and accommodate the demands of a growing population; for example, public water supply is estimated to lose 23 million m^3 of clean drinking water each day, or 14 percent of all that is used, through leaky pipes in need of repair.[25]

In the United States and other wealthy countries, the main role of privatization has still been to introduce competition into the water services market through allowing different firms to compete to provide services on the existing delivery network, or allowing private concessions or agreements to manage all or part of a water utility. Management and regulation of this form or privatization has to be done carefully to avoid declines in the quality of service or overall network performance.[26] In Santiago, Chile, this was accomplished by establishing a public water utility that is financially independent from the government, which then contracted out private concessions for water billing and collection as well as the replacement and repair of pipelines. The result was improved cost recovery and water conservation as well as reduced illegal connections and broken water meters.[27]

In many high-income countries, in an effort to control the financial burden on governments of rising investment costs, there has been increasing use of private contractors to design and build water treatment and supply facilities that are then managed and operated by municipalities after completion. In some cases, the private entity continues to operate the facility, or does so for a long initial period (e.g., thirty years) and then transfers ownership to a public utility. Evidence from the United States suggests that the latter model of ownership is much more effective in generating cost savings than the conventional approach of private construction followed by public operation.[28]

In developing countries, there has been a shift to public–private partnerships (PPPs) in providing water and sanitation services, especially to expand coverage in urban areas to residents lacking access to these services. However, the performance of these partnerships has been mixed.[29] Although there have been some successes, PPPs have often failed due to the ambitious scope and hasty design of many concessions, susceptibility to economic volatility, and weak governance leading to political opportunism.

The contrasting experiences of India and China with PPPs are instructive.[30] The share of the Chinese population served by PPPs grew from 8 percent in 1989 to nearly 40 percent by 2008. In comparison, over the same period, there has been little development of PPPs in India. This difference is attributed largely to the economic, governance and institutional climate in both countries. In China, the expansion of PPPs for providing water and sanitation services was facilitated by water tariff reform, strong support and oversight from the national government, and the availability of credible and effective regulatory mechanisms to safeguard development and sustainability of PPPs. In India, these factors were largely absent.

Evidence of how privatization has impacted water-saving innovation is rare. However, a selection of studies mainly of the experience of privatization of public water utilities in a handful of countries—France, Germany, Spain, the United Kingdom and the United States—has found that the switch to private ownership has enabled technological innovation but not changed significantly the rate of efficiency improvements in the water supply infrastructure and delivery networks.[31] For example, in 1989 the public utilities for water and sanitation services in England and Wales were fully privatized and turned into regulated private monopolies. Although technical change improved after privatization, productivity growth did not improve, and this was attributable to efficiency losses as the private water utilities appear to have struggled to keep up with technical advances after privatization and the excessive scale of the regional monopolies may have impacted overall productivity growth.[32]

In sum, if implemented correctly, privatization and increased competition in water services and infrastructure benefits may lead to improved cost recovery, greater water conservation and extended coverage, but the assumption that private ownership will spur water-saving innovation has yet to be proven.

Corporate Initiatives

There is increasing evidence that private companies are taking note of the increased risks and costs associated with water scarcity. In 2016, water scarcity resulted in more than $14 billion of costs to business operations worldwide, including fines, loss of production, new treatment systems and securing water from new sources.[33] Seventy percent of the world's largest companies have identified water scarcity as a substantial risk, either in their direct operations or in their supply chains.[34] Investors and corporate clients are also requiring that companies disclose such impacts. As of June 2018, 639 institutional investors with assets of $69 trillion and 34 purchasing organizations with a combined spend of $1 trillion on their global supply chains have been requesting information on corporate water security and risk to inform investment decisions and catalyze change.[35] In addition, the threat posed by climate change is contributing to these concerns, as it is increasingly motivating companies to undertake steps to avoid water-related impacts, such as investments and contingency plans to overcome water shortfalls or chronic scarcity due to more variable climate.[36]

These rising costs and risks, as well as the demand by investors and corporate clients to disclose such impacts, are motivating companies to improve internal accounting for the costs that rising water scarcity may impose on their investments and operations. In addition, the internal cost accounting and the need to improve environmental performance are encouraging companies to innovate to reduce their water use.

Increasingly, companies are incorporating water valuation tools for internal accounting purposes that provide them with a "shadow" water price they can use to estimate these impacts of water scarcity.[37] Shadow pricing, or internal cost accounting, has proven especially valuable in helping companies raise awareness of the potential economic costs of their water use and risks. Such accounting also helps companies plan for the possibility of higher water prices, in anticipation of future policy initiatives to improve cost recovery and conserve water. For example, in 2017 fifty-three companies reported using internal water pricing that accounts for the economic and environmental costs of their water use in anticipation of possible higher water prices and regulatory changes.[38]

China Water Risk, for example, a leading non-government organization in east Asia on water-related issues, uses these tools to apply shadow water prices to assist major power producers in the region to understand and value water risks.[39] The UK alcoholic beverage company Diageo, the world's largest producer of spirits and a key beer producer, uses internal cost pricing to estimate the full cost of water to a given plant, which allows the company to plan for the financial impact of price or tariff increases and supports its overall goal of improving water use efficiency by 50 percent from 2015 to 2020.[40] Internal water pricing by companies has proven to be a spur to the spread of innovations such as smart meters, which provide real-time data on water use and water losses, and can give businesses information they need to conserve water, thereby lowering their water bills.[41]

In 2017, companies committed $23.4 billion across more than a thousand projects to tackle water risks in ninety-one countries.[42] Box 7.2 provides examples of some of these projects which involve substantial corporate investments in water-saving innovations and new technologies. As these

Box 7.2 Corporate Initiatives in Water-Saving Innovations

In its 2017 Global Water Report, CDP (formerly the Carbon Disclosure Project) cites a number of corporate projects resulting in major water-saving innovations. Some examples are:

• ITC Limited of India has invested nearly $9 million in water interventions in that country, constructing over 10,000 water harvesting units and using demonstration farms to share best practice in efficient irrigation and soil conservation.

• Taiwanese technology company AU Optronics has invested $49.7 million in improving water use efficiency across all sites by increasing water recycling to 90 percent, aiming for zero discharge of processing water and securing its supply in case of drought.

• Flavor and fragrance producer Symrise of Germany has invested $12 million, with a further $47 million approved, in new equipment and technology to increase synthetic menthol production as an alternative to natural mint oils, which are highly water-intensive to produce. The substitution reduces Symrise's water footprint and its impact on groundwater resources.

• US mining company Alcoa invested $115 million in its Australian operations for a filtration system that reduces freshwater use by 317 million gallons annually, and which also reduces effluent discharge.

• Personal care company Kimberly-Clark of the United States is investing $9 million in a new wastewater treatment system at one of its facilities in Peru. The new system will use recycling to reduce water use and reduce wastewater discharge. In addition, Kimberly-Clark is using internal pricing to calculate the actual costs of water in procurement, consumption and wastewater treatment to obtain financing for other water reduction and recycling projects.

Source: CDP (2017), *A Turning Tide: Tracking Corporate Action on Water Security* (London: CDP Worldwide), available at https://www.cdp.net/en/research/global-reports/global-water-report-2017 (accessed June 20, 2018).

initiatives suggest, many corporations are taking a risk-averse approach to water scarcity, anticipating the potential for rising demand and rising prices for water. Consequently, companies are increasingly setting ambitious targets and goals to reduce their impact on water resources and are using investments in water-saving innovations to achieve these objectives.

However, as long as water remains cheap, with corporations and other users paying below the costs of supplying it, then the incentive to make further investments in water-saving technologies is reduced. As we have seen in this chapter, a comprehensive strategy for promoting and disseminating water-saving innovations requires a combination of technology-push policies that induce greater private R&D and learning-by-doing, pricing and market-based policies that increase the returns to investments in water-efficient technologies, and policies targeting barriers to adoption of these technologies.

8

MANAGING A GLOBAL RESOURCE

As we saw in Chapter 4, two pressing global issues are potential conflicts over transboundary water resources and "water grabbing." These are two important challenges emerging from the current water paradox. As water becomes increasingly scarce and valuable, and countries fail to manage competing uses, they are increasingly looking outside their borders to obtain additional supplies.

A major complication in global water management is that many countries share their sources of water, as river basins, large lakes, aquifers and other freshwater bodies often cross national boundaries. Such transboundary water sources are an important, and growing, source of water for many people, countries and regions. Although there are currently more than 300 international freshwater agreements, many shared water resources still lack any type of joint management structure, and some existing international agreements need to be updated or improved.[1] Cooperation to resolve disputes over water is becoming increasingly problematic, and compounding these difficulties is the number of countries that share multiple water resources.[2] Modification of freshwater ecosystems and watersheds and global environmental threats such as climate change will also make management of transboundary water resources increasingly difficult.

Many countries with scarce water resources, large populations and sufficient wealth are meeting their current and future food security needs through "water grabbing"—investing in other countries to acquire fertile land and water resources.[3] Water grabbing could have adverse impacts on food production and even be a cause of malnourishment in targeted countries, many of which are developing economies.[4] If future land and water acquisitions continue to occur mainly in poor economies, they could generate disputes and conflict over the legality of the expropriation, the basis of compensation, meeting the needs of local people for water, protecting the environmental integrity of ecosystems, and ensuring food security in targeted countries.[5]

Consequently, the failure to resolve disputes over transboundary water resources and water grabbing could become a source of civil unrest and international conflict. This chapter will discuss how such adverse outcomes could be avoided through better global management, which should be a priority for the international community.

Managing Transboundary Water Resources[6]

In Chapter 4, we noted that there are two major transboundary management issues that need to be addressed urgently. First, many international river basins and other shared water resources still lack any type of joint management structure, and some existing international agreements need to be updated or improved. This problem is especially critical in shared river basins in which countries are planning major infrastructure projects to meet future water needs, yet there are no formal agreements with neighbors on management (see Table 4.1).[7]

Second, even where water sharing agreements exist, they may not account adequately for possible future disruptions caused by water scarcity and climate change. For example, when multiple countries share a river or other water body, the competition over available water resources will intensify if the climate is more variable and causes periodic water shortages. Under such conditions, satisfying rising freshwater demand while at the same time adhering to past agreements could be a major challenge for policy makers.[8]

For transboundary water bodies that lack an agreement, an important first step is to determine which shared water resources should be priorities for negotiating agreements. Based on analyzing past river basin treaties, Jennifer Song and Dale Whittington suggest several lessons for guiding the international community in formulating new water sharing agreements.[9]

First, providing international assistance to help countries negotiate and conclude transboundary water agreements is difficult, expensive and time-consuming. As multilateral organizations have limited political and administrative resources to provide such assistance, they must be selective in which international water negotiations should receive priority. Song and Whittington suggest two criteria for making this selection:

- *Low-hanging fruit*: rivers and other transboundary water resources that are most likely to yield a successful international agreement relatively quickly and through only a modest amount of assistance from the international community.
- *High risk of conflict*: rivers and other transboundary water resources that have high risk of future conflict, yet, because countries sharing these waters are unlikely on their own to reach agreement, they have the most need of international assistance and will provide potentially the greatest returns.

As we saw in Chapter 4, the basins with high risk of conflict are of most concern. Table 8.1 combines the analysis from Table 4.1 and Song and Whittington's selection of shared river basins with high risk of political conflict. As it indicates, the vulnerable basins are largely in developing countries— several in southeast Asia, south Asia, Central America, the northern part of South America, the southern Balkans and across Africa. These basins are already in areas of considerable political tension, and, in some cases, are the sites of past conflicts. Thus, directing international assistance to these countries to negotiate treaties should be a priority.

A second challenge is to determine to what extent water scarcity and climate change are likely to hinder successful negotiation of transboundary water treaties. In the case of water scarcity, the general presumption has been that an increase makes it more difficult for countries sharing a freshwater resource to cooperate on a negotiated agreement for joint management. However, as indicated in Box 8.1, the more likely case is that there will be an "inverted-U-shaped"

Table 8.1 Priority River Basins for Transboundary Agreements

River basin	Riparian countries	Region
Bei Jiang/Hsi	China, Vietnam	East Asia
Ca/Song-Koi	Laos, Vietnam	East Asia
Ma	Laos, Vietnam	East Asia
Red/Song Hong	China, Laos, Vietnam	East Asia
Saigon	Cambodia, Vietnam	East Asia
Salween	China, Myanmar, Thailand	East Asia
Irrawaddy	China, India, Myanmar	East & South Asia
Kura-Araks	Armenia, Azerbaijan, Georgia, Iran, Russia, Turkey	Central Asia
Tarim	Afghanistan, China, Kazakhstan, Kyrgyzstan, Tajikistan	Central Asia
Drin	Albania, Macedonia, Montenegro, Serbia	Eastern Europe
Krka	Bosnia & Herzegovina, Croatia	Eastern Europe
Neretva	Bosnia & Herzegovina, Croatia	Eastern Europe
Vardar	Bulgaria, Greece, Macedonia, Serbia	Eastern Europe
Chiriqui	Costa Rica, Panama	Latin America
Mira	Colombia, Ecuador	Latin America
San Juan	Costa Rica, Nicaragua	Latin America
Benito/Ntem	Cameroon, Gabon, Equatorial Guinea	Sub-Saharan Africa
Congo/Zaire	Angola, Central African Republic, Congo, Democratic Republic of Congo, Tanzania, Zambia	Sub-Saharan Africa
Juba-Shibeli	Ethiophia, Kenya, Somalia	Sub-Saharan Africa
Lake Turkana	Ethiopia, Kenya, South Sudan, Uganda	Sub-Saharan Africa
Mono	Benin, Togo	Sub-Saharan Africa
Ogooue	Cameroon, Congo, Gabon, Equatorial Guinea	Sub-Saharan Africa
Sabi	Mozambique, Zimbabwe	Sub-Saharan Africa
Sanaga	Cameroon, Central African Republic, Nigeria	Sub-Saharan Africa
Thukela	Lesotho, South Africa	Sub-Saharan Africa

Source: L. De Stefano, Jacob D. Petersen-Perlman, Erica A. Sproles, Jim Eynard and Aaron T. Wolf (2017), "Assessment of Transboundary River Basins for Potential Hydro-Political Tensions," *Global Environmental Change* 45, 35–46; and Jennifer Song and Dale Whittington (2004), "Why Have Some Countries on International Rivers Been Successful Negotiating Treaties? A Global Perspective," *Water Resources Research* 40:5, W05S06.

relationship between cooperation and scarcity. That is, if countries sharing transboundary water have abundant supplies, then a treaty to manage jointly the resource is unnecessary. At the other extreme, if water is highly scarce, then the conditions for cooperation break down, as there already likely to be political tension and possibly conflict over sharing the resource. It is only in the intermediate case, when countries are experiencing moderate water scarcity, that they may have the greatest incentive to cooperate on reaching an agreement on shared management.

Box 8.1 also highlights two other important ways for facilitating cooperation on transboundary water management, which are *side payments* and *issue linkage*.[10] Wealthier states sometimes provide incentives, in the form of side payments or financial inducements, to get other countries to cooperate on sharing and managing freshwater resources. Issue linkage occurs when countries sharing a water resource are able to link an agreement to some additional issue of mutual interest, such as strengthening trade and other economic benefits, political links and technology transfers.

Side payments are common in successful international treaties governing shared river basins. For example, a country upstream can unilaterally alter the water quantity and quality available to downstream countries. If such activities lead to better stream flow regulation or reduced pollution, then the downstream nations may benefit without paying. However,

Box 8.1 Scarcity and Cooperation over Transboundary Water

Shlomi Dinar and colleagues have found that increasing water scarcity is not always detrimental to cooperation over shared water resources. Instead, transboundary water-sharing agreements are more likely to emerge when scarcity is moderate rather than very low or high. As shown in the graph below, this suggests that there is likely to be an "inverted-U-shaped" relationship between increasing water scarcity and cooperation. When water is relatively abundant, there is little need for countries to cooperate on shared management. At the other extreme, when scarcity is very high, there is likely to be conflict and tensions over water from the shared resource. However, with moderate water scarcity, the countries will have the incentive and motivation to cooperate on water sharing, and thus the likelihood of an agreement is high. Dinar and colleagues also find that cooperation is enhanced by good governance, diplomatic relations and trade, and whether wealthier states are able to provide incentives to developing countries to facilitate an international agreement.

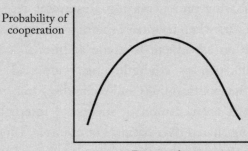

Probability of cooperation

Degree of water scarcity

Source: Shlomi Dinar (2009), "Scarcity and Cooperation along International Rivers," *Global Environmental Politics* 9:1, 108–135; Shlomi Dinar, Ariel Dinar and Pradeep Kurukulasuriya (2011), "Scarcity and Cooperation along International Rivers: An Empirical Assessment of Bilateral Treaties," *International Studies Quarterly* 55:3, 809–833.

more often than not, the upstream country's activities lead to less water and more pollution downstream, in which case conflicts can occur over shared water use. A downstream country that is richer, has a strong military or contains a large population can exercise more influence on joint management negotiations, or is able to reduce some of the risks and costs associated with a transboundary water agreement. But, often, it is easier and quicker for the wealthier downstream country to offer financial inducements to the poorer upstream country to cooperate on shared management.

However, side payments do not always lead to increased cooperation by upstream and downstream countries.[11] Instead, they can result in the classic *victim pays* outcome, as the downstream countries are essentially bribing the upstream countries to share water or improve its quality. Upstream countries would prefer not to share or improve water, as it is always costly to do so, whereas downstream countries would rather not offer a side payment, not only because it is costly to do so but also because they appear as a "weak negotiator." As a consequence, each party has an incentive to cheat if it believes that the other party will choose cooperation, which results in mutual defection from any initial agreement and lower payoffs.

Increasingly, agreements on water sharing involve issue linkages, given the potential for mutual gain by all countries. For example, an analysis of 145 treaties found that 30 percent have some form of economic linkage, such as trade and other economic incentive, 4 percent have land linkages, 1 percent are linked to political concessions, and 7 percent exhibit other linkages.[12]

Linking additional economic benefits to a water-sharing agreement is often an important incentive. In central Asia, the Syr Darya River basin crosses Kyrgyzstan, Uzbekistan, Tajikistan and Kazakhstan. Successive agreements among these four countries include sharing of both water and energy. The upstream country, Kyrgyzstan, withdraws water for a series of hydropower dams, whereas the downstream countries in the basin would like to use the water for more irrigation. Under current agreements, Kyrgyzstan curtails some hydropower production to release more water downstream. In turn, Uzbekistan and Kazakhstan increase fuel deliveries to Kyrgyzstan as compensation, and Tajikistan increases its hydropower production and transfers to Kyrgyzstan.[13]

As noted in Table 8.1, a number of river basins that require treaties in east Asia involve a dominant and powerful country—China—and a number of smaller neighbors in southeast and south Asia. Because of its military, economic and political power, China as the upstream country can dictate the terms of sharing water with its smaller downstream neighbors. The potential for high risk of conflict and political tension is great. Despite this situation, issue linkage involving mutual gains in trade and possibly other economic benefits could still lead to cooperation.

A good example may be how current agreements for the Mekong River basin may be evolving. The river is shared by two countries in the upper basin, China and Myanmar, and four lower-basin countries, Thailand, Laos, Cambodia and Vietnam. In 1995, the four downstream nations signed the Mekong Agreement and formed the Mekong River Commission to promote development and joint projects in the lower basin, especially sharing hydropower production and water for irrigation. To date, China has shown little interest in participating in the agreement, as it can expand its upstream hydropower capacity and water abstraction without cooperating with the lower-basin countries. However, this could change, if trade and other economic benefits are linked with a basin-wide agreement on water sharing. If the agreement led to cooperation on hydropower generation, trade, agriculture and ecosystem benefits involving the four lower-basin countries, China, and possibly even Myanmar, then all six countries would gain considerably.[14]

In some cases, the desire for better relations with neighboring countries can lead to cooperation. If two countries sharing a river basin wish to maintain favorable political relations with one another, then the upstream country will care about the impacts of its water diversion on the downstream country's welfare. If the desire for better political relations is strong enough, it may overcome the tendency of the richer and more populous upstream country to withdraw water unilaterally without any consideration of the impacts on the downstream country. This important rationale may explain why, after years of failing to resolve water-sharing issues over the Ganges River, India and Bangladesh were able to sign in 1996 the Ganges River Treaty on water sharing, which is still in force today despite both countries' growing demands for water.[15]

Perhaps the most intriguing example of issue linkage in a conflict-ridden region is the Israeli-Palestinian sharing of the Mountain Aquifer in Israel.[16] Access to the aquifer is unequal, because the West Bank of Palestine is at a much higher elevation that requires high pumping costs to reach the lower groundwater table in the mountains. In contrast, the groundwater table of the aquifer is shallower at sea level, where Israel is located, making access easier and cheaper. As the Palestinian Authority has no other water resources, it relies on Israel extracting less water from the Mountain Aquifer to prevent lowering the water table further in the mountains and driving up the costs of extraction for Palestine. Remarkably, despite the frequent conflicts, tension and even periodic warfare with Palestine, Israel still adheres to this water-sharing arrangement. The main reason is that Israel needs the Palestine Authority to cooperate on other issues of mutual benefit, such as control of smuggling, reducing sewage contamination of the aquifer, restricting refugees and agricultural trade.

Fluctuations in water variability due to climate change will pose an additional challenge to transboundary water management. Recent evidence suggests that the likely consequences for cooperation over water sharing are similar to those depicted for increasing water scarcity in Box 8.1.[17] Up to a point, high variability is likely to drive countries to cooperate on water sharing, but, beyond a certain threshold, cooperation may be negatively impacted.

An important implication is that there should be concern about the impacts of climate change on transboundary resources in regions that are already displaying very high water variability, periodic shortages and frequent drought. Especially vulnerable are the Nile, Niger, Okavango and Zambezi river basins and Lake Chad, and the Euphrates–Tigris, Kura–Araks, Colorado and Rio Grande river basins. The Kura–Araks river basin is already identified as a priority for an agreement, given its high risk of conflict (See Table 8.1). Existing agreements for managing these resources will need to take into account and develop mechanisms for addressing the likely impact of climate change on water availability, which should be supported by more analysis of the resulting effects.

One such study, for example, examines how the uncertainties caused by climate change may affect transboundary water sharing between Burkina Faso and Ghana in the Volta River basin of west Africa.[18] The study finds that linking the water agreement with energy sharing could be the key to overcoming the potential impacts of climate change on water variability. In this case, the linkage concerns the trade of hydroelectric power generated in the downstream country, Ghana, to the upstream country, Burkina Faso. For example, Ghana could offer trade concessions on its exports of hydroelectricity as an incentive for Burkina Faso to cooperate on water sharing, especially during periods of increasing variance of water flow in the Volta basin due to climate change. This suggests strongly that such a direct water-energy linkage has the likelihood of strengthening cooperation between Burkina Faso and Ghana, even with the uncertainties arising from climate change.

Managing Water Grabbing

As we saw in Chapter 4, water grabbing is on the rise globally. In addition, almost all the targeted countries are low- and middle-income economies (see Table 4.3), and the majority of countries responsible for water grabbing are high-income economies (see Table 4.4). This has raised concerns about problems of governance, conflict, adequate compensation, local water needs, environmental protection and food security in the targeted countries.[19] In addition, there is evidence that wealthier countries may be acquiring cheaper land and water resources for agriculture overseas to avoid the consequences, and possibly rising costs, of inefficient water management at home.[20]

To a large extent, the problems associated with water grabbing have their roots in the mismanagement of water globally. If adequate institutions, incentives and innovation for managing freshwater were adopted worldwide, then acquiring land and water resources overseas by water-scarce countries may not have such negative consequences.

By acquiring land in regions that have more abundant freshwater resources, countries in which freshwater is scarce can ease the demand on their water supplies for growing food. The result could alleviate water scarcity and at the same time improve food security.[21] If the country with less freshwater saves on water and obtains food more cheaply, acquiring land in water-abundant regions can lead to more efficient use of water and land for agricultural production globally. Equally, water-abundant regions would only sell their water if the price included any impacts on local water needs and food security, if they received adequate compensation, and if there was little risk of political strife or conflict. But this outcome presumes that all countries are pricing their water effectively, recovering the costs of supply and compensating for any environmental damages, and allocating their water efficiently among competing uses.

Effective transboundary agreements on sharing water could also reduce the incentive for powerful countries to target weaker neighbors for water grabbing. For example, Kim Hang Pham Do and Ariel Dinar maintain that China joining the Mekong Agreement would deter it from meeting its water and agricultural needs by expanding land and water acquisitions in the lower basin countries.[22]

However, acquiring water and land resources overseas still needs international regulation and monitoring, especially for targeted low- and middle-income economies. One way to do this is for countries that are currently responsible for much of the water grabbing worldwide to collaborate with the main targeted countries to form an international body for over-seeing large-scale global water and land acquisitions. Such an international committee for monitoring and regulating these acquisitions could comprise the major developing and developed countries that are responsible for much of the water grabbing worldwide (see Table 8.2).

The main purpose of the international body would be to formulate a set of principles governing large-scale acquisitions of water and land globally. These principles should

Table 8.2 Countries Concerned with Global Water Grabbing

Top water-grabbed countries

Argentina, Australia, Brazil, Cameroon, Democratic Republic of Congo, Ethiopia, Gabon, Indonesia, Liberia, Madagascar, Morocco, Mozambique, Nigeria, Pakistan, Papua New Guinea, Philippines, Republic of Congo, Russia, Sierra Leone, Sudan, Tanzania, Uganda, Ukraine, Uruguay

Top water-grabbing countries

Argentina, Brazil, Canada, China, Egypt, France, Germany, India, Israel, Italy, Kazakhstan, Malaysia, Portugal, Qatar, Russia, Saudi Arabia, Singapore, South Africa, South Korea, Sudan, Sweden, United Arab Emirates, United Kingdom, United States

Note: Argentina, Brazil, Russia and Sudan are both top water-grabbed and top water-grabbing countries.
Source: Tables 4.3 and 4.4 in this volume.

embody the conditions under which such acquisitions would lead to a fair and efficient outcome for both parties—sellers and buyers. In addition, the body should monitor and evaluate acquisitions occurring in developing countries to ensure that any concerns about governance, conflict, adequate compensation, local water needs, environmental protection and food security in the targeted countries are adequately addressed.

Overall, the purpose of such international regulation and monitoring is to minimize any potential negative impacts of acquiring land and water resources overseas by water-scarce countries, which is essential to a strategy of managing global water resources efficiently and equitably.

9

THE FUTURE OF WATER

Two Visions of the Future

Throughout history, humankind has treated freshwater as a resource that is always there to be exploited. Since the Agricultural Transition ten thousand years ago, our perception of water has been that it is abundant, freely available and easily accessible. Our approach to water has been straightforward: by developing better and cheaper ways of tapping, transporting and using water, we can sustain our growing human populations and economies. As a result, economic progress has always been linked with increased water appropriation, control and use, and, in turn, increased utilization of water has meant greater prosperity and human welfare.

The Industrial Revolution dramatically changed our ability to harness water resources, as it generated considerable technological, economic and energy resources to capture, exploit and convey water in substantially large quantities. These resources have allowed us to design and build massive, sophisticated engineering structures—dams, dykes, pipelines and reservoirs—to move water from where it is abundant, and sometimes unwanted, to cities, farms and populations that have growing demands. We treat, recycle and redistribute wastewater to prevent contamination of natural sources of freshwater and to extend its consumption. These water developments, in turn, have fostered significant expansion of agriculture, industries and cities, helped cement the relationship between increased economic prosperity and water use, and improved the health and wellbeing of billions of people through advances in safe drinking water and sanitation.

This paradigm of water development has become the "hydraulic mission" of the modern era. Its aim is to meet every new demand for water—whether it is for agricultural or municipal and industrial use, for domestic food production or expanding exports to other countries—by obtaining and utilizing new supplies of freshwater. As a consequence, in today's economies, water use management, and its accompanying institutions, incentives and innovations, is dominated by the "hydraulic mission" of finding and exploiting more freshwater resources.

But what works in an era of freshwater abundance is detrimental in an age of increasing water scarcity. That is why, as argued throughout this book, the global water crisis today is predominantly a crisis of inadequate and poor water management. Institutions, incentives and innovations that are geared toward providing more freshwater supplies to meet growing demands are incapable of mitigating water scarcity.

As a consequence, there are two possible paths for managing water. First, if the world continues with inadequate governance and institutions, incorrect market signals and insufficient innovations to improve efficiency and manage competing demands, most chronic water and scarcity problems will continue to worsen. Current projections indicate that the global population will continue to rise rapidly over the next few decades, from just under 7 billion in 2010 to 8.3 billion in 2030 and nearly 9.4 billion by 2050.[1] If we continue to meet the rising demand for water by finding new supplies, then this hydraulic mission commits us to a path of increasing global water utilization as populations rise. As we saw in Chapter 3, by the time the world population tops 9 billion in 2050, annual water withdrawals will have risen from 3,000 billion m^3 to 4,300 billion m^3 (see Figure 3.1). Will it even be possible by 2050 to withdraw 4,300 billion m^3 of water annually, and can that level of water use be sustained, or even expanded, as the world's population approaches 10 or 11 billion people by the end of the twenty-first century?

Most projections of future water supply and demand suggest that this current path will not alleviate chronic water and scarcity problems. Currently, between 1.6 and 2.4 billion people are estimated to be living within watersheds exposed to water scarcity. With no change in our institutions, incentives and innovations for managing this scarcity, by 2050 the number of people affected could rise to between 3.1 and 4.3 billion. Climate change could increase this number by an additional 0.5 to 3.1 billion.[2] These projections suggest that, in the best-case scenario, we could see around 40 percent of the world's population in 2050 facing water scarcity, but, in the worst-case scenario, this share could double.

If we continue to persist with institutions, incentives and innovations that chronically underprice water, then as water scarcity afflicts more and more of the world's population we will see a future of declining water security, freshwater ecosystem degradation, and increasing disputes and conflicts over remaining water resources. At some point over the coming decades, the resulting rise in economic, social and environmental costs will force drastic changes in our approach to managing global water. But the social and economic costs of such a transformation will be abrupt, expensive and highly disruptive. Human societies and economies may be totally unprepared for such unanticipated and chaotic changes.

Even if we are able to handle crises, the problem of addressing rising economic, social and environmental costs remains. Under the current management paradigm, we will be probably relying mainly on regulation and restrictions on water use, and possibly even rationing, to control these costs. This may do the trick in terms of controlling competing uses and rising costs, but such regulatory solutions are themselves inefficient and thus costly in the long run.

The alternative path to managing water is the one offered by this book. If in anticipation of the coming decades of increasing water scarcity we are able to develop appropriate governance and institutions for water management, instigate market and policy reforms, and address global management issues, then improved innovation and investments in new water technologies and better protection of freshwater ecosystems should secure sufficient beneficial water use for a growing world population.

In the Introduction, we described how the current system of incentives, institutions and innovations has become a vicious cycle (see Figure 0.2). Existing governance and institutions are geared toward the ongoing hydraulic mission that is focused on solving growing water problems by finding and exploiting more freshwater resources. Our incentives and innovations remain guided by the assumption that water is still abundant, and not scarce.

However, if in anticipation of rising water scarcity, we respond with the correct institutions, policies and technological innovations to avert this crisis, then there could be a "virtuous cycle" of managing water use and scarcity. This virtuous cycle is depicted in Figure 9.1. It starts with water governance regimes and institutions that are suitable for managing the rapidly changing conditions of water availability and competing demands, including the threat posed by climate change. Ending the underpricing of water also requires reforms to markets and policies to ensure that they adequately capture the rising economic costs of exploiting water resources. These costs include not only the full cost recovery of water infrastructure supply but also environmental damages from degrading ecosystems and any social impacts of inequitable distribution. Incorporating these costs will ensure that all water developments will minimize environmental and social impacts, which in turn will lead to more water conservation, control of pollution and ecosystem protection. The result will be efficient allocation of water among its competing uses, fostering of water-saving innovations, and further mitigation of water scarcity and its costs.

Implementing such solutions is not easy. As noted in Chapter 6, the pricing of water is contentious, and designing and implementing a marketing mechanism for a resource that has long been underpriced is a major challenge. But rising scarcity and the growing threat of water crises mean that it is time to grapple with this challenge and view pricing and markets as the basis for a new paradigm in water management.

Figure 9.1 The Virtuous Cycle of Managing Water Use and Scarcity

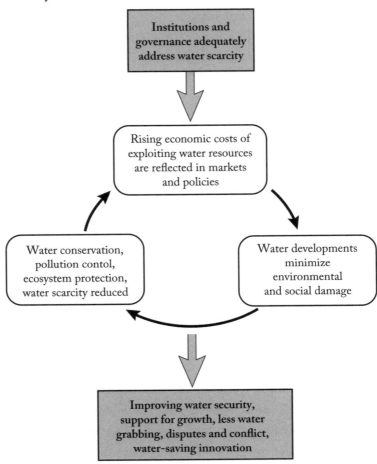

Ultimately, ending the underpricing of water means resolving the water paradox. Only through developing efficient, fair and sustainable institutions, incentives and innovations can we adequately manage water in a world of growing freshwater scarcity.

NOTES

Introduction

1. Nick Squires (2017), "Rome Turns Off Its Historic 'Big Nose' Drinking Fountains as Drought Grips Italy," *The Telegraph*, June 29, http://www.telegraph.co.uk/news/2017/06/29/rome-turns-historic-big-nose-drinking-fountains-drought-grips/ (accessed June 7, 2018).
2. See Steven Solomon (2010), *Water: The Epic Struggle for Wealth, Power, and Civilization* (New York: Harper), ch. 4; David Sedlak (2014), *Water 4.0: The Past, Present, and Future of the World's Most Vital Resource* (New Haven and London: Yale University Press), ch. 1.
3. Squires (2017).
4. World Economic Forum (2016), *The Global Risks Report 2016*, 11th ed. (Geneva: World Economic Forum), available at http://www3.weforum.org/docs/GRR/WEF_GRR16.pdf (accessed June 7, 2018).
5. OECD (2012), *OECD Environmental Outlook to 2050: The Consequences of Inaction* (Paris: OECD).
6. Arjen Y. Hoekstra, Mesfin M. Mekonnen, Ashok K. Chapagain, Ruth E. Mathews and Brian D. Richter (2012), "Global Monthly Water Scarcity: Blue Water Footprints Versus Blue Water Availability," *PLoS ONE* 7:2, e32688.
7. UNICEF and WHO (2015), *Progress on Sanitation and Drinking Water: 2015 Update and MDG Assessment* (Geneva: WHO Press).
8. Mark W. Rosegrant, Claudia Ringler and Tingju Zhu (2009), "Water for Agriculture: Maintaining Food Security under Growing Scarcity," *Annual Review of Environmental and Resources* 34, pp. 205–22.

9. Igor A. Shiklomanov (1993), "World Fresh Water Resources," in Peter H. Gleick, ed., *Water in Crisis: A Guide to the World's Fresh Water Resources* (New York: Oxford University Press), pp. 13–24.
10. Hoekstra et al. (2012); OECD (2012); Nels Johnson, Carmen Revenga and Jaime Echeverria (2001), "Managing Water for People and Nature," *Science* 292:5519, pp. 1071–2; C. Revenga, I. Campbell, R. Abell, P. de Villiers and M. Bryer (2005), "Prospects for Monitoring Freshwater Ecosystems towards the 2010 Targets," *Philosophical Transactions of the Royal Society B-Biological Sciences* 360:1454, pp. 397–413; Charles J. Vörösmarty, Peter B. McIntyre, Mark O. Gessner, David Dudgeon, Alexander Prusevich, et al. (2012), "Global Threats to Human Water Security and River Biodiversity," *Nature* 467, pp. 555–61.
11. W. R. T. Darwall, K. Smith, D. Allen, M. Seddon, G. McGregor Reid, et al. (2008), "Freshwater Biodiversity: A Hidden Resource under Threat," in J.-C. Vié, C. Hilton-Taylor and S. N. Stuart, eds., *The 2008 Review of the IUCN Red List of Threatened Species* (Gland, Switzerland: IUCN); David Dudgeon, Angela H. Arthington, Mark O. Gessner, Zen-Ichiro Kawabata, Duncan J. Knowler, et al. (2006), "Freshwater Biodiversity: Importance, Threats, Status and Conservation Challenges," *Biological Review* 81:2, pp. 163–82; Johnson et al. (2001); OECD (2012); Vörösmarty et al. (2012).
12. See, for example, Darwall et al. (2008); Dudgeon et al. (2006); Revenga et al. (2005); Vörösmarty et al. (2012).
13. Johnson et al. (2001).
14. Revenga et al. (2005). As indicated in Table 0.1, high water stress is associated with annual water withdrawals amounting to 40–80 percent of annual available freshwater supplies, and extreme water stress is associated with annual water withdrawals exceeding 80 percent of annual supplies.
15. UNDP (2006), *Human Development Report 2006: Beyond Scarcity—Power, Poverty and the Global Water Crisis* (Basingstoke, England: Palgrave Macmillan).
16. Hoekstra et al. (2012).
17. Johnson et al. (2001); OECD (2012); Vörösmarty et al. (2012).
18. WWAP (World Water Assessment Programme) (2012), *The United Nations World Water Development Report 4, vol. 1: Managing Water under Uncertainty and Risk* (Paris: UNESCO); and WWAP (2015), *The United Nations World Water Development Report 2015: Water for a Sustainable World* (Paris: UNESCO).
19. Hydrologists generally distinguish two concepts of water use: water withdrawal and water consumption. Withdrawal refers to water removed or extracted from a freshwater source and used for human purposes (i.e., industrial, agricultural or domestic water use). However, some of this water may be returned to the original source, albeit with changes in quality and quantity. In contrast, consumption refers to the water that is withdrawn from a source and actually consumed or lost to seepage, contamination or a "sink" where it cannot economically be reused. Thus water consumption is the proportion of water withdrawal that is "irretrievably lost" after human use. Throughout this book, I will follow common practice of using the more general term "water use" and, where necessary, clarify whether I mean either water withdrawal or water consumption.

20. WWAP (2012).
21. OECD (2012), p. 216.
22. UNEP (2007), *Global Environment Outlook 4: Environment for Development* (Nairobi: UNEP).
23. Meena Palaniappan and Peter H. Gleick (2009), "Peak Water," in Peter H. Gleick, ed., *The World's Water 2008–9: The Biennial Report on Freshwater Resources* (Washington, DC: Island Press), p. 8.
24. J. S. Famiglietti, (2014), "The Global Groundwater Crisis," *Nature Climate Change* 4:11, pp. 946–8. See also Palaniappan and Gleick (2009).
25. Ibid.
26. Famiglietti (2014).
27. Edward B. Barbier (2004), "Water and Economic Growth," *Economic Record* 80:248, pp. 1–16; Edward B. Barbier (2015b), "Water and Growth in Developing Countries," in Ariel Dinar and Kurt Schwabe, eds., *Handbook of Water Economics* (Cheltenham, England: Edward Elgar), pp. 500–12; David Grey and Claudia W. Sadoff (2007), "Sink or Swim? Water Security for Growth and Development," *Water Policy* 9:6, pp. 545–71.
28. Barbier (2015b); Cesare Dosi and K. William Easter (2003), "Water Scarcity: Market Failure and the Implications for Markets and Privatization," *International Journal of Public Administration* 26:3, pp. 265–90; Grey and Sadoff (2007); Karina Schoengold and David Zilberman (2007), "The Economics of Water, Irrigation, and Development," in Robert Evenson and Prabhu Pingali, eds., *Handbook of Agricultural Economics, vol. 3* (Amsterdam: Elsevier), pp. 2933–77.
29. UNICEF and WHO (2015).
30. UNDP (2006).
31. Edward B. Barbier and Anik Bhaduri (2015), "Transboundary Water Resources," in Robert Halvorsen and David F. Layton, eds., *Handbook on the Economics of Natural Resources* (Cheltenham, England: Edward Elgar), pp. 502–28.
32. Aaron T. Wolf (2007), "Shared Waters: Conflict and Cooperation," *Annual Review of Environment and Resources* 32, pp. 241–69.
33. UNDP (2006).
34. Anik Bhaduri and Edward B. Barbier (2008a), "International Water Transfer and Sharing: The Case of the Ganges River," *Environment and Development Economics* 13:1, pp. 29–51.
35. Barbier and Bhaduri (2015).
36. Edith Brown Weiss (2012), "The Coming Water Crisis: A Common Concern of Humankind," *Transnational Environmental Law* 1:1, pp. 153–68; Arjen Y. Hoekstra and Mesfin M. Mekonnen (2012), "The Water Footprint of Humanity," *Proceedings of the National Academy of Sciences* 109:9, pp. 3232–7; Maria Cristina Rulli, Antonio Saviori and Paolo D'Odorico (2013), "Global Land and Water Grabbing," *Proceedings of the National Academy of Sciences* 110:3, pp. 892–7.
37. Rulli et al. (2013).
38. Hoekstra and Mekonnen (2012).
39. Brown Weiss (2012).
40. Although this quote is widely attributed to H. L. Mencken, it is most likely a restatement of what he actually wrote in his essay "The Divine

Afflatus," published in the collection *Prejudices: Second Series* (1920): "There is always a well-known solution to every human problem—neat, plausible, and wrong." See "H. L. Mencken," Wikiquote, https://en.wikiquote.org/wiki/H._L._Mencken; Quote Investigator, http://quoteinvestigator.com/2016/07/17/solution/ (both accessed June 11, 2018).

1. Water as an Economic Good

1. Available at http://www.wmo.int/pages/prog/hwrp/documents/english/icwedece.html (accessed June 11, 2018).
2. Ronald C. Griffin (2006), *Water Resource Economics: The Analysis of Scarcity, Policies, and Projects* (Cambridge, MA: MIT Press), p. 7.
3. Meena Palaniappan and Peter H. Gleick (2009), "Peak Water," in Peter H. Gleick, ed., *The World's Water 2008–9: The Biennial Report on Freshwater Resources* (Washington, DC: Island Press), p. 13.
4. W. Michael Hanemann (2006), "The Economic Conception of Water," in Peter P. Rogers, M. Ramón Llamas and Luis Martínez-Cortina, eds., *Water Crisis: Myth or Reality?* (London: Routledge), pp. 77–8.
5. Of course, underground sources of oil are often large and it may be hard to determine how much oil is contained in these deposits. Extraction of oil may mean less available for use by others, so such oil reserves are still rival. However, unless exclusive right of extraction is given to a single user, it may be difficult to exclude other entities from drilling and extracting oil. In such circumstances, the oil fields are not strictly a private good, but considered a common pool resource—extraction and use is rival but not exclusive. See also the next note and further discussion of water as a common pool resource later in this chapter.
6. This occurs when consumption or use of a good is either rival or exclusive but not both. For example, according to Hanemann (2006), p. 62: "In addition to private and public goods, there is an intermediate case where there is rivalry in consumption but not excludability. These are known as common pool resources. Examples include fisheries, forests, grazing grounds, and oil fields. The other intermediate case, sometimes called club goods or quasi-public goods, is where there is non-rivalry combined with the possibility of exclusion. Examples include television frequencies, public libraries, and bridges, for each of which it is possible to exclude access. Furthermore, there may be non-rivalry at low levels of aggregate consumption of a club good, but rivalry at a high level of consumption once the item becomes congested—this can happen, for example, with parks and bridges."
7. Gary D. Libecap (2011), "Institutional Path Dependence in Climate Adaptation: Coman's 'Some Unsettled Problems of Irrigation'," *American Economic Review* 101:1, pp. 64–80, at p. 70.
8. Edward B. Barbier and Anik Bhaduri (2015), "Transboundary Water Resources," in Robert Halvorsen and David F. Layton, eds., *Handbook on the Economics of Natural Resources* (Cheltenham, England: Edward Elgar), pp. 502–28; Aaron T. Wolf (2007), "Shared Waters: Conflict and Cooperation," *Annual Review of Environment and Resources* 32, pp. 214–69.

2. Humankind and Water

1. Steven Solomon (2010), *Water: The Epic Struggle for Wealth, Power, and Civilization* (New York: Harper), p. 15. Several recent books have also traced the role of water and economic development throughout human history. See, for example, Brian Fagan (2011), *Elixir: A History of Water and Humankind* (New York: Bloomsbury Press); David Sedlak (2014), *Water 4.0: The Past, Present, and Future of the World's Most Vital Resource* (New Haven and London: Yale University Press); Terje Tvedt (2016), *Water and Society: Changing Perceptions of Societal and Historical Development* (London: I. B. Tauris).

2. Paul A. David (1994), "Why Are Institutions the 'Carriers of History'? Path Dependence and the Evolution of Conventions, Organizations and Institutions," *Structural Change and Economic Dynamics* 5:2, pp. 205–20. The term "path dependence" is often used in economics and economic history to denote the dependence of economic outcomes on the path of previous outcomes, rather than simply on current conditions. Institutions and processes of technological change (i.e., innovation) are subject to widespread path dependence, because, once they are created, they tend to evolve very slowly. "Path dependence is more than the incremental process of institutional evolution in which yesterday's institutional framework provides the opportunity set for today's organizations and individual entrepreneurs (political or economic). The institutional matrix consists of an interdependent web of institutions and consequent political and economic organizations that are characterized by massive increasing returns. That is, the organizations owe their existence to the opportunities provided by the institutional framework." (Douglass C. North (1991), "Institutions," *Journal of Economic Perspectives* 5:1, pp, 97–112, at p. 109.)

3. Edward B. Barbier (2011a), *Scarcity and Frontiers: How Economies Have Developed through Natural Resource Exploitation* (Cambridge, England: Cambridge University Press), ch. 1; Solomon (2010), ch. 1.

4. Arnold Toynbee (1978), *Mankind and Mother Earth* (London: Granada), pp. 40–1.

5. Steven Mithen (2003), *After the Ice: A Global Human History: 20,000–5000 BC* (Cambridge, MA: Harvard University Press), p. 3. Note that "BC" in this quote refers to the traditional BC (Before Christ) / AD (Anno Domini, In the Year of Our Lord) system for historical dates, in which 1 AD is designated as Jesus Christ's birth year.

6. For further details and discussion, see Barbier (2011a), ch. 1; Mithen (2003); Peter Bellwood (2005), *The First Farmers: The Origins of Agricultural Societies* (Oxford: Blackwell); Bruce D. Smith (1995), *The Emergence of Agriculture* (New York: Scientific American Library).

7. This is often referred to as the "oasis theory," which was first proposed in V. Gordon Childe (1936), *Man Makes Himself* (London: Watts). Childe suggested that climate change at the end of the last glacial age led to dry conditions that forced humans and animals together in isolated "oases," especially in the Fertile Crescent, eventually fostering domestication. Childe also maintained that "the concentration of fertile land in alluvial basins and oases limited its supply, but made it amenable to improvements by irrigation," as quoted in Andrew Sherratt (1997), *Economy and Society*

in Prehistoric Europe: Changing Perspectives (Princeton: Princeton University Press), p. 59. See also Bellwood (2005); Smith (1995).

8. See Smith (1995), pp. 207–14.

9. For further discussion and examples see Bellwood (2005).

10. Arie S. Issar and Marranyah Zohar (2004), *Climate Change: Environment and Civilization in the Middle East* (Berlin: Springer), p. 132.

11. See, for example, Mark Elvin (1993), "Three Thousand Years of Unsustainable Growth: China's Environment from Archaic Time to the Present," *East Asian History* 6, pp. 7–46; Mark Elvin and Liu Ts'ui-jung, eds. (1998), *Sediments of Time: Environment and Society in Chinese History*, 2 vols. (Cambridge, England: Cambridge University Press); Li Liu (1996), "Settlement Patterns, Chiefdom Variability, and the Development of Early States in North China," *Journal of Anthropological Archaeology* 15:3, pp. 237–88; John R. McNeill (1998), "Chinese Environmental History in World Perspective," in Elvin and Liu, eds. (1998), vol. 1, pp. 31–49.

12. According to McNeill (1998), pp. 32–4, the role of water-based transportation in Imperial China cannot be overlooked: "Taken together, these waterways form a gigantic fishhook, a huge fertile crescent united by cheap and safe transport. Countless capillaries—small rivers and feeder canals—connected the main arteries to a broad hinterland . . . No inland waterway system in world history approaches this one as a device for integrating large and productive spaces . . . With its waterways the Chinese state from the Song times forward kept under its control (most of the time) a huge diversity of ecological zones with a broad array of useful natural resources . . . Consequently, the Chinese state had available great stocks and wide varieties of timber, grains, fish, fibers, salt, metals, building stone, and occasionally livestock and grazing land." See also Solomon (2010), ch. 5.

13. William H. McNeill (1999), *A World History*, 4th ed. (New York: Oxford University Press), ch. 4.

14. Karl A. Wittfogel (1957), *Oriental Despotism: A Comparative Study of Total Power* (New Haven and London: Yale University Press). See also Karl A. Wittfogel (1955), "Developmental Aspects of Hydraulic Civilizations," in Julian H. Steward, ed., *Irrigation Civilizations: A Comparative Study—A Symposium on Method and Result in Cross Cultural Regularities* (Washington, DC: Pan American Union).

15. For a reassessment of Wittfogel's hydraulic hypothesis as well as its limitations, see William P. Mitchell (1973), "The Hydraulic Hypothesis: A Reappraisal," *Current Anthropology* 14:5, pp. 532–4; David H. Price (1994), "Wittfogel's Neglected Hydraulic/Hydroagricultural Distinction," *Journal of Anthropological Research* 50:2, pp, 187–204; Michael J. Harrower (2009), "Is the Hydraulic Hypothesis Dead Yet? Irrigation and Social Change in Ancient Yemen, *World Archaeology* 41:1, pp. 58–72.

16. See, in particular, Issar and Zohar (2004), ch. 4–6 on the role of climate change in shaping the ancient environmental history of the Middle East.

17. Sing C. Chew (2001), *World Ecological Degradation: Accumulation, Urbanization, and Deforestation 3000 BC–AD 2000* (Walnut Creek, CA: Altamira Press); Issar and Zohar (2004), ch. 4–6.

18. Arnold Toynbee (1934), *A Study of History, vol. 3: The Growths of Civilizations* (London: Oxford University Press).
19. George Modelski and William R. Thompson (1999), "The Evolutionary Pulse of the World-System: Hinterland Incursion and Migrations 4000 BC to 1500 AD," in P. Nick Kardulias, ed., *World-Systems Theory in Practice: Leadership, Production and Exchange* (Lanham, MD: Rowman and Littlefield), pp. 241–74.
20. See Solomon (2010), ch. 5.
21. K. N. Chaudhuri (1990), *Asia before Europe: Economy and Civilization of the Indian Ocean from the Rise of Islam to 1750* (Cambridge, England: Cambridge University Press); Elvin (1993); Eric L. Jones (1988), *Growth Recurring: Economic Change in World History*, new ed. (Oxford: Clarendon Press); McNeill (1998).
22. Solomon (2010), p. 85.
23. Solomon (2010), ch. 4. See also Sedlak (2014), ch. 1.
24. See Sedlak (2014) ch. 1, where he refers to the Roman water supply and sewage system as "Water 1.0" in the chronology of urban water developments.
25. Chaudhuri (1990); Andrew Watson (1983), *Agricultural Innovation in the Early Islamic World: The Diffusion of Crops and Farming Techniques 700–1100* (Cambridge, England: Cambridge University Press).
26. Chaudhuri (1990), p. 244.
27. Watson (1983), p. 110.
28. Robert Bartlett (1993), *The Making of Europe: Conquest, Colonization, and Cultural Change 950–1350* (Princeton: Princeton University Press).
29. Eric L. Jones (1987), *The European Miracle: Environments, Economies, and Geopolitics in the History of Europe and Asia*, 2nd ed. (Cambridge, England: Cambridge University Press); Tvedt (2016), ch. 2.
30. Bartlett (1993), p. 143. See also Joshua Getzler (2004), *A History of Water Rights at Common Law* (Oxford: Oxford University Press), ch. 1; Fagan (2011), ch. 16.
31. David Herlihy (1997), *The Black Death and the Transformation of the West* (Cambridge, MA: Harvard University Press). See also Getzler (2004), ch. 1.
32. Getzler (2004). See also Thomas V. Cech (2010), *Principles of Water Resources: History, Development, Management, and Policy*, 3rd ed. (Hoboken, NJ: John Wiley), ch. 8.
33. The key implication of this evolution in water law was to recognize that flowing water is a public good that is common to everyone and thus can only be the object of rights of use—a principle that began under Roman common law and still exists today. This is nicely summarized by Michael W. Hanemann: "The public good nature of water in situ, historically associated with navigation, has been a decisive influence on the legal status of water. In Roman Law and, subsequently, in English and American common law, and to an extent in Civil Law systems, flowing waters are treated as common to everyone (*res communis omnium*), and are not capable of being owned. These waters can only be the object of rights of use (usufructuary rights), but not of rights of ownership." (Michael W. Hanemann (2006), "The Economic Conception of Water," in Peter P. Rogers, M.

Ramón Llamas and Luis Martínez-Cortina, eds., *Water Crisis: Myth or Reality?* (London: Routledge, 2006), p. 73.)

34. "Riparian" is from the Latin *ripa*, which means "bank" or "shore." Thus, as outlined by Cech (2010), p. 251, "The riparian doctrine states that water in a stream belongs to the public for use by fishers and for navigation, and cannot be controlled by private individuals. However, the owner of land along a stream owns the property to the water's edge and in some cases may own the underlying property to the center of the stream. The riparian landowner was allowed to make de minimis (reasonable) use of water in the stream for milling, domestic, and agricultural purposes as long as navigation was not injured. A riparian landowner was required to return any diverted water back to the stream unchanged in quantity or quality."

35. See, especially, Getzler (2004), ch. 1.

36. Getzler (2004), p. 37. See also Tvedt (2016), ch. 2 for a compelling discussion of why Britain's water resource endowment was more conducive for promoting such innovations to jump-start industrialization compared to the endowments of the two largest and richest agricultural-based empires of the mid-eighteenth century, China and India.

37. See, for example, Edward B. Barbier (2015a), *Nature and Wealth: Overcoming Environmental Scarcity and Inequality* (Basingstoke, England: Palgrave Macmillan); Gregory Clark (2007), *A Farewell to Alms: A Brief Economic History of the World* (Princeton: Princeton University Press); Ronald Findlay and Kevin H. O'Rourke (2007), *Power and Plenty: Trade, War, and the World Economy in the Second Millennium* (Princeton: Princeton University Press); M. W. Flinn (1978), "Technical Change as an Escape from Resource Scarcity: England in the 17th and 18th Centuries," in William N. Parker and Antoni Mączak, eds., *Natural Resources in European History* (Washington, DC: Resources for the Future), pp. 139–59; Jones (1987); David Landes (1998), *The Wealth and Poverty of Nations: Why Some Are So Rich and Some So Poor* (New York: W. W. Norton); Angus Maddison (2003), *The World Economy: Historical Statistics* (Paris: OECD); Joel Mokyr, ed. (1999), *The British Industrial Revolution: An Economic Perspective*, 2nd ed. (Boulder, CO: Westview Press); Patrick K. O'Brien (1986), "Do We Have a Typology for the Study of European Industrialization in the XIXth Century?" *Journal of European Economic History* 15:2, pp. 291–333; P. H. H. Vries (2001), "Are Coal and Colonies Really Crucial? Kenneth Pomeranz and the Great Divergence," *Journal of World History* 12:2, pp. 407–46.

38. Tvedt (2016), p. 35.

39. Fagan (2011), p. 328.

40. Barbier (2015a); Robert J. Gordon (2016), *The Rise and Fall of American Growth: The U.S. Standard of Living since the Civil War* (Princeton: Princeton University Press).

41. Fagan (2011), p. 329.

42. Walter P. Webb (1964), *The Great Frontier* (Lincoln: University of Nebraska Press), p. 13. See also William H. McNeill (1982), *The Great Frontier: Freedom and Hierarchy in Modern Times* (Princeton: Princeton University Press); Barbier (2011a), ch. 5; Jones (1987).

43. See Barbier (2011a), ch. 7; Findlay and O'Rourke (2007); W. Arthur Lewis (1978), *Growth and Fluctuations 1870–1913* (London: George Allen and Unwin); Jeffrey G. Williamson (2002), "Land, Labor, and Globalization in the Third World 1870–1940," *Journal of Economic History* 62:1, pp. 55–85; Jeffrey G. Williamson (2006), *Globalization and the Poor Periphery before 1950* (Cambridge, MA: MIT Press).
44. Barbier (2011a), Table 7.5, pp. 382–3.
45. For example, in 1860 the United States accounted for only 7.2 percent of world manufacturing output, but by 1913 its share was 32.0 percent. In contrast, in 1860 the United Kingdom was the leading world manufacturer, with 19.9 percent of world output, but by 1913 its share had fallen to 13.6 percent. See Barbier (2011a), Table 7.8, p. 391.
46. See, especially, Solomon (2010), ch. 11.
47. Solomon (2010), p. 267.
48. Cech (2010), ch. 8.
49. John C. Weaver (2003), *The Great Land Rush and the Making of the Modern World 1650–1900* (Montreal: McGill-Queen's University Press).
50. Fagan (2011), p. 325.
51. Sedlak (2014). David Sedlak refers to this revolution in treating urban drinking water as "Water 2.0."
52. Getzler (2004), pp. 350–1.
53. For a comprehensive history of large-scale federal dam development in the United States, see David P. Billington, Donald C. Jackson and Martin V. Melosi (2005), *The History of Large Federal Dams: Planning, Design, and Construction* (Denver: U.S. Department of Interior, Bureau of Reclamation), available at https://www.usbr.gov/history/HistoryofLargeDams/LargeFederalDams.pdf (accessed June 12, 2018).

3. Water in the Modern Era

1. FAO (2012), *Coping with Water Scarcity: An Action Framework for Agriculture and Food Security* (Rome: FAO).
2. Mark W. Rosegrant, Claudia Ringler and Tingju Zhu (2009), "Water for Agriculture: Maintaining Food Security under Growing Scarcity," *Annual Review of Environmental and Resources* 34, pp. 205–22.
3. The sectoral water use depicted in Figure 3.3 is based on the AQUASTAT main database of the Food and Agriculture Organization of the United Nations (FAO). In their sectoral classification of water use, the FAO defines "municipal water use" as the annual quantity of water withdrawn primarily for direct use by the population, and it is usually computed as the total water withdrawn by the public distribution network, i.e., total public-supply water use. "Municipal water use" is sometimes used interchangeably with "domestic water use," but the latter focuses more specifically on human/household needs (drinking, cooking, cleaning, sanitation), whereas "municipal" includes all that is connected to the public distribution network (households, shops, services, some urban industries, some urban agriculture, etc.). In contrast, the FAO distinguishes "industrial water use" as the annual quantity of self-supplied water withdrawn for industrial

uses, and "agricultural water use" as the annual quantity of self-supplied water withdrawn for irrigation, livestock and aquaculture purposes.

4. Molly A. Maupin, Joan F. Kenny, Susan S. Hutson, John K. Lovelace, Nancy L. Barber and Kristin S. Linsey (2014), *Estimated Use of Water in the United States in 2010* (Washington, DC: U.S. Department of Interior/ U.S. Geological Survey).
5. Melissa S. Kearney, Benjamin H. Harris, Elisa Jácome and Gregory Nantz (2014), *In Times of Drought: Nine Economic Facts about Water in the United States* (Washington, DC: Hamilton Project, Brookings Institution).
6. Kearney et al. (2014).
7. Miina Porkka, Dieter Gerten, Sibyll Schaphoff, Stefan Siebert and Matti Kummu (2016), "Causes and Trends of Water Scarcity in Food Production," *Environmental Research Letters* 11:1, 015001.
8. Upali A. Amarasinghe and Vladimir Smakhtin (2014), *Global Water Demand Projections: Past, Present and Future* (Colombo, Sri Lanka: International Water Management Institute), pp. 15–19.
9. Rosegrant et al. (2009). See also Edward B. Barbier (2015b), "Water and Growth in Developing Countries," in Ariel Dinar and Kurt Schwabe, eds., *Handbook of Water Economics* (Cheltenham, England: Edward Elgar), pp. 500–12.
10. Rosegrant et al. (2009), p. 217.
11. See, for example, J. A. Allan (2003), "Virtual Water: The Water, Food, and Trade Nexus—Useful Concept or Misleading Metaphor?" *Water International* 28:1, pp. 106–13; Peter Debaere (2014), "The Global Economics of Water: Is Water a Source of Comparative Advantage?" *American Economic Journal: Applied Economics* 6:2, pp. 32–48; Andrea Fracasso (2014), "A Gravity Model of Virtual Water Trade," *Ecological Economics* 108, pp. 215–28; Arjen Y. Hoekstra and Ashok K. Chapagain (2008), *Globalization of Water: Sharing the Planet's Freshwater Resources* (Oxford: Blackwell); Graham K. MacDonald, Kate A. Brauman, Shipeng Sun, Kimberly M. Carlson, Emily S. Cassidy, et al. (2015), "Rethinking Agricultural Trade Relationships in an Era of Globalization," *BioScience* 65:3, pp. 275–89; Jeffrey J. Reimer (2012), "On the Economics of Virtual Water Trade," *Ecological Economics* 75, pp. 135–9; Rosegrant et al. (2009); H. H. J. Savenije, A. Y. Hoekstra and P. van der Zaag (2014), "Evolving Water Science in the Anthropocene," *Hydrology and Earth System Sciences* 18:1, pp. 319–32.
12. Carole Dalin, Megan Konar, Naota Hanasaki, Andrea Rinaldo and Ignacio Rodriguez-Iturbe (2012), "Evolution of the Global Virtual Water Trade Network," *Proceedings of the National Academy of Sciences* 109:16, pp. 5989–94.
13. Dalin et al. (2012); Debaere (2014); Arjen Y. Hoekstra (2010), "The Relation between International Trade and Freshwater Scarcity," Staff Working Paper ERSD-2010-05, World Trade Organization, January; MacDonald et al. (2015).
14. Hoekstra (2010). See also Allan (2003), who has long argued that the import of water-intensive commodities by Middle Eastern countries has helped alleviate water shortages in that region.
15. Hoekstra (2010); Manfred Lenzen, Daniel Moran, Anik Bhaduri, Keiichiro Kanemoto, Maksud Bekchanov, et al. (2013), "International Trade of Scarce Water," *Ecological Economics* 94, pp. 78–85.

16. Lenzen et al. (2013).
17. Dalin et al. (2012); Debaere (2014); Hoekstra (2010); Hoekstra and Chapagain (2008); MacDonald et al. (2015).
18. Debaere (2014), p. 42.
19. Carole Dalin, Yoshihide Wada, Thomas Kastner and Michael J. Puma (2017) "Groundwater Depletion Embedded in International Food Trade," *Nature* 543, pp. 700–5.
20. Population Reference Bureau (2009), "Urbanization," in *Human Population: Lesson Plans*, http://www.prb.org/Publications/Lesson-Plans/HumanPopulation/Urbanization.aspx (accessed June 13, 2018).
21. UN DESA (2014), "2014 Revision of World Urbanization Prospects," available at https://esa.un.org/unpd/wup/Publications/ (accessed July 17, 2018).
22. UN DESA (2014).
23. Amarasinghe and Smakhtin (2014), p. 12.
24. Robert I. McDonald, Katherine Weber, Julie Padowski, Martina Flörke, Christof Schneider, et al. (2014), "Water on an Urban Planet: Urbanization and the Reach of Urban Water Infrastructure," *Global Environmental Change* 27, pp. 96–105. This study focused on water use of a sample of urban agglomerations greater than 750,000.
25. McDonald et al. (2014).
26. David Sedlak (2014), *Water 4.0: The Past, Present, and Future of the World's Most Vital Resource* (New Haven and London: Yale University Press). Sedlak refers to this revolution in water-borne sewage treatment as "Water 3.0."
27. Sedlak (2014), pp. 118–19.
28. This evolving water resource management ethos that emerged from the Industrial Revolution is described succinctly by H. H. G. Savenije and colleagues: "The increased exploitation of freshwater and the related development of societies has been made possible by increasing knowledge of water engineering, large-scale water supply, flood mitigation and irrigation ... Equipped with new technological powers, a new generation of engineers emerged that had a new hydraulic mission: that of 'taming' nature and making it orderly ... During the last decades of the nineteenth century and the first decades of the twentieth century, the water landscape was transformed in various places, including but not limited to India, Sudan, Mali, Egypt, the USA, Brazil, Spain and the Netherlands. These developments, associated with large and powerful water bureaucracies ... allowed for unprecedented growth in the production of agricultural commodities and energy and confirmed the belief that man could fully control water and be the master of nature." (Savenije et al. (2014), pp. 320–1).
29. Ronald C. Griffin (2012), "The Origins and Ideals of Water Resource Economics in the United States," *Annual Reviews of Resource Economics* 4, pp. 353–77. See also David Grey and Claudia W. Sadoff (2007), "Sink or Swim? Water Security for Growth and Development," *Water Policy* 9:6, pp. 545–71.
30. Michael D. Young (2014a), "Designing Water Abstraction Regimes for an Ever-Changing and Ever-Varying Future," *Agricultural Water Management* 145, pp. 32–38.

31. Edward B. Barbier and Anita M. Chaudhry (2014), "Urban Growth and Water," *Water Resources and Economics* 6, pp. 1–17.

32. UNICEF and WHO (World Health Organization) (2015), *Progress on Sanitation and Drinking Water: 2015 Update and MDG Assessment* (Geneva: WHO Press).

33. See the International Commission on Large Dams (ICOLD) register, available at http://www.icold-cigb.org/.

34. Troy Sternberg (2016), "Water Megaprojects in Deserts and Drylands," *International Journal of Water Resources Development* 32:2, pp. 301–20. As noted by the author (pp. 301–2), "In the recent past schemes promoted 'man over nature,' 'conquer the virgin lands' and 'westward expansion' across arid regions, steppes and prairies driven by 'new' groundwater resources. The mantra has shifted to economic progress, water security, anti-desertification efforts and the idea of deserts as environments to be managed by expanding populations. This has led to today's era of megaprojects where basic water needs and desires have exponentially expanded with technology and funding to 'bring the resource to the people' rather than situating people 'where the water is.' Deserts and semi-deserts, home to 2 billion people and covering about 40% of the Earth . . . are the clearest manifestation of this trend . . . A focus on desert environments encapsulates the how water resources are (mis)used in today's globalized world."

35. Michael Hanemann (2002), "The Central Arizona Project," CUDARE Working Paper 937, University of California, Berkeley; Sternberg (2016).

36. Sternberg (2016), p. 301.

4. A Global Crisis in Water Management

1. Simon N. Gosling and Nigel W. Arnell (2016), "A Global Assessment of the Impact of Climate Change on Water Scarcity," *Climatic Change* 134:3, pp. 371–85. Note, however, that the authors stress that there is substantial uncertainty in the projections of the impact of climate change on water scarcity in south and east Asia, which in turn suggests considerable uncertainty in the global-scale effect. Thus, the authors conclude (p. 371): "Most of the world will see an increase in exposure to water scarcity than a decrease due to climate change but this is not consistent across all climate change patterns." Other assessments of the impact of climate change on water scarcity are less cautious; see, for example, Jacob Schewe, Jens Heinke, Dieter Gerten, Ingjerd Haddeland, Nigel W. Arnell, et al. (2014), "Mutimodel Assessment of Water Scarcity under Climate Change," *Proceedings of the National Academy of Sciences* 111:9, pp. 3245–50.

2. Joshua Elliott, Delphine Deryang, Christoph Müller, Katja Frieler, Markus Konzmann, et al. (2014), "Constraints and Potentials of Future Irrigation Water Availability on Agricultural Production under Climate Change," *Proceedings of the National Academy of Sciences* 111:9, pp. 3239–44.

3. Robert I. McDonald, Pamela Green, Deborah Balk, Balazs M. Fekete, Carmen Revenga, et al. (2011), "Urban Growth, Climate Change, and Freshwater Availability," *Proceedings of the National Academy of Sciences* 108:15, pp. 6312–17.

4. OECD (2012), *OECD Environmental Outlook to 2050: The Consequences of Inaction* (Paris: OECD), p. 216.

5. J. A. Allan (2003), "Virtual Water: The Water, Food, and Trade Nexus— Useful Concept or Misleading Metaphor?" *Water International* 28:1, pp. 106–13; Arjen Y. Hoekstra (2010), "The Relation between International Trade and Freshwater Scarcity," Staff Working Paper ERSD-2010-05, World Trade Organization, January.

6. Edward B. Barbier (2004), "Water and Economic Growth," *Economic Record* 80:248, pp. 1–16.

7. Souha El Khanji and John Hudson (2016), "Water Utilization and Water Quality in Endogenous Economic Growth," *Environment and Development Economics* 21:5, pp. 626–48.

8. Gosling and Arnell (2016).

9. Edward B. Barbier (2015b), "Water and Growth in Developing Countries," in Ariel Dinar and Kurt Schwabe, eds., *Handbook of Water Economics* (Cheltenham, England: Edward Elgar), pp. 500–12; Cesare Dosi and K. William Easter (2003), "Water Scarcity: Market Failure and the Implications for Water Markets and Privatization," *International Journal of Public Administration* 26:3, pp. 265–90; R. Quentin Grafton, Jamie Pittock, Richard Davis, John Williams, Guobin Fu, et al. (2013), "Global Insights into Water Resources, Climate Change and Governance," *Nature Climate Change* 3:4, pp. 315–21; David Grey and Claudia W. Sadoff (2007), "Sink or Swim? Water Security for Growth and Development," *Water Policy* 9:6, pp. 545–71; R. Maria Saleth and Ariel Dinar (2005), "Water Institutional Reforms: Theory and Practice," *Water Policy* 7:1, pp. 1–19; Céline Nauges and Dale Whittington (2010), "Estimation of Water Demand in Developing Countries: An Overview," *World Bank Research Observer* 25:2, pp. 263–94; Karina Schoengold and David Zilberman (2007), "The Economics of Water, Irrigation, and Development," in Robert Evenson and Prabhu Pingali, eds., *Handbook of Agricultural Economics, vol. 3* (Amsterdam: Elsevier), pp. 2933–77; Dale Whittington, W. Michael Hanemann, Claudia Sadoff and Marc Jeuland (2008), "The Challenge of Improving Water Sanitation Services in Less Developed Countries," *Foundations and Trends in Microeconomics* 4:6–7, pp. 469–609.

10. Schoengold and Zilberman (2007).

11. Barbier (2015b).

12. Jacob D. Petersen-Perlman, Jennifer C. Veilleux and Aaron T. Wolf (2017), "International Water Conflict and Cooperation: Challenges and Opportunities," *Water International* 42:2, pp. 105–20.

13. UNDP (2006), *Human Development Report 2006: Beyond Scarcity—Power, Poverty and the Global Water Crisis* (Basingstoke, England: Palgrave Macmillan).

14. E. Stephen Draper and James E. Kundell (2007), "Impact of Climate Change on Transboundary Water Sharing," *Journal of Water Resources Planning and Management* 133:5, pp. 405–15.

15. Richard E. Just and Sinaia Netanyahu (1998), "International Water Resource Conflicts: Experience and Potential," in Richard E. Just and Sinaia Netanyahu, eds., *Conflict and Cooperation on Trans-Boundary Water Resources* (Boston: Kluwer Academic), pp. 1–26.

16. Edward B. Barbier and Anik Bhaduri (2015), "Transboundary Water Resources," in Robert Halvorsen and David R. Layton, eds., *Handbook on the Economics of Natural Resources* (Cheltenham, England: Edward Elgar), pp. 502–28.

17. Jennifer Song and Dale Whittington (2004), "Why Have Some Countries on International Rivers Been Successful Negotiating Treaties? A Global Perspective," *Water Resources Research* 40:5, W05S06.

18. Meredith A. Giordano and Aaron T. Wolf (2003), "Sharing Waters: Post-Rio International Water Management," *Natural Resources Forum* 27:2, pp. 163–71; Aaron T. Wolf (2007), "Shared Waters: Conflict and Cooperation," *Annual Review of Environment and Resources* 32, pp. 241–69. See also UNEP (2002), *Atlas of International Freshwater Agreements* (Nairobi: UNEP), available at https://wedocs.unep.org/handle/20.500.11822/8182 (accessed June 15, 2018).

19. Wolf (2007).

20. Song and Whittington (2004).

21. UNDP (2006).

22. Anik Bhaduri and Edward B. Barbier (2008a), "International Water Transfer and Sharing: The Case of the Ganges River," *Environment and Development Economics* 13:1, pp. 29–51.

23. L. De Stefano, Jacob D. Petersen-Perlman, Eric A. Sproles, Jim Eynard and Aaron T. Wolf (2017), "Assessment of Transboundary River Basins for Potential Hydro-Political Tensions," *Global Environmental Change* 45, pp. 35–46.

24. J. S. Famiglietti (2014), "The Global Groundwater Crisis," *Nature Climate Change* 4:11, pp. 946–8.

25. Famiglietti (2014).

26. Marguerite de Chaisemartin, Robert G. Varady, Sharon B. Megdal, Kirstin I. Conti, Jac van der Gun, et al. (2017), "Addressing the Groundwater Governance Challenge," in Eiman Karar, ed., *Freshwater Governance for the 21st Century* (London: SpringerOpen), pp. 205–27.

27. Carole Dalin, Yoshihide Wada, Thomas Kastner and Michael J. Puma (2017), "Groundwater Depletion Embedded in International Food Trade," *Nature* 543, pp. 700–5.

28. Robert I. McDonald, Katherine Weber, Julie Padowski, Martina Flörke, Christof Schneider, et al. (2014), "Water on an Urban Planet: Urbanization and the Reach of Urban Water Infrastructure," *Global Environmental Change* 27, pp. 96–105. This study focused on water use of a sample of urban agglomerations greater than 750,000.

29. Edith Brown Weiss (2012), "The Coming Water Crisis: A Common Concern of Humankind," *Transnational Environmental Law* 1:1, pp. 153–68; Arjen Y. Hoekstra and Mesfin M. Mekonnen (2012), "The Water Footprint of Humanity," *Proceedings of the National Academy of Sciences* 109:9, pp. 3232–7; Maria Cristina Rulli, Antonio Saviori and Paolo D'Odorico (2013), "Global Land and Water Grabbing," *Proceedings of the National Academy of Sciences* 110:3, pp. 892–7.

30. See, for example: Allan (2003); Peter Debaere (2014), "The Global Economics of Water: Is Water a Source of Comparative Advantage?"

American Economic Journal: Applied Economics 6:2, pp. 32–48; Andrea Fracasso (2014), "A Gravity Model of Virtual Water Trade," *Ecological Economics* 108, pp. 215–28; Arjen Y. Hoekstra and Ashok K. Chapagain (2008), *Globalization of Water: Sharing the Planet's Freshwater Resources* (Oxford: Blackwell); Graham K. MacDonald, Kate A. Brauman, Shipeng Sun, Kimberly M. Carlson, Emily S. Cassidy, et al. (2015), "Rethinking Agricultural Trade Relationships in an Era of Globalization," *BioScience* 65:3, pp. 275–89; Jeffrey J. Reimer (2012), "On the Economics of Virtual Water Trade," *Ecological Economics* 75, pp. 135–9; Mark W. Rosegrant, Claudia Ringler and Tingju Zhu (2009), "Water for Agriculture: Maintaining Food Security under Growing Scarcity," *Annual Review of Environmental and Resources* 34, pp. 205–22; H. H. G. Savenije, A. Y. Hoekstra and P. van der Zaag (2014), "Evolving Water Science in the Anthropocene," *Hydrology and Earth System Sciences* 18, pp. 319–32.

31. Rulli et al. (2013).
32. Brown Weiss (2012).
33. Hoekstra and Mekonnen (2012).
34. Hoekstra (2010); Manfred Lenzen, Daniel Moran, Anik Bhaduri, Keiichiro Kanemoto, Maksud Bekchanov, et al. (2013), "International Trade of Scarce Water," *Ecological Economics* 94, pp. 78–85.

5. Reforming Governance and Institutions

1. Michael D. Young (2014a), "Designing Water Abstraction Regimes for an Ever-Changing and Ever-Varying Future," *Agricultural Water Management* 145, pp. 32–8.
2. As noted in Chapter 3, the term "hydraulic mission" was coined and described by H. H. G. Savenije, A. Y. Hoekstra and P. van der Zaag (2014), "Evolving Water Science in the Anthropocene," *Hydrology and Earth System Sciences* 18, pp. 319–32.
3. Jonathan Lautze, Sanjiv de Silva, Mark Giordano and Luke Sanford (2011), "Putting the Cart before the Horse: Water Governance and IWRM," *Natural Resources Forum* 35:1, pp. 1–8.
4. R. Maria Saleth and Ariel Dinar (2005), "Water Institutional Reforms: Theory and Practice," *Water Policy* 7:1, pp. 1–19.
5. Sheila M. Olmstead (2014), "Climate Change Adaptation and Water Resource Management: A Review of the Literature," *Energy Economics* 46, pp. 500–9; Young (2014a).
6. Edith Brown Weiss (2012), "The Coming Water Crisis: A Common Concern of Humankind," *Transnational Environmental Law* 1:1, pp. 153–68; Marguerite de Chaisemartin, Robert G. Varady, Sharon B. Megdal, Kirstin I. Conti, Jac van der Gun, et al. (2017), "Addressing the Groundwater Governance Challenge," in Eiman Karar, ed., *Freshwater Governance for the 21st Century* (London: SpringerOpen), pp. 205–27; Maria Cristina Rulli, Antonio Saviori and Paolo D'Odorico (2013), "Global Land and Water Grabbing," *Proceedings of the National Academy of Sciences* 110:3, pp. 892–97; FAO (2016), *Global Diagnostic on Groundwater Governance* (Rome: FAO).

7. Peter Rogers, Radhika De Silva and Ramesh Bhatia (2002), "Water Is an Economic Good: How to Use Prices to Promote Equity, Efficiency, and Sustainability," *Water Policy* 4:1, pp. 1–17.

8. R. Quentin Grafton, Jamie Pittock, Richard Davis, John Williams, Guobin Fu, et al. (2013), "Global Insights into Water Resources, Climate Change and Governance," *Nature Climate Change* 3:4, pp. 315–21.

9. As noted in Alice Cohen and Seanna Davidson (2011), "An Examination of the Watershed Approach: Challenges, Antecedents, and the Transition from Technical Tool to Governance Unit," *Water Alternatives* 4:1, pp. 1–14. The terms "watershed" and "river basin" are hydrologically distinct units that are nevertheless frequently used interchangeably in the literature. For example, as Cohen and Davidson point out (p. 1), a "watershed" is "an area of land draining into a common body of water such as a lake, river, or ocean. 'Watershed' is the most common North American term for such a unit, but these are also labelled variously as 'river basins' and 'catchments' throughout the world." Similarly, the US Geological Survey indicates that "a watershed is an area of land that drains all the streams and rainfall to a common outlet such as the outflow of a reservoir, mouth of a bay, or any point along a stream channel. The word watershed is sometimes used interchangeably with drainage basin or catchment" ("What Is a Watershed?" https://water.usgs.gov/edu/watershed.html, accessed June 15, 2018). For ease of terminology, the term "river basin" will be used here as a shorthand for a river system and its entire watershed catchment that drains via the river into some common outlet. In other words, for simplicity, "river basin" will also imply a "watershed," "drainage basin," "catchment," "catchment basin" or "catchment area." Strictly speaking this is not accurate, as there are some important hydrological differences between a river basin and a watershed. For a good explanation of this distinction, see "Difference between River Basin and Watershed," Difference Between, http://www.differencebetween.net/science/nature/difference-between-river-basin-and-watershed/ (accessed June 15, 2018).

10. UNEP (2012), *Status Report on the Application of Integrated Approaches to Water Resources Management* (Nairobi: UNEP).

11. See, for example, Asit K. Biswas (2008), "Integrated Water Resources Management: Is It Working?" *International Journal of Water Resources Development* 24:1, pp. 5–22; Mark Giordano and Tushaar Shah (2014), "From IWRM Back to Integrated Resources Management," *International Journal of Water Resources Development* 30:3, pp. 364–76; François Molle (2009), "River Basin Planning and Management: The Social Life of a Concept," *Geoforum* 40:3, pp. 484–94.

12. Frank G. W. Jaspers (2003), "Institutional Arrangements for Integrated River Basin Management," *Water Policy* 5:1, pp. 77–90; Molle (2009).

13. Dan Shrubsole, Dan Walters, Barbara Veale and Bruce Mitchell (2017), "Integrated Water Resources Management in Canada: The Experience of Watershed Agencies," *International Journal of Water Resources Development* 33:3, pp. 349–59, at p. 350.

14. Shrubsole et al. (2017), p. 350.

15. See, for example, Giordano and Shah (2014), which cites the various treaties governing the Columbia River, which is shared between Canada and

the United States. Because the treaties focus on providing flood control and hydroelectricity, there has never been any discussion of the need to use a "basin-scale approach" to manage these two services for the mutual benefit of the two countries.

16. Cohen and Davidson (2011).
17. Grafton et al. (2013).
18. The following discussion of governance and institutional developments in managing the Murray–Darling river basin draws on Grafton et al. (2013); R. Quentin Grafton, James Horne and Sarah Ann Wheeler (2016), "On the Marketisation of Water: Evidence from the Murray–Darling Basin, Australia," *Water Resources Management* 30:3, pp. 913–26; Barry T. Hart (2016a), "The Australian Murray–Darling Basin Plan: Challenges in Its Implementation (Part 1)," *International Journal of Water Resources Development* 32:6, pp. 819–34; Barry T. Hart (2016b), "The Australian Murray–Darling Basin Plan: Challenges in Its Implementation (Part 2)," *International Journal of Water Resources Development* 32:6, pp. 835–52; James Horne (2014), "The 2012 Murray–Darling Basin Plan: Issues to Watch," *International Journal of Water Resources Development* 30:1, pp. 152–63; Michael D. Young (2014b), "Trading into Trouble? Lessons from Australia's Mistakes in Water Policy Reform Sequencing," in K. William Easter and Qiuqiong Huang, eds., *Water Markets for the 21st Century: What Have We Learned?* (Dordrecht, Netherlands: Springer), pp. 203–14.
19. Young (2014b).
20. Hart (2016b); Horne (2014).
21. Hart (2016a); Hart (2016b); Horne (2016).
22. Young (2014b).
23. See, for example, Grafton et al. (2013); Elke Herrfahrdt-Pühle (2014), "Applying the Concept of Fit to Water Governance Reforms in South Africa," *Ecology and Society* 19:1, p. 25; Richard Meissner, Sabine Stuart-Hill and Zakariya Nakhooda (2017), "The Establishment of Catchment Management Agencies in South Africa with Reference to the *Flussgebietsgemeinschaft Elbe*: Some Practical Considerations," in Eiman Karar, ed., *Freshwater Governance for the 21st Century* (London: SpringerOpen), pp. 15–26; Barbara van Koppen and Barbara Schreiner (2014), "Moving Beyond Integrated Water Resource Management: Developmental Water Management in South Africa," *International Journal of Water Resources Development* 30:3, pp. 543–58.
24. Koppen and Schreiner (2014).
25. Cecilia Tortajada (2001), "Institutions for Integrated River Basin Management in Latin America," *International Journal of Water Resources Development* 17:3, pp. 289–301.
26. Adrian Cashman (2017), "Why Isn't IWRM Working in the Caribbean?" *Water Policy* 19:4, pp. 587–600.
27. Frank Hüesker and Timothy Moss (2017), "The Politics of Multi-Scalar Action in River Basin Management: Implementing the EU Water Framework Directive (WFD)," *Land Use Policy* 42, pp. 38–47; Meissner et al. (2017); Nikolaos Voulvoulis, Karl Dominic Arpon and Theodoros Giakoumis (2017), "The EU Water Framework Directive: From Great Expectations to Problems with Implementation," *Science of the Total Environment* 575, pp. 358–66.

28. Voulvoulis et al. (2017).
29. Voulvoulis et al. (2017).
30. Hüesker and Moss (2017).
31. Groundwater Governance (2015), *Shared Global Vision for Groundwater Governance 2030 and a Call-for-Action*, available at http://www.groundwatergovernance.org/fileadmin/user_upload/groundwatergovernance/docs/GWG_VISION_EN.pdf (accessed June 22, 2018).
32. Groundwater Governance (2016), *Global Diagnostic on Groundwater Governance*, March, available at http://www.groundwatergovernance.org/fileadmin/user_upload/groundwatergovernance/docs/GWG_DIAGNOSTIC.pdf (accessed June 22, 2018).
33. Groundwater Governance (2016). See also Sharon B. Megdal, Andrea K. Gerlak, Robert G. Varady and Ling-Yee Huang (2015), "Groundwater Governance in the United States: Common Priorities and Challenges" *Groundwater* 53:5, pp. 677–84.
34. Chaisemartin et al. (2017); Carole Dalin, Yoshihide Wada, Thomas Kastner and Michael J. Puma (2017), "Groundwater Depletion Embedded in International Food Trade," *Nature* 543, pp. 700–5; J. S. Famiglietti (2014), "The Global Groundwater Crisis," *Nature Climate Change* 4:11, pp. 946–8; Christine J. Kirchhoff and Lisa Dilling (2016), "The Role of U.S. States in Facilitating Effective Water Governance under Stress and Change," *Water Resources Research* 52:4, pp. 2951–64; Groundwater Governance (2016); Megdal et al. (2015).
35. The following discussion of the Netherlands is from Chaisemartin et al. (2017).
36. The following discussion of Texas and Maryland is from Kirchhof and Dilling (2016).
37. See, for example, Olmstead (2014).

6. Ending the Underpricing of Water

1. Michael D. Young (2014a), "Designing Water Abstraction Regimes for an Ever-Changing and Ever-Varying Future," *Agricultural Water Management* 145, pp. 32–8.
2. As noted in Chapter 3, this "hydraulic mission" began in the United States during the last decades of the nineteenth century and the early twentieth century, and has been adopted throughout the rest of the world ever since. For an excellent summary of the US history and experience, see Ronald C. Griffin (2012), "The Origins and Ideals of Water Resource Economics in the United States," *Annual Review of Resource Economics* 4, pp. 353–77.
3. W. Michael Hanemann (2006), "The Economic Conception of Water," in Peter P. Rogers, M. Ramón Llamas and Luis Martínez-Cortina, eds., *Water Crisis: Myth or Reality?* (London: Routledge), pp. 61–91; Sheila M. Olmstead (2010a), "The Economics of Managing Scarce Water Resources," *Review of Environmental Economics and Policy* 4:2, pp. 179–98.
4. R. Quentin Grafton (2017), "Responding to the 'Wicked Problem' of Water Insecurity," *Water Resources Management* 31:10, pp. 3023–41; Peter Rogers, Radhika De Silva and Ramesh Bhatia (2002), "Water Is an

Economic Good: How to Use Prices to Promote Equity, Efficiency, and Sustainability," *Water Policy* 4:1, pp. 1–17; Olmstead (2010a).

5. See, for example, Frank J. Convery (2013), "Reflections: Shaping Water Policy—What Does Economics Have to Offer?" *Review of Environmental Economics and Policy* 7:1, pp. 156–74; Peter Debaere, Brian D. Richter, Kyle Frankel Davis, Melissa S. Duvall, Jessica Ann Gephart, et al. (2014), "Water Markets as a Response to Scarcity," *Water Policy* 16:4, pp. 625–49; Ariel Dinar, Victor Pochat and José Albiac-Murillo, eds. (2015), *Water Pricing Experiences and Innovations* (Cham, Switzerland: Springer); K. William Easter and Qiuqiong Huang, eds. (2014b), *Water Markets for the 21st Century: What Have We Learned?* (Dordrecht, Netherlands: Springer); R. Quentin Grafton, Gary Libecap, Samuel McGlennon, Clay Landry and Bob O'Brien (2011), "An Integrated Assessment of Water Markets: A Cross-Country Comparison," *Review of Environmental Economics and Policy* 5:2, pp. 219–39; Olmstead (2010a); Young (2014a).

6. See, for example, Jedidiah Brewer, Robert Glennon, Alan Ker and Gary Libecap (2008), "Water Markets in the West: Prices, Trading, and Contractual Forms," *Economic Inquiry* 46:2, pp. 91–112, which finds that the median price of agricultural-to-agricultural leases of water in the western United States is $8 per 10^3 cubic metres (m^3), whereas the median price of agriculture-to-urban leases is $32 per 10^3 m^3.

7. Convery (2013).

8. See Gary D. Libecap (2011), "Institutional Path Dependence in Climate Adaptation: Coman's 'Some Unsettled Problems of Irrigation'," *American Economic Review* 101, pp. 64–80, which describes how the prior appropriation water rights contributed to the present-day difficulty of creating water markets in the western United States for reallocating water from irrigation agriculture to other higher-valued uses in the economy as well as to allow more flexible responses to climate change, period drought and other hydrological uncertainties in the region. For a broad review of the policy responses to climate change impact on water resource management, see Sheila M. Olmstead (2014), "Climate Change Adaptation and Water Resource Management: A Review of the Literature," *Energy Economics* 46, pp. 500–9.

9. See, for example, Edward B. Barbier (2011b), "Transaction Costs and the Transition to Environmentally Sustainable Development," *Environmental Innovation and Societal Transitions* 1:1, pp. 58–69; Kerry Krutilla (1999), "Environmental Policy and Transactions Costs," in Jeroen C. J. M. van den Bergh, ed., *Handbook of Environmental and Resource Economics* (Cheltenham, England: Edward Elgar); Laura McCann, Bonnie Colby, K. William Easter, Alexander Kasterine and K. V. Kuperan (2005), "Transaction Cost Measurement for Evaluating Environmental Policies," *Ecological Economics* 52:4, pp. 527–42.

10. Olmstead (2010a). For a thorough examination of the multitude of transaction costs in creating water markets and trading, see Laura McCann and K. William Easter (2004), "A Framework for Estimating the Transaction Costs of Alternative Mechanisms for Water Exchange and Allocation," *Water Resources Research* 40:9.

11. McCann and Easter (2004), p. 2.

12. For a comprehensive analysis of how transaction costs have impacted market-based allocations for environmental benefits in the Columbia River basin of the western United States, see Dustin Garrick and Bruce Aylward (2012), "Transaction Costs and Institutional Performance in Market-Based Environmental Water Allocation," *Land Economics* 88:3, pp. 536–60.

13. Bonnie Colby (1990), "Enhancing Instream Flow Benefits in an Era of Water Marketing," *Water Resources Research* 26:6, pp. 1113–20.

14. The following discussion of creating water markets in the Murray–Darling river basin draws on Henning Bjornlund and Jennifer McKay (2002), "Aspects of Water Markets for Developing Countries: Experiences from Australia, Chile, and the US," *Environment and Development Economics* 7:4, pp. 769–95; Debaere et al. (2014); Dustin Garrick, Stuart M. Whitten and Anthea Coggan (2013), "Understanding the Evolution and Performance of Water Markets and Allocation Policy: A Transaction Costs Analysis Framework," *Ecological Economics* 88, pp. 195–205; R. Quentin Grafton and James Horne (2014), "Water Markets in the Murray–Darling Basin," *Agricultural Water Management* 145, pp. 61–71; Grafton et al. (2011); R. Quentin Grafton, James Horne and Sarah Ann Wheeler (2016), "On the Marketisation of Water: Evidence from the Murray–Darling Basin, Australia," *Water Resources Management* 30:3, pp. 913–26; Barry T. Hart (2016a), "The Australian Murray–Darling Basin Plan: Challenges in Its Implementation (Part 1)," *International Journal of Water Resources Development* 32:6, pp. 819–34; Barry T. Hart (2016b), "The Australian Murray–Darling Basin Plan: Challenges in Its Implementation (Part 2)," *International Journal of Water Resources Development* 32:6, pp. 835–52; James Horne (2014), "The 2012 Murray–Darling Basin Plan: Issues to Watch," *International Journal of Water Resources Development* 30:1, pp. 152–63; S. Wheeler, A. Loch, A. Zuo and H. Bjornlund (2014), "Reviewing the Adoption and Impact of Water Markets in the Murray–Darling Basin, Australia," *Journal of Hydrology* 518:A, pp. 28–41; Michael D. Young (2014b), "Trading into Trouble? Lessons from Australia's Mistakes in Water Policy Reform Sequencing," in K. William Easter and Qiuqiong Huang, eds., *Water Markets for the 21st Century: What Have We Learned?* (Dordrecht, Netherlands: Springer), pp. 203–14.

15. The following discussion of creating water markets in Chile draws on Carl J. Bauer (2005), "In the Image of the Market: The Chilean Model of Water Resource Management," *International Journal of Water* 3:2, pp. 146–65; Carl J. Bauer (2013), "The Experience of Water Markets and the Market Model in Chile," in Josefina Maestu, ed., *Water Trading and Global Water Scarcity: International Experiences* (Abingdon, England: RFF Press), pp. 130–43; Bjornlund and McKay (2002); Convery (2013); Debaere et al. (2014); Guillermo Donoso (2013), "The Evolution of Water Markets in Chile," in Josefina Maestu, ed., *Water Trading and Global Water Scarcity: International Experiences* (Abingdon, England: RFF Press), pp. 111–29; Grafton et al. (2011); Robert R. Hearne and Guillermo Donoso (2014), "Water Markets in Chile: Are They Meeting Needs?" in K. William Easter and Qiuqiong Huang, eds., *Water Markets for the 21st Century:*

What Have We Learned? (Dordrecht, Netherlands: Springer), pp. 103–26; Robert R. Hearne and K. William Easter (1997), "The Economic and Financial Gains from Water Markets in Chile," *Agricultural Economics* 15:3, pp. 187–99.

16. Bauer (2005), p. 160.

17. The following discussion of creating water markets in the western United States draws on Edward B. Barbier and Anita M. Chaudhry (2014), "Urban Growth and Water," *Water Resources and Economics* 6, pp. 1–17; Bjorlund and McKay (2002); Brewer et al. (2008); Craig D. Broadbent, David S. Brookshire, Don Coursey and Vince Tisdell (2017), "Futures Contracts in Water Leasing: An Experimental Analysis Using Basin Characteristics of the Rio Grande, NM," *Environmental and Resource Economics* 68:3, pp. 569–94; David S. Brookshire, Bonnie Colby, Mary Ewers and Philip T. Ganderton (2004), "Market Prices for Water in the Semiarid West of the United States," *Water Resources Research* 40:9; Convery (2013); Peter W. Culp, Robert Glennon and Gary Libecap (2014), *Shopping for Water: How the Market Can Mitigate Water Scarcity in the American West* (Washington, DC: Hamilton Project); Debaere et al. (2014); Garrick et al. (2013); Christopher Goemans and James Pritchett (2014), "Western Water Markets: Effectiveness and Efficiency," in K. William Easter and Qiuqiong Huang, eds., *Water Markets for the 21st Century: What Have We Learned?* (Dordrecht, Netherlands: Springer), pp. 305–30; Grafton et al. (2011); Griffin (2012); and Olmstead (2010a).

18. These estimates of various water uses in the western United States are from Culp et al. (2014).

19. Brewer et al. (2008).

20. Goemans and Pritchett (2014).

21. Libecap (2011), p. 76.

22. These two examples are from Culp et al. (2014).

23. As explained in Culp et al. (2014), p. 24, across the western United States, the failure to control unlimited "open access" to groundwater is highly detrimental to efforts to establish water markets: "The failure of some states to regulate groundwater use has created an ongoing open-access resource problem causing widespread ecological degradation, property damage, and continuing erosion of private property rights in both land and surface water . . . In addition, open access to groundwater substantially impedes the development of markets for water (both in groundwater and with respect to other water resources) because a prospective water user frequently has the option of access to free groundwater in lieu of paying for access to a more sustainable but comparatively expensive, scarce, and tightly regulated supply of surface water. Open access to groundwater thus inhibits the development of real markets for water and distorts the prices we pay."

24. See Javier Calatrava and David Martínez-Granados (2017), "The Limited Success of Formal Water Markets in the Segura River Basin, Spain," *International Journal of Water Resources Development*. https://doi.org/10.108 0/07900627.2017.1378628 (accessed June 18, 2018); Vanessa Casado-Pérez (2015), "Missing Water Markets: A Cautionary Table of Governmental Failure," *New York University Environmental Law Journal* 23:2, pp. 157–244;

David Zetland (2011), "Water Markets in Europe," *Water Resources IMPACT* 13:5, pp. 15–18.

25. K. William Easter and Qiuqiong Huang (2014), "The New Role for Water Markets in the Twenty-First Century," in K. William Easter and Qiuqiong Huang, eds., *Water Markets for the 21st Century: What Have We Learned?* (Dordrecht, Netherlands: Springer), p. 336.

26. Bjorlund and McKay (2002); R. Maria Saleth (2014), "Water Markets in India: Extent and Impact," in K. William Easter and Qiuqiong Huang, eds., *Water Markets for the 21st Century: What Have We Learned?* (Dordrecht, Netherlands: Springer), pp. 239–61.

27. Saleth (2014), p. 259.

28. Min Jiang (2018), *Towards Tradable Water Rights: Water Law and Policy Reform in China* (Cham, Switzerland: Springer); Scott M. Moore (2015), "The Development of Water Markets in China: Progress, Peril, and Prospects," *Water Policy* 17:2, pp. 253–67; Jinxia Wang, Lijuang Zhang, Qiuqiong Huang, Jikun Huang and Scott Rozelle (2014), "Assessment of the Development of Groundwater Markets in Rural China," in K. William Easter and Qiuqiong Huang, eds., *Water Markets for the 21st Century: What Have We Learned?* (Dordrecht, Netherlands: Springer), pp. 263–81.

29. Moore (2015), p. 257.

30. See, for example, Convery (2013); K. William Easter (2009), "Demand Management, Privatization, Water Markets, and Efficient Water Allocation in Our Cities," in L. A. Baker, ed., *The Water Environment of Cities* (New York: Springer), pp. 259–74; Grafton (2017); Olmstead (2010a); Rogers et al. (2002).

31. This discussion of the two-part pricing scheme is based on Easter (2009).

32. Easter (2009), p. 262. Easter (2009) also suggests that the pricing scheme can be easily adjusted for the seasonal variability of water supplies and demand, as has been implemented in Phoenix, Arizona: "For seasonal variability, peak load or seasonal pricing can be used. In this case the prices or charges per unit would be raised during periods of high water demand and/or low supplies. For the United States this tends to mean high rates in the summer and low rates in the winter. For example, the rate might be only $1/1,000 gallons in the winter, $4 in the summer, and $2 in the fall and spring. It might also be set lower for part of the spring season since in northern climates this is usually a period of high rainfall and snow melt. In Phoenix, Arizona, a city in the dry southwest, they charge $1.65 per ccf from December through March; $1.97 for April, May, October, and November; and $2.50 from June through September."

33. Sheila M. Olmstead and Robert N. Stavins (2009), "Comparing Price and Nonprice Approaches to Urban Water Conservation," *Water Resources Research* 45:4, W04301.

34. Jaroslav Mysiak, Fabio Farinosi, Lorenzo Carrera, Francesca Testella, Margaretha Breil and Antonio Massaruto (2015), "Residential Water Pricing in Italy," in Manuel Lago, Jaroslav Mysiak, Carlos M. Gómez, Gonzalo Delacámara and Alexandros Maziotis, eds., *Use of Economic Instruments in Water Policy: Insights from International Experience* (Cham, Switzerland: Springer), pp. 105–19.

35. Dajun Shen and Juan Wu (2017), "State of the Art Review: Water Pricing Reform in China," *International Journal of Water Resources Development* 33:2, pp. 198–232.

36. Diego Fernández (2015), "Water Pricing in Colombia: From Bankruptcy to Full Cost Recovery," in Ariel Dinar, Victor Pochat and José Albiac-Murillo, eds., *Water Pricing Experiences and Innovations* (Cham, Switzerland: Springer), pp. 117–38.

37. UNICEF and WHO (2015), *Progress on Sanitation and Drinking Water: 2015 Update and MDG Assessment* (Geneva: WHO Press).

38. Ephias M. Makaudze and Gregory M. Gelles (2015), "The Challenges of Providing Water and Sanitation to Urban Slum Settlements in South Africa," in Quentin Grafton, Katherine A. Daniell, Céline Nauges, Jean-Daniel Rinaudo and Noel Wai Wah Chan, eds., *Understanding and Managing Urban Water in Transition* (Dordrecht, Netherlands: Springer), pp. 121–33.

39. Dale Whittington, W. Michael Hanemann, Claudia Sadoff and Marc Jeuland (2008), "The Challenge of Improving Water and Sanitation Services in Less Developed Countries," *Foundations and Trends in Microeconomics* 4:6–7, pp. 469–609.

40. For further details on these and other examples see Jennifer Möller-Gulland, Manuel Lago, Katriona McGlade and Gerardo Anzaldua (2015), "Effluent Tax in Germany," in Manuel Lago, Jaroslav Mysiak, Carlos M. Gómez, Gonzalo Delacámara and Alexandros Maziotis, eds., *Use of Economic Instruments in Water Policy: Insights from International Experience* (Cham, Switzerland: Springer), pp. 21–38; Sheila M. Olmstead (2010b), "The Economics of Water Quality," *Review of Environmental Economics and Policy* 4:1, pp. 44–62; Rogers et al. (2002); Shen and Wu (2017); James Shortle (2017), "Policy Nook: 'Economic Incentives for Water Quality Protection'," *Water Economics and Policy* 3:2.

41. Möller-Gulland et al. (2015).

42. Shen and Wu (2017).

43. James Shortle (2013), "Economics and Environmental Markets: Lessons from Water-Quality Trading," *Agricultural and Resource Economics Review* 42:1, pp. 57–74; Richard D. Horan and James S. Shortle (2011), "Economic and Ecological Rules for Water Quality Trading," *Journal of the American Water Resources Association* 47:1, pp. 59–69.

44. James Shortle and Richard D. Horan (2017), "Nutrient Pollution: A Wicked Challenge for Economic Instruments," *Water Economics and Policy* 3:2. For the difficulty of controlling nutrient pollution from agricultural sources through water quality trading, see Kurt Stephenson and Leonard Shabman (2017), "Can Water Quality Trading Fix the Agricultural Nonpoint Source Problem?" *Annual Review of Resource Economics* 9, pp. 95–116.

45. Olmstead (2010b).

46. Tiho Ancev and M. S. Samad Azad (2015), "Evaluation of Salinity Offset Programs in Australia," in Manuel Lago, Jaroslav Mysiak, Carlos M. Gómez, Gonzalo Delacámara and Alexandros Maziotis, eds., *Use of Economic Instruments in Water Policy: Insights from International Experience* (Cham, Switzerland: Springer), pp. 235–48.

47. Olmstead (2010b); Shortle (2013).
48. J. Medellín-Azuara, R. E. Howitt and J. J. Harou (2012), "Predicting Farmer Responses to Water Pricing, Rationing and Subsidies Assuming Profit-Maximizing Investment in Irrigation Technology," *Agricultural Water Management* 108, pp. 73–82.
49. OECD (2010), *Sustainable Management of Water Resources in Agriculture* (Paris: OECD).
50. This example from India is based on Kuppannan Palanisami, Kadiri Mohan, Mark Giordano and Chris Charles (2011), "Measuring Irrigation Subsidies in Andhra Pradesh and Southern India: An Application of the GSI Method for Quantifying Subsidies," International Institute for Sustainable Development, March, available at http://indiaenvironmentportal.org.in/files/irrig_india.pdf (accessed June 19, 2018); and Kuppannan Palanisami, Krishna Reddy Kakumanu and Ravinder P. S. Malik (2015), "Water Pricing Experiences in India: Emerging Issues," in Ariel Dinar, Victor Pochat and José Albiac-Murillo, eds., *Water Pricing Experiences and Innovations* (Cham, Switzerland: Springer), pp. 161–80.
51. Shen and Wu (2017).
52. This means that for every dollar earned in revenues by OECD farms, 18 cents came from some kind of agricultural subsidy (OECD (2014), *Agricultural Policy Monitoring and Evaluation 2014: OECD Countries* (Paris: OECD)). The OECD member countries then comprised: Australia, Austria, Belgium, Canada, Chile, Czech Republic, Denmark, Estonia, Finland, France, Germany, Greece, Hungary, Iceland, Ireland, Israel, Italy, Japan, South Korea, Luxembourg, Mexico, Netherlands, New Zealand, Norway, Poland, Portugal, Slovakia, Slovenia, Spain, Sweden, Switzerland, Turkey, United Kingdom and United States. In fact, the agricultural subsidy rate for some individual countries is extremely high. According to OECD (2014), in the European Union, producer support is around 20 percent of gross farm receipts, and the share is even larger for Japan (56 percent), South Korea (53 percent), Norway (53 percent), Switzerland (49 percent), and Iceland (41 percent). The European Union (EU) estimate excludes Croatia, which joined on July 1, 2013. The other EU members included in the estimate by OECD (2014) are: Austria, Belgium, Bulgaria, Cyprus, Czech Republic, Denmark, Estonia, Finland, France, Germany, Greece, Hungary, Ireland, Italy, Latvia, Lithuania, Luxembourg, Malta, Netherlands, Poland, Portugal, Romania, Slovakia, Slovenia, Spain, Sweden and United Kingdom.
53. Grant Potter (2014), "Agricultural Subsidies Remain a Staple in the Industrial World," Vital Signs, February 28, http://vitalsigns.worldwatch.org/vs-trend/agricultural-subsidies-remain-staple-industrial-world (accessed June 19, 2018).
54. Potter (2014). In addition, it is the mainly rich and large emerging market economies in Asia, Europe and North America that account for 94 percent of global agricultural subsidies, with only 6 percent spent in the rest of the world. Thus the subsidies are highly inequitable.

7. Supporting Innovations

1. See, for example, P. D. Aher, J. Adinarayana, S. D. Gorantiwar and S. A. Sawant (2014), "Information System for Integrated Watershed Management Using Remote Sensing and GIS," in Prashant K. Srivastava, Saumitra Mukherjee, Manika Gupta and Tanvir Islam, eds., *Remote Sensing Applications in Environmental Research* (Cham, Switzerland: Springer), pp. 17–34; Stephanie C. J. Palmer, Tiit Kutser and Peter D. Hunter (2015), "Remote Sensing of Inland Waters: Challenges, Progress and Future Directions," *Remote Sensing of Environment* 157, pp. 1–8; Elena Lopez-Gunn and Manuel Ramón Llamas (2008), "Re-thinking Water Scarcity: Can Science and Technology Solve the Global Water Crisis?" *Natural Resources Forum* 32, pp. 228–38; A. Shakoor, A. Shehzad and M. N. Ashgar (2006), "Application of Remote Sensing Techniques for Water Resources Planning and Management," International Conference on Advances in Space Technologies, Islamabad, Pakistan, 2–3 September.

2. See, for example, A. AghaKouchak, A. Farahmand, F. S. Melton, J. Teixeira, M. C. Anderson, et al. (2015), "Remote Sensing of Drought: Progress, Challenges and Opportunities," *Reviews of Geophysics* 53:2, pp. 452–80; Joshua Elliott, Delphine Deryng, Christoph Müller, Katja Frieler, Markus Konzmann, et al. (2014), "Constraints and Potentials of Future Irrigation Water Availability on Agricultural Production under Climate Change," *Proceedings of the National Academy of Sciences* 111:9, pp. 3239–44; Khurrum Ahmed Khan and Mansoor A. Hashmi (2006), "Drought Mitigation and Preparedness Planning Using RS and GIS," 2006 International Conference on Advances in Space Technologies, Islamabad, Pakistan, 2–3 September.

3. See, for example, Bonnie Colby, Lana Jones and Michael O'Donnell (2014), "Supply Reliability under Climate Change: Forbearance Agreements and Measurement of Water Conserved," in K. William Easter and Qiuqiong Huang, eds., *Water Markets for the 21st Century: What Have We Learned?* (Dordrecht, Netherlands: Springer), pp. 57–82; Elliott et al. (2014); Lopez-Gunn and Llamas (2008); Palmer et al. (2015).

4. Elliott et al. (2014).

5. Claudia Kuenzer and Kim Knauer (2013), "Remote Sensing of Rice Crop Areas," *International Journal of Remote Sensing* 34:6, pp. 2101–39.

6. See, for example, Leila Hassan-Esfahani, Alfonso Torres-Rua and Mac McKee (2015), "Assessment of Optimal Irrigation Water Allocation for Pressurized Irrigation System Using Water Balance Approach, Learning Machines, and Remotely Sensed Data," *Agricultural Water Management* 153, pp. 42–50; David J. Mulla (2013), "Twenty Five Years of Remote Sensing in Precision Agriculture: Key Advances and Remaining Knowledge Gaps," *Biosystems Engineering* 114:4, pp. 358–71.

7. Mulla (2013), p. 359.

8. Cameron M. Pittelkow, Xinqiang Liang, Bruce A. Linquist, Kees Jan van Groenigen, Juhwan Lee, et al. (2015), "Productivity Limits and Potentials of the Principles of Conservation Agriculture," *Nature* 517:7534, pp. 365–8.

9. Lopez-Gunn and Llamas (2008).

10. J. E. Ayars, Alan Fulton and Brock Taylor (2015), "Subsurface Drip Irrigation in California: Here to Stay?" *Agricultural Water Management* 157, pp. 39–47; International Water Management Institute (IWMI) (2017), *IWMI 2016 Annual Report: Water Solutions for a Changing World* (Colombo, Sri Lanka: IWMI).

11. David Sedlak (2014), *Water 4.0: The Past, Present, and Future of the World's Most Vital Resource*. (New Haven and London: Yale University Press).

12. See, for example, Fei Li and Eran Feitelson (2017), "To Desalinate or Divert? A Comparative Supply Cost Analysis for North Coastal China," *International Journal of Water Resources Development* 33:1, pp. 93–110; Sedlak (2014); Dong Zhou, Lijing Zhu, Yinyi Fu, Minghe Zhu and Lixin Xue (2015), "Development of Lower Cost Seawater Desalination Processes Using Nanofiltration Technologies: A Review," *Desalination* 376, pp. 109–16; Jadwiga R. Ziolkowska (2015), "Is Desalination Affordable? Regional Cost and Price Analysis," *Water Resources Management* 29:5, pp. 1385–97.

13. Li and Feitelson (2017).

14. See, for example, Daron Acemoglu, Philippe Aghion, Leonardo Bursztyn and David Hemous (2012), "The Environment and Directed Technical Change," *American Economic Review* 102:1, pp. 131–66; Edward B. Barbier (2015c), "Are There Limits to Green Growth?" *World Economics* 16:3, pp. 163–92; Edward B. Barbier (2016), "Building the Green Economy," *Canadian Public Policy* 42:S1, S1–S9; Sam Fankhauser, Alex Bowen, Raphael Calel, Antoine Dechezleprêtre, James Rydge and Misato Sato (2013), "Who Will Win the Green Race? In Search of Environmental Competitiveness and Innovation," *Global Environmental Change* 23:5, pp. 902–13; Lawrence H. Goulder (2004), *Induced Technological Change and Climate Policy* (Arlington, VA: Pew Center on Global Climate Change); Dani Rodrik (2014), "Green Industrial Policy," *Oxford Review of Economic Policy* 30:3, pp. 469–91.

15. See Barbier (2015c); Barbier (2016). Goulder (2004) refers to these type of policies as "technology-pull" policies.

16. See Barbier (2015c); Barbier (2016); Goulder (2004).

17. See, for example, Hunt Allcott and Nathan Wozny (2014), "Gasoline Prices, Fuel Economy, and the Energy Paradox," *Review of Economics and Statistics* 96:5, pp. 779–95; Jasmin Ansar and Roger Sparks (2009), "The Experience Curve, Option Value, and the Energy Paradox," *Energy Policy* 37:3, pp. 1012–20; Kenneth Gillingham, Richard Newell and Karen Palmer (2006), "Energy Efficiency Policies: A Retrospective Examination," *Annual Review of Environment and Resources* 31, pp. 161–82; Nigel Jollands, Paul Waide, Mark Ellis, Takao Onoda, Jens Laustsen, et al. (2010), "The 25 Energy Efficiency Policy Recommendations to the G8 Gleneagles Plan of Action," *Energy Policy* 38:11, pp. 6409–18; Tom Tietenberg (2009), "Reflections: Energy Efficiency Policy–Pipe Dream or Pipeline to the Future?" *Review of Environmental Economics and Policy* 3:2, pp. 304–20.

18. J. A. Rodríguez-Díaz, L. Pérez-Urrestarazu, E. Comacho-Poyato and P. Montesinos (2011), "The Paradox of Irrigation Scheme Modernization: More Efficient Water Use Linked to Higher Energy Demand," *Spanish Journal of Agricultural Research* 9:4, pp. 1000–8.

19. Maria A. Garcia-Valiñas, Roberto Martínez-Espiñeira and Hang To (2015), "The Use of Non-Pricing Instruments to Manage Water Demand: What Have We Learned?" in Quentin Grafton, Katherine A. Daniell, Céline Nauges, Jean-Daniel Rinaudo and Noel Wai Wah Chan, eds., *Understanding and Managing Urban Water in Transition* (Dordrecht, Netherlands: Springer), pp. 269–80.
20. IWMI (2017).
21. Garcia-Valiñas et al. (2015).
22. Garcia-Valiñas et al. (2015).
23. IWMI (2017). In Pakistan, there has also been ongoing devolvement of irrigation from the government to farmer organizations and collectives. The result has been a unique set of informational, market and technological barriers to collective management that need to be overcome to improve irrigation productivity and efficiency. See Aatika Nagrah, Anita M. Chaudhry and Mark Giordano (2016), "Collective Action in Decentralized Irrigation Systems: Evidence from Pakistan," *World Development* 84, pp. 282–98.
24. K. William Easter (2009). "Demand Management, Privatization, Water Markets, and Efficient Water Allocation in Our Cities," in L. A. Baker, ed., *The Water Environment of Cities* (New York: Springer), pp. 259–74.
25. Edward B. Barbier and Anita M. Chaudhry (2014), "Urban Growth and Water," *Water Resources and Economics* 6, pp. 1–17.
26. François Destandau and Serge Garcia (2014), "Service Quality, Scale Economies and Ownership: An Econometric Analysis of Water Supply Costs," *Journal of Regulatory Economics* 46:2, pp. 152–82.
27. Easter (2009).
28. Easter (2009).
29. See, for example, Okke Braadbaart (2005), "Privatizing Water and Wastewater in Developing Countries: Assessing the 1990s' Experiments," *Water Policy* 7:4, pp. 329–44; Sheila M. Olmstead (2010a), "The Economics of Managing Scarce Water Resources," *Review of Environmental Economics and Policy* 4:2, pp. 179–98; Xun Wu, R. Schuyler House and Ravi Peri (2016), "Public-Private Partnerships (PPPs) in Water and Sanitation in India: Lessons from China," *Water Policy* 18:S1, pp. 153–76.
30. Wu et al. (2016).
31. See, for example, Richard Allan, Paul Jeffrey, Martin Clarke and Simon Pollard (2013), "The Impact of Regulation, Ownership and Business Culture on Managing Corporate Risk within the Water Industry," *Water Policy* 15:3, pp. 458–78; Arunava Bhattacharyya, Thomas R. Harris, Rangesan Narayanan and Kambiz Raffiee (1995), "Specification and Estimation of the Effect of Ownership on the Economic Efficiency of the Water Utilities," *Regional Science and Urban Economics* 25:6, pp. 759–84; Sophia Ruester and Michael Zschille (2010), "The Impact of Governance Structure on Firm Performance: An Application to the German Water Distribution Sector," *Utilities Policy* 18:3, pp. 154–62; David S. Saal, David Parker and Tom Weyman-Jones (2007), "Determining the Contribution of Technical Change, Efficiency Change and Scale Change to Productivity Growth in the Privatized English and Welsh Water and Sewerage Industry, 1985–2000," *Journal of Productivity Analysis* 28:1–2, pp. 127–39.

32. Saal et al. (2007).
33. CDP (2016), *Thirsty Business: Why Water Is Vital to Climate Action* (London: CDP Worldwide), https://www.cdp.net/en/research/global-reports/global-water-report-2016 (accessed June 20, 2018).
34. Peter W. Culp, Robert Glennon and Gary Libecap (2014), *Shopping for Water: How the Market Can Mitigate Water Scarcity in the American West* (Washington, DC: Hamilton Project).
35. CDP (2017), *A Turning Tide: Tracking Corporate Action on Water Security* (London: CDP Worldwide), https://www.cdp.net/en/research/global-reports/global-water-report-2017 (accessed June 20, 2018).
36. Edward B. Barbier and Joanne C. Burgess (2017), "Innovative Corporate Initiatives to Reduce Climate Risk: Lessons from East Asia," *Sustainability* 10:1, art. 13.
37. Natural Capital Declaration (2015), *Towards Including Natural Resource Risks in Cost of Capital: State of Play and the Way Forward* (Geneva: UNEP Finance Initiative / Oxford: Global Canopy Programme), available at http://www.unepfi.org/fileadmin/documents/NCD-NaturalResourceRisksScopingStudy.pdf (accessed June 20, 2018).
38. CDP (2017).
39. Barbier and Burgess (2018).
40. CDP (2017).
41. Barbier and Burgess (2018).
42. CDP (2017).

8. Managing a Global Resource

1. Meredith A. Giordano and Aaron T. Wolf (2003), "Sharing Waters: Post-Rio International Water Management," *Natural Resources Forum* 27:2, pp. 163–71; Aaron T. Wolf (2007), "Shared Waters: Conflict and Cooperation," *Annual Review of Environment and Resources* 32, pp. 241–69. See also UNEP (2002), *Atlas of International Freshwater Agreements* (Nairobi; UNEP), available at https://wedocs.unep.org/handle/20.500.11822/8182 (accessed June 15, 2018).
2. Jennifer Song and Dale Whittington (2004), "Why Have Some Countries on International Rivers Been Successful Negotiating Treaties? A Global Perspective," *Water Resources Research* 40:5, W05S06; Wolf (2007).
3. Edith Brown Weiss (2012), "The Coming Water Crisis: A Common Concern of Humankind," *Transnational Environmental Law* 1:1, pp. 153–68; Arjen Y. Hoekstra and Mesfin M. Mekonnen (2012), "The Water Footprint of Humanity," *Proceedings of the National Academy of Sciences* 109:9, pp. 3232–7; Maria Cristina Rulli, Antonio Saviori and Paolo D'Odorico (2013), "Global Land and Water Grabbing," *Proceedings of the National Academy of Sciences* 110:3, pp. 892–7.
4. Rulli et al. (2013).
5. Brown Weiss (2012).
6. For further discussion of the economic, governance and institutional issues surrounding transboundary water management, see Edward B. Barbier and Anik Bhaduri (2015), "Transboundary Water Resources," in Robert Halvorsen and David F. Layton, eds., *Handbook on the Economics of Natural*

Resources (Cheltenham, England: Edward Elgar), pp. 502–28; Shlomi Dinar (2009), "Scarcity and Cooperation along International Rivers," *Global Environmental Politics* 9:1, pp. 108–35; Shlomi Dinar, Ariel Dinar and Pradeep Kurukulasuriya (2011), "Scarcity and Cooperation along International Rivers: An Empirical Assessment of Bilateral Treaties," *International Studies Quarterly* 55:3, pp. 809–33; Anton Earle and Marian J. Neal (2017), "Inclusive Transboundary Water Governance," in Eiman Karar, ed., *Freshwater Governance for the 21st Century* (London: SpringerOpen), pp. 145–58; Jacob D. Petersen-Perlman, Jennifer C. Veilleux and Aaron T. Wolf (2017), "International Water Conflict and Cooperation: Challenges and Opportunities," *Water International* 42:2, pp. 105–20; Song and Whittington (2004); Jos Timmerman, John Matthews, Sonja Koeppel, Daniel Valensuela and Niels Vlaanderen (2017), "Improving Governance in Transboundary Cooperation in Water and Climate Change Adaptation," *Water Policy* 19:6, pp. 1014–29; Wolf (2007); Mark Zeitoun, Marisa Goulden and David Tickner (2013), "Current and Future Challenges Facing Transboundary River Basin Management," *WIREs Climate Change* 4:5, pp. 331–49.

7. L. De Stefano, Jacob D. Petersen-Perlman, Eric A. Sproles, Jim Eynard and Aaron T. Wolf (2017), "Assessment of Transboundary River Basins for Potential Hydro-Political Tensions," *Global Environmental Change* 45, pp. 35–46.

8. Barbier and Bhaduri (2015); Shlomi Dinar, David Katz, Lucia De Stefano and Brian Blankespoor (2015), "Climate Change, Conflict, and Cooperation: Global Analysis of the Effectiveness of International River Treaties in Addressing Water Variability," *Political Geography* 45, pp. 55–66; Sheila M. Olmstead (2014), "Climate Change Adaptation and Water Resource Management: A Review of the Literature," *Energy Economics* 46, pp. 500–9; Petersen-Perlman et al. (2017); Timmerman et al. (2017).

9. Song and Whittington (2004).

10. See, for example, Barbier and Bhaduri (2015); Lynne L. Bennett, Shannon E. Ragland and Peter Yolles (1998), "Facilitating International Agreements through an Interconnected Game Approach: The Case of River Basins, in Richard E. Just and Sinaia Netanyahu, eds., *Conflict and Cooperation on Trans-Boundary Water Resources* (Boston: Kluwer Academic), pp. 61–85; Shlomi Dinar (2008), *International Water Treaties: Negotiation and Cooperation along Transboundary Rivers* (London: Routledge); Ines Dombrowsky (2007), *Conflict, Cooperation and Institutions in International Water Management: An Economic Analysis* (Cheltenham, England: Edward Elgar); Kim Hang Pham Do, Ariel Dinar and Daene McKinney (2012), "Transboundary Water Management: Can Issue Linkage Help Mitigate Externalities?" *International Game Theory Review* 14:1; Richard E. Just and Sinaia Netanyahu (2004), "Implications of 'Victim Pays' Infeasibilities for Interconnected Games with an Illustration for Aquifer Sharing under Unequal Access Costs," *Water Resources Research* 40:5, W05S02.

11. Bennett et al. (1998); Just and Netanyahu (2004).

12. Aaron T. Wolf (1999), "The Transboundary Freshwater Dispute Database Project," *Water International* 24:2, pp. 160–3.
13. Rebecca L. Teasley and Daene C. McKinney (2011), "Calculating the Benefits of Transboundary River Basin Cooperation: Syr Darya Basin," *Journal of Water Resources Planning and Management* 137:6, pp. 481–90.
14. Kim Hang Pham Do and Ariel Dinar (2014), "The Role of Issue Linkage in Managing Noncooperating Basins: The Case of the Mekong," *Natural Resource Modeling* 27:4, pp. 492–517.
15. Anik Bhaduri and Edward B. Barbier (2008b), "Political Altruism of Transboundary Water Sharing," *B.E. Journal of Economic Analysis & Policy* 8:1, art. 32. Although India is broadly adhering to the Ganges Treaty, it still uses its dominant position as an upstream country to withdraw water unilaterally during critical dry-season periods. See Kimberley Anh Thomas (2017), "The Ganges Water Treaty: 20 Years of Cooperation, on India's Terms," *Water Policy* 19:4, pp. 724–40. Note that full basin-wide agreement for managing the Ganges River would require the cooperation of Nepal, which is the furthest upstream country. This could be accomplished through linking the current Ganges River Treaty to potential water transfers from Nepal to augment the lower basin flow, which could be paid for jointly by India and Bangladesh. See Anik Bhaduri and Edward B. Barbier (2008a), "International Water Transfer and Sharing: The Case of the Ganges River," *Environment and Development Economics* 13:1, pp. 29–51.
16. Just and Netanyahu (2004).
17. S. Dinar et al. (2015).
18. Anik Bhaduri, Utpal Manna, Edward Barbier and Jens Liebe (2011), "Climate Change and Cooperation in Transboundary Water Sharing: An Application of Stochastic Stackelberg Differential Games in Volta River Basin," *Natural Resource Modeling* 24:4, pp. 409–44.
19. Brown Weiss (2012).
20. Arjen Y. Hoekstra(2010), "The Relation between International Trade and Freshwater Scarcity," Staff Working Paper ERSD–2010–05, World Trade Organization, January; Manfred Lenzen, Daniel Moran, Anik Bhaduri, Keiichiro Kanemoto, Maksud Bekchanov, et al. (2013), "International Trade of Scarce Water," *Ecological Economics* 94, pp. 78–85.
21. See, for example, J. A. Allan (2003), "Virtual Water: The Water, Food, and Trade Nexus—Useful Concept or Misleading Metaphor?" *Water International* 28:1, pp. 106–13; Peter Debaere (2014), "The Global Economics of Water: Is Water a Source of Comparative Advantage?" *American Economic Journal: Applied Economics* 6:2, pp. 32–48; Andrea Fracasso (2014), "A Gravity Model of Virtual Water Trade," *Ecological Economics* 108, pp. 215–28; Arjen Y. Hoekstra and Ashok K. Chapagain (2008), *Globalization of Water: Sharing the Planet's Freshwater Resources* (Oxford: Blackwell); Graham K. MacDonald, Kate A. Brauman, Shipeng Sun, Kimberly M. Carlson, Emily S. Cassidy, et al. (2015), "Rethinking Agricultural Trade Relationships in an Era of Globalization," *BioScience* 65:3, pp. 275–89; Jeffrey J. Reimer (2012), "On the Economics of Virtual Water Trade," *Ecological Economics* 75, pp. 135–9; Mark W. Rosegrant, Claudia Ringler and Tingju Zhu (2009), "Water for Agriculture: Maintaining

Food Security under Growing Scarcity," *Annual Review of Environment and Resources* 34, pp. 205–22; H. H. J. Savenije, A. Y. Hoekstra and P. van der Zaag (2014), "Evolving Water Science in the Anthropocene," *Hydrology and Earth System Sciences* 18:1, pp. 319–32.

22. Pham Do and Dinar (2014).

9. The Future of Water

1. U.S. Census Bureau, International Data Base, available at https://www. census.gov/data-tools/demo/idb/informationGateway.php (accessed July 17, 2018).

2. Simon N. Gosling and Nigel W. Arnell (2016), "A Global Assessment of the Impact of Climate Change on Water Scarcity," *Climatic Change* 134:3, pp. 371–85. Note, however, that the authors stress that there is substantial uncertainty in the projections of the impact of climate change on water scarcity: "Most of the world will see an increase in exposure to water scarcity than a decrease due to climate change but this is not consistent across all climate change patterns" (p. 371). Other assessments of the impact of climate change on water scarcity are less cautious; see, for example, Jacob Schewe, Jens Heinke, Dieter Gerten, Ingjerd Haddeland, Nigel W. Arnell, et al. (2014), "Mutimodel Assessment of Water Scarcity under Climate Change," *Proceedings of the National Academy of Sciences* 111:9, pp. 3245–50.

SELECT BIBLIOGRAPHY

Allan, J. A. (2003), "Virtual Water: The Water, Food, and Trade Nexus—Useful Concept or Misleading Metaphor," *Water International* 28:1, pp. 106–13.

Baker, L.A., ed. (2009), *The Water Environment of Cities* (New York: Springer).

Barbier, Edward B. (2004), "Water and Economic Growth," *Economic Record* 80:248, pp. 1–16.

Barbier, Edward B. (2011a), *Scarcity and Frontiers: How Economics Have Exploited Natural Resources for Economic Development* (Cambridge, England: Cambridge University Press).

Barbier, Edward B. (2011b), "Transaction Costs and the Transition to Environmentally Sustainable Development," *Environmental Innovation and Societal Transitions* 1:1, pp. 58–69.

Barbier, Edward B. (2015a), *Nature and Wealth: Overcoming Environmental Scarcity and Inequality* (Basingstoke, England: Palgrave Macmillan).

Barbier, Edward B. (2015b), "Water and Growth in Developing Countries," in Ariel Dinar and Kurt Schwabe, eds., *Handbook of Water Economics* (Cheltenham, England: Edward Elgar), pp. 500–12.

Barbier, Edward B. and Anik Bhaduri (2015), "Transboundary Water Resources," in Robert Halvorsen and David F. Layton, eds., *Handbook on the Economics of Natural Resources* (Cheltenham: Edward Elgar), pp. 502–28.

Barbier, Edward B. and Joanne C. Burgess (2017), "Innovative Corporate Initiatives to Reduce Climate Risk: Lessons from East Asia," *Sustainability* 10:1, art. 13.

Barbier, Edward B. and Anita M. Chaudhry (2014), "Urban Growth and Water," *Water Resources and Economics* 6, pp. 1–17.

Biswas, Asit K. (2008), "Integrated Water Resources Management: Is It Working?" *International Journal of Water Resources Development* 24:1, pp. 5–22.

264

Braadbaart, Okke (2005), "Privatizing Water and Wastewater in Developing Countries: Assessing the 1990s' Experiments," *Water Policy* 7:4, pp. 329–44.

Brewer, Jedidiah, Robert Glennon, Alan Ker and Gary Libecap (2008), "Water Markets in the West: Prices, Trading, and Contractual Forms," *Economic Inquiry* 46:2, pp. 91–112.

Brown Weiss, Edith (2012), "The Coming Water Crisis: A Common Concern of Humankind," *Transnational Environmental Law* 1:1, pp. 153–68.

CDP (2017), *A Turning Tide: Tracking Corporate Action on Water Security* (London: CDP Worldwide), https://www.cdp.net/en/research/global-reports/global-water-report-2017 (accessed June 20, 2018).

Cech, Thomas V. (2010), *Principles of Water Resources: History, Development, Management, and Policy*, 3rd ed. (New York: John Wiley).

Chew, Sing C. (2001), *World Ecological Degradation: Accumulation, Urbanization, and Deforestation 3000 BC–AD 2000* (Walnut Creek, CA: Altamira Press).

Convery, Frank J. (2013), "Reflections: Shaping Water Policy—What Does Economics Have to Offer?" *Review of Environmental Economics and Policy* 7:1, pp. 156–74.

Culp, Peter W., Robert Glennon and Gary Libecap (2014), *Shopping for Water: How the Market Can Mitigate Water Scarcity in the American West* (Washington, DC: Hamilton Project).

Dalin, Carole, Megan Konar, Naota Hanasaki, Andrea Rinaldo and Ignacio Rodriguez-Iturbe (2012), "Evolution of the Global Virtual Water Trade Network," *Proceedings of the National Academy of Sciences* 109:16, pp. 5989–94.

Dalin, Carole, Yoshihide Wada, Thomas Kastner and Michael J. Puma (2017), "Groundwater Depletion Embedded in International Food Trade," *Nature* 543, pp. 700–5.

Darwall, W. R. T., K. Smith, D. Allen, M. Seddon, G. McGregor Reid, et al. (2008), "Freshwater Biodiversity: A Hidden Resource Under Threat," in J.-C. Vié, C. Hilton-Taylor and S. N. Stuart, eds., *The 2008 Review of the IUCN Red List of Threatened Species* (Gland, Switzerland: IUCN).

De Stefano, L., Jacob D. Petersen-Perlman, Eric A. Sproles, Jim Eynard and Aaron T. Wolf (2017), "Assessment of Transboundary River Basins for Potential Hydro-Political Tensions," *Global Environmental Change* 45, pp. 35–46.

Debaere, Peter (2014), "The Global Economics of Water: Is Water a Source of Comparative Advantage?" *American Economic Journal: Applied Economics* 6:2, pp. 32–48.

Debaere, Peter, Brian D. Richter, Kyle Frankel Davis, Melissa S. Duvall, Jessica Ann Gephart, et al. (2014), "Water Markets as a Response to Scarcity," *Water Policy* 16:4, pp. 625–49.

Dinar, Ariel and Kurt Schwabe, eds. (2015), *Handbook of Water Economics* (Cheltenham, England: Edward Elgar).

Dinar, Shlomi (2008), *International Water Treaties: Negotiation and Cooperation along Transboundary Rivers* (Abingdon, England: Routledge).

Dinar, Shlomi, David Katz, Lucia De Stefano and Brian Blankespoor (2015), "Climate Change, Conflict, and Cooperation: Global Analysis of the Effectiveness of International River Treaties in Addressing Water Variability," *Political Geography* 45, pp. 55–66.

Dosi, Cesare and K. William Easter (2003), "Water Scarcity: Market Failure and the Implications for Markets and Privatization," *International Journal of Public Administration* 26:3, pp. 265–90.

Draper, E. Stephen and James E. Kundell (2007), "Impact of Climate Change on Trans-Boundary Water Sharing," *Journal of Water Resources Planning and Management* 133:5, pp. 405–15.

Dudgeon, David, Angela H. Arthington, Mark O. Gessner, Zen-Ichiro Kawabata, Duncan J. Knowler, et al. (2006), "Freshwater Biodiversity: Importance, Threats, Status and Conservation Challenges," *Biological Review* 31, pp. 163–82.

Easter, K. William (2009), "Demand Management, Privatization, Water Markets, and Efficient Water Allocation in Our Cities," in L. A. Baker, ed., *The Water Environment of Cities* (New York: Springer), pp. 259–74.

Easter, K. William and Qiuqiong Huang, eds. (2014), *Water Markets for the 21st Century: What Have We Learned?* (Dordrecht, Netherlands: Springer).

Elliott, Joshua, Delphine Deryang, Christoph Müller, Katja Frieler, Markus Konzmann, et al. (2014), "Constraints and Potentials of Future Irrigation Water Availability on Agricultural Production under Climate Change," *Proceedings of the National Academy of Sciences* 111:9, pp. 3239–44.

Fagan, Brian M. (2011), *Elixir: A History of Water and Humankind* (New York: Bloomsbury Press).

Famiglietti, J. S. (2014), "The Global Groundwater Crisis," *Nature Climate Change* 4:11, pp. 946–8.

FAO (2012), *Coping with Water Scarcity: An Action Framework for Agriculture and Food Security* (Rome: FAO).

Garrick, Dustin and Bruce Aylward (2012), "Transaction Costs and Institutional Performance in Market-Based Environmental Water Allocation," *Land Economics* 88:3, pp. 536–60.

Getzler, Joshua (2004), *A History of Water Rights at Common Law* (Oxford: Oxford University Press).

Giordano, Meredith A. and Aaron T. Wolf (2003), "Sharing Waters: Post-Rio International Water Management," *Natural Resources Forum* 27:2, pp. 163–71.

Gosling, Simon N. and Nigel W. Arnell (2016), "A Global Assessment of the Impact of Climate Change on Water Scarcity," *Climatic Change* 134:3, pp. 371–85.

Grafton, R. Quentin (2017), "Responding to the 'Wicked Problem' of Water Insecurity," *Water Resources Management* 31:10, pp. 3023–41.

Grafton, R. Quentin, James Horne and Sarah Ann Wheeler (2016), "On the Marketisation of Water: Evidence from the Murray–Darling Basin, Australia," *Water Resources Management* 30:3, pp. 913–26.

Grafton, R. Quentin, Gary Libecap, Samuel McGlennon, Clay Landry and Bob O'Brien (2011), "An Integrated Assessment of Water Markets: A Cross-Country Comparison," *Review of Environmental Economics and Policy* 5:2, pp. 219–39.

Grafton, R. Quentin, Jamie Pittock, Richard Davis, John Williams, Guobin Fu, et al. (2013), "Global Insights into Water Resources, Climate Change and Governance," *Nature Climate Change* 3:4, pp. 315–21.

Grey, David and Claudia W. Sadoff (2007), "Sink or Swim? Water Security for Growth and Development," *Water Policy* 9:6, pp. 545–71.

Griffin, Ronald C. (2006), *Water Resource Economics: The Analysis of Scarcity, Policies, and Projects* (Cambridge, MA: MIT Press).

Griffin, Ronald C. (2012), "The Origins and Ideals of Water Resource Economics in the United States," *Annual Review of Resource Economics* 4, pp. 353–77.

Hanemann, W. Michael (2006), "The Economic Conception of Water," in Peter P. Rogers, M. Ramón Llamas and Luis Martínez-Cortina, eds., *Water Crisis: Myth or Reality?* (London: Routledge), pp. 77–8.

Hoekstra, Arjen Y. and Ashok K. Chapagain (2008), *Globalization of Water: Sharing the Planet's Freshwater Resources* (Oxford: Blackwell).

Hoekstra, Arjen Y. and Mesfin M. Mekonnen (2012), "The Water Footprint of Humanity," *Proceedings of the National Academy of Sciences* 109:9, pp. 3232–7.

Hoekstra, Arjen Y., Mesfin M. Mekonnen, Ashok K. Chapagain, Ruth E. Mathews and Brian D. Richter (2012), "Global Monthly Water Scarcity: Blue Water Footprints Versus Blue Water Availability," *PLoS ONE* 7:2, e32688.

Jaspers, Frank G. W. (2003), "Institutional Arrangements for Integrated River Basin Management," *Water Policy* 5:1, pp. 77–90.

Johnson, Nels, Carmen Revenga and Jaime Echeverria (2001), "Managing Water for People and Nature," *Science* 292:5519, pp. 1071–2.

Jones, Eric L. (1987), *The European Miracle: Environments, Economics and Geopolitics in the History of Europe and Asia*, 2nd ed. (Cambridge, England: Cambridge University Press).

Just, Richard E. and Sinaia Netanyahu, eds. (1998), *Conflict and Cooperation on Trans-Boundary Water Resources* (Boston: Kluwer Academic).

Karar, Eiman, ed. (2017), *Freshwater Governance for the 21st Century* (London: SpringerOpen).

Kearney, Melissa S., Benjamin H. Harris, Elisa Jácome and Gregory Nantz (2014), *In Times of Drought: Nine Economic Facts about Water in the United States* (Washington, DC: Hamilton Project, Brookings Institution).

Lenzen, Manfred, Daniel Moran, Anik Bhaduri, Keiichiro Kanemoto, Maksud Bekchanov, et al. (2013), "International Trade of Scarce Water," *Ecological Economics* 94, pp. 78–85.

Libecap, Gary D. (2011), "Institutional Path Dependence in Climate Adaptation: Coman's 'Some Unsettled Problems of Irrigation'," *American Economic Review* 101, pp. 64–80.

Lopez-Gunn, Elena and Manuel Ramon Llamas (2008), "Re-thinking Water Scarcity: Can Science and Technology Solve the Global Water Crisis?" *Natural Resources Forum* 32, pp. 228–38.

McCann, Laura and K. William Easter (2004), "A Framework for Estimating the Transaction Costs of Alternative Mechanisms for Water Exchange and Allocation," *Water Resources Research* 40:9.

MacDonald, Graham K., Kate A. Brauman, Shipeng Sun, Kimberly M. Carlson, Emily S. Cassidy, et al. (2015), "Rethinking Agricultural Trade Relationships in an Era of Globalization," *BioScience* 65:3, pp. 275–89.

McDonald, Robert I., Pamela Green, Deborah Balk, Balazs M. Fekete, Carmen Revenga, et al. (2011), "Urban Growth, Climate Change, and Freshwater Availability," *Proceedings of the National Academy of Sciences* 108:15, pp. 6312–17.

McDonald, Robert I., Katherine Weber, Julie Padowski, Martina Flörke, Christof Schneider, et al. (2014), "Water on an Urban Planet: Urbanization and the Reach of Urban Water Infrastructure," *Global Environmental Change* 27, pp. 96–105.

Nauges, Céline and Dale Whittington (2010), "Estimation of Water Demand in Developing Countries: An Overview," *World Bank Research Observer* 25:2, pp. 263–94.

OECD (2010), *Sustainable Management of Water Resources in Agriculture* (Paris: OECD).

OECD (2012), *OECD Environmental Outlook to 2050: The Consequences of Inaction* (Paris: OECD).

Olmstead, Sheila M. (2010a), "The Economics of Managing Scarce Water Resources," *Review of Environmental Economics and Policy* 4:1, pp. 44–62.

Olmstead, Sheila M. (2010b), "The Economics of Water Quality," *Review of Environmental Economics and Policy* 4:1, pp. 44–62.

Olmstead, Sheila M. (2014), "Climate Change Adaptation and Water Resource Management: A Review of the Literature," *Energy Economics* 46, pp. 500–9.

Olmstead, Sheila M. and Robert N. Stavins (2009), "Comparing Price and Nonprice Approaches to Urban Water Conservation," *Water Resources Research* 45:4, W04301.

Palaniappan, Meena and Peter H. Gleick (2009), "Peak Water," in Peter H. Gleick, ed., *The World's Water 2008–9: The Biennial Report on Freshwater Resources* (Washington, DC: Island Press).

Petersen-Perlman, Jacob D., Jennifer C. Veilleux and Aaron T. Wolf (2017), "International Water Conflict and Cooperation: Challenges and Opportunities," *Water International* 42:2, pp. 105–20.

Pittelkow, Cameron M., Xinqiang Liang, Bruce A. Linquist, Kees Jan van Groenigen, Juhwan Lee, et al. (2015), "Productivity Limits and Potentials of the Principles of Conservation Agriculture," *Nature* 517:7534, pp. 365–8.

Revenga, C., I. Campbell, R. Abell, P. de Villiers and M. Bryer (2005), "Prospects for Monitoring Freshwater Ecosystems towards the 2010 Targets," *Philosophical Transactions of the Royal Society B-Biological Sciences* 360:1454, pp. 397–413.

Rogers, Peter, Radhika de Silva and Ramesh Bhatia (2002), "Water Is an Economic Good: How to Use Prices to Promote Equity, Efficiency, and Sustainability," *Water Policy* 4:1, pp. 1–17.

Rogers, Peter P., M. Ramón Llamas and Luis Martínez-Cortina, eds. (2006), *Water Crisis: Myth or Reality?* (London: Routledge).

Rosegrant, Mark W., Claudia Ringler and Tingju Zhu (2009), "Water for Agriculture: Maintaining Food Security under Growing Scarcity," *Annual Review of Environment and Resources* 34, pp. 205–22.

Rulli, Maria Cristina, Antonio Saviori and Paolo D'Odorico (2013), "Global Land and Water Grabbing," *Proceedings of the National Academy of Sciences* 110:3, pp. 892–7.

Saleth, R. Maria and Ariel Dinar (2005), "Water Institutional Reforms: Theory and Practice," *Water Policy* 7:1, pp. 1–19.

Savenije, H. H. G., A. Y. Hoekstra and P. van der Zaag (2014), "Evolving Water Science in the Anthropocene," *Hydrology and Earth System Sciences* 18:1, pp. 319–32.

Schoengold, Karina and David Zilberman (2007), "The Economics of Water, Irrigation, and Development," in Robert Evenson and Prabhu Pingali, eds., *Handbook of Agricultural Economics, vol. 3* (Amsterdam: Elsevier), pp. 2933–77.

Sedlak, David (2014), *Water 4.0: The Past, Present, and Future of the World's Most Vital Resource* (New Haven and London: Yale University Press).

Shiklomanov, Igor A. (1993), "World Fresh Water Resources," in Peter H. Gleick, ed., *Water in Crisis: A Guide to the World's Fresh Water Resources* (New York: Oxford University Press), pp. 13–24.

Shortle, James (2013), "Economics and Environmental Markets: Lessons from Water-Quality Trading," *Agricultural and Resource Economics Review* 42:1, pp. 57–74.

Solomon, Steven (2010), *Water: The Epic Struggle for Wealth, Power, and Civilization* (New York: Harper).

Song, Jennifer and Dale Whittington (2004), "Why Have Some Countries on International Rivers Been Successful Negotiating Treaties? A Global Perspective," *Water Resources Research* 40:5, W05S06.

Squires, Nick (2017), "Rome Turns Off Its Historic 'Big Nose' Drinking Fountains as Drought Grips Italy," *The Telegraph*, June 29, http://www.telegraph.co.uk/news/2017/06/29/rome-turns-historic-big-nose-drinking-fountains-drought-grips/ (accessed June 7, 2018).

Sternberg, Troy (2016), "Water Megaprojects in Deserts and Drylands," *International Journal of Water Resources Development* 32:2, pp. 301–20.

Timmerman, Jos, John Matthews, Sonja Koeppel, Daniel Valensuela and Niels Vlaanderen (2017), "Improving Governance in Transboundary Cooperation in Water and Climate Change Adaptation," *Water Policy* 19:6, pp. 1014–29.

Tvedt, Terje (2016), *Water and Society: Changing Perceptions of Societal and Historical Development* (London: I. B. Tauris).

UNDP (2006), *Human Development Report 2006: Beyond Scarcity—Power, Poverty and the Global Water Crisis* (Basingstoke, England: Palgrave Macmillan).

UNEP (2012), *Status Report on the Application of Integrated Approaches to Water Resources Management* (Nairobi: UNEP).

UNICEF and WHO (2015), *Progress on Sanitation and Drinking Water: 2015 Update and MDG Assessment* (Geneva: WHO Press).

Vié, J.-C., C. Hilton-Taylor and S. N. Stuart, eds. (2008), *The 2008 Review of the IUCN Red List of Threatened Species* (Gland, Switzerland: IUCN).

Vörösmarty, Charles J., Peter B. McIntyre, Mark O. Gessner, David Dudgeon, Alexander Prusevich, et al. (2012), "Global Threats to Human Water Security and River Biodiversity," *Nature* 467, pp. 555–61.

Whittington, Dale, W. Michael Hanemann, Claudia Sadoff and Marc Jeuland (2008), "The Challenge of Improving Water and Sanitation Services in Less Developed Countries," *Foundations and Trends in Microeconomics* 4: 6–7, pp. 469–609.

Wittfogel, Karl A. (1955), "Developmental Aspects of Hydraulic Civilizations," in Julian H. Steward, ed., *Irrigation Civilizations: A Comparative Study—A Symposium on Method and Result in Cross Cultural Regularities* (Washington, DC: Pan American Union).

Wolf, Aaron T. (1999), "The Transboundary Freshwater Dispute Database Project," *Water International* 24:2, pp. 160–3.

Wolf, Aaron T. (2007), "Shared Waters: Conflict and Cooperation," *Annual Review of Environment and Resources* 32, pp. 241–69.

World Economic Forum (2016), *The Global Risks Report 2016*, 11th ed. (Geneva: World Economic Forum), available at http://www3.weforum.org/docs/GRR/WEF_GRR16.pdf (accessed June 7, 2018).

Young, Michael D. (2014a), "Designing Water Abstraction Regimes for an Ever-Changing and Ever-Varying Future," *Agricultural Water Management* 145, pp. 32–8.

Young, Michael D. (2014b), "Trading into Trouble? Lessons from Australia's Mistakes in Water Policy Reform Sequencing," in K. William Easter and Qiuqiong Huang, eds., *Water Markets for the 21st Century: What Have We Learned?* (Dordrecht, Netherlands: Springer), pp. 203–14.

INDEX

Locations for tables and boxes are entered in *italics*.